D0266842

SCREENWRITING

Lew Hunter has two master's degrees (from UCLA and Northwestern University) and has worked for Columbia, Lorimar, Paramount, Disney, NBC, ABC, and CBS as a writer, producer, and executive. Between semesters of his Screenwriting 434 course at UCLA, where he is chairman of the screenwriting department, he travels around the world conducting workshops for thousands of aspiring screenwriters. He lives in Burbank, California.

Screenwriting

LEW HUNTER

ROBERT HALE • LONDON

© Lew Hunter Productions 1993
First published in Great Britain 1994

ISBN 0 7090 5444 0

Robert Hale Limited
Clerkenwell House
Clerkenwell Green
London ECIR OHT

The right of Lew Hunter to be identified as author of this work has been asserted by him in accordance with the Copyright, Designs and Patents Act, 1988.

Manufactured in Malta by Interprint Ltd.

2 4 6 8 10 9 7 5 3

Garlands and potted plants to my beloved students,
Bill Froug, and my wife, Pamela.
All beloved but not in that order.

ACKNOWLEDGMENTS

Super Editor, Steve Ross
The World's Greatest Agent,
Richard Curtis
Rubin Carson
Richard Ray Walter
Andrea Rich
Gil Cates
Howard Suber
Robert Rosen
Bob Gray
Ruth Schwartz
John Young
Jorge Preloran
Jerzy Antczak
Alex Ayres
Stephanie Riseley
Edgar Bravo
Tony Caballero

Deanne Barkley, Harve Bennett, Dick Berman, John Ray Bernstein, Mel Bloom, Steven Bochco, Ray Bradbury, Richard Brenne, Stan Canter, Bruce Cowgill, James Dalessandro, Ken Dancyger, Lon Diamond, Barry Diller, Walt Disney, Dick Donner, Genevieve Ebsen, Michael Eisner, Jules Epstein, Maggie Field, Christine Foster, Len Goldberg, John Graves, Peter Guber, Bill Haber, Dean Hunter, Esther L. Hunter, Joe Hunter, Ray Lewis Hunter, Scott Hunter, Paul Jensen, Terry Keegan, Robert Lewis, Paul Lucey, John McMahon, Mike Medavoy, Shannon Morris, Steve Mills, Janet Neipris, Richard Newton, Dennis Olson, Jr., Michelle Olson, Michael Ovitz, Alex Petry, Frank Price, Stan Robertson, Stu Robinson, Ed Ropolo, Bill Sackheim, Jeff Sagansky, Bill Self, Michael Severid, Aaron Spelling, Eileen Rae Hunter-Sweeney, Brandon Tartikoff, Sam Thomas, Grant Tinker, Godbrother David Titcher,

Card Walker, Lew Weitzman, Larry White, John Wilder, and the UCLA Writers Block.

A tremendous *merci beaucoup* to the above *and the names in the index* for their inspirational roles in my screen and book writing and professing careers.

Lewis Ray Hunter
Superior, Nebraska

CONTENTS

FADE IN

I have been teaching the 434 graduate screenwriting classes at UCLA since 1979. Prior to then, I guest lectured at universities across the contiguous United States. Since then, I have molested creative minds with workshops and lectures in Israel, England, China, South America, France, Australia, and oh, literally, around the world. In every university, the cry is consistent. "Our weakest link is writing." Not so at UCLA. Why? Let me speak just for myself.

My personal teaching bent is not to dispense excessive theory or hypothetical situations and exercises in screenwriting. I like to get with a small group of well-educated, highly motivated people, roll up our figurative sleeves, and start developing screenplays, from idea through story and script to notes for the rewrite. At the end of that creative tunnel is an original creation: a script that will develop that person's potential many steps closer to being the finest writer he or she can be. Not a "Hollywood" writer but a writer who can apply quality talent to any possible screen around the globe. From Hollywood to Nairobi. From TV to esoteric video experiments.

Out of my lectures and writings have come many thoughts and passions about screenwriting. Some from fellow writers, some from me, some from clippings about writing I have accumulated, and some from just the mutual hard work between student and professor.

It eventually occurred to me that the current screenwriting volumes do not really grasp the aspiring screenwriter by the hand and lead them through the beat-by-beat journey of driving a worthy idea through the rewrite of the first draft. The books talk and theorize about writing characters, dialogue, plot, and scripts but most readers afterward still feel somewhat panicked sitting before that blank page or phosphorus screen. That's a good reason for a book. One that would take you step by step and demystify the process, yet simultaneously suggest the profundity of it all. Like my 434 class.

My favorite American play is *Our Town* by Thornton Wilder. It is so simple it can be performed by junior high classes throughout the world as verily it has been translated into multiple languages. Yet *Our Town* is so profound that it's a staple in the repertoire of the Royal Shakespeare Company. Ergo, "434: Becoming a Screenwriter" is designed to be simple, yet not simplistic. I mean to give you vision, hope, confidence, and a beacon light to shine upon your own special creativity.

What you will be experiencing is no more and no less than what my graduate students receive on a quarterly basis. We tabulate that since 1980, one out of two who write in our three-year program become writers that make their living before keyboards. What you will be reading has demonstrated a batting average of validity that way surpasses Ty Cobb's record-breaking accomplishments. And writing screenplays may be *almost* as meaningful to life as baseball.

People often say, "We believe anything you write will be beautiful because . . . *you* are beautiful." That hoary phrase of the sixties suggests that structure is secondary to "your own thing." To counter, I almost gleefully suggest on the first day of 434 that "you are not beautiful. You are ugly, misshapen and not dissimilar to a swamp frog. But . . . you are about to be kissed by a princess called the UCLA writing program and a prince who thinks he is visually Robert Redford but periodically confesses to being Lew Hunter."

I submit you put down your hard- or easy-earned dollars to learn TO WRITE A SCREENPLAY. That is what this book will be about. I and no one can teach you talent. You *can* be taught screenwriting. But before you close this book weakly murmuring, "I can't write," I quote you my own UCLA screenwriting professor of the fifties, Arthur Ripley. He used to suggest to such people they write him a letter telling him they can't write.

You can do it, Charlie, Jane, Mel, Mary. *All* of you. You do have to want to, though. It's called "seat" writing: seat of pants to seat of chair.

The Old Testament says, "God sometimes chooses the strangest vessels from which to pour the sweetest wine." I do consider myself to be a vessel. A vessel of thirty-plus years of trying to persuade audiences to laugh and cry. A vessel of hundreds of writers I have known and brilliant strangers I have voraciously read. I have a reasonable amount of intelligence and a maximum amount of passion. This book aims to merge all these ingredients for wine to make you drunk with inspiration, creativity, and effectiveness.

I am a camera, a vessel, Robert Redford, a farm boy from Guide Rock, Nebraska, who ran out of town to catch a pop fly and never got back. *Most of all I am you.* Another swamp frog. Let us join together and be kissed by the prince and princesses in the following pages. Ribbit.

FILMS TO SEE

Books on screenwriting use a blizzard of film titles as examples of their authors' profundity. There are so many that you often feel left out of the discussion when a point is made. You just know if you could correlate the insight with having seen the film, you'd snare the meaning to life, screenwriting, and sex.

Since I fully expect you to glean from this book your unraveling of all three of these human mysteries, I want you to have a viewing relationship with a mere five movies available at your neighborhood video store. I strongly suggest running the ones you have not yet seen before turning this page. I will mention other movies but they are not "must sees."

The fantastic five are, in zero order of preference or significance are:

Citizen Kane
Casablanca
Butch Cassidy and the Sundance Kid
Fallen Angel
(my 1981 TV movie)
E.T.

Chapter 1

IDEAS

When the cave people were sitting around the fire eating hot pterodactyl wings, someone said, "Irving, tell us a story." Irving was always the one chosen because he had the ideas that best held their attention through laughter, tears, and the good stuff in between. The first storyteller, if you will.

In my opening 434 graduate class, I bring in a gaggle of storytellers, small figures from countries my wife, Pamela, and I have visited around the world. I started this collection when I first visited Africa. In Nairobi, I found a wooden man with his finger in the air, as if he were telling a story, and from there my collection grew. I often look at the figures as I write and contemplate my (and their) stories:

A young Russian boy holds a fish and clearly gestures with his free hand about the "one that got away." Buddha strums a mandolin to communicate his tale. A laughing Fiji god can drop his pants to reveal his phallic self on the punch line of an obvious joke. An Aztec god from Mexico City coolly has his hand drawn to his chest, pausing in his drama. A Maori warrior sticks out his tongue for story emphasis. A hula girl rolls her story from supple hips.

For a quotient of reality, all of my storytellers face a plaster of paris Notre Dame gargoyle, his elbows on a ledge, his grotesque chin resting in cupped palms. He is the Audience. An audience that wants your ideas. Your *good* ideas. Ideas that can move them to take their chins out of their hands and tilt that chin forward in anticipation of comedy, drama, excitement, inspiration, escape.

THE ANATOMY OF SCREEN IDEAS

Where do you get your ideas?" That's easily the query most fielded by professional writers from "normal" people. If I am in a particularly off-center mood, I'll tell them:

"You want a wonderful idea? Let me tell you *exactly* where to go. Every Monday morning get to the Thrifty Drugstore on the corner of Hollywood Way and Magnolia in Burbank. Go around to the alley, in the back. There are two black guys on the loading dock. Every Monday morning at 9 o'clock, these guys give out ideas. You be there."

As silly as this story seems, I submit the question is equally silly. And everybody really knows it. In life, *you are the most important person in your world.* So it is for screenwriting. Look within *you* for creation, for inspiration, for ideas.

Someone once suggested to author Willa Cather that Nebraska, her home state, "surely couldn't be much of a storehouse for literary material." Cather strongly responded, "Of course Nebraska is a storehouse of literary material. Everywhere is a storehouse of literary material. If a true artist were born in a pigpen and raised in a sty, he would still find plenty of inspiration for his work. The only need is the eye to see."

Studio chief/professor Peter Guber tells his UCLA students. "God is in the details." To be a quality screenwriter, you must *see* the emotional and physical details of your human race.

See the man absently scratching his scrotum while talking to his minister. See the frustration in a woman twisting her wedding ring when her husband goes on and on to others about nothing. See a ringbearer child pick boogers at his sister's wedding. See the embarrassment in a woman trying to conceal her box of extra-large Kotex in the middle of her overflowing shopping cart. See how Willa Cather saw: read her masterpiece, *My Antonia.* See how John Steinbeck saw: read *Grapes of Wrath.* See how Hemingway, F. Scott Fitzgerald, et al., saw. Get the screenplays of *Citizen Kane, Butch Cassidy and the Sundance Kid, E.T.,* and see how their screenwriters Herman Mankiewicz and Orson Welles and William Goldman and Melissa Mathison saw. The ideas are out there and right under your nose and inside of you. *You must develop* the eye to see. You can do it. Even more than you already do.

John Gardner once wrote: "A story with a stupid central idea, no matter how brilliantly the story is told, will be a stupid story."

What are the criteria for your good idea?

1. Conflict

The idea must promise CONFLICT. That's the heart *and* soul of screenwriting. In his book *Adventures in the Screen Trade,* screenwriter William Goldman *(Butch Cassidy and the Sundance Kid, Misery)* repeatedly says screenplays are most importantly "structure." I say, "Yes, and also most importantly, screenplays are conflict." One of the goals of my 434 class is to demystify the writing of screenplays and not to cloak the process in a spiritual-academic-psycho-babble-guruish fog. Conflict. Is that demystifying enough? In short, never put two people in the same scene who agree with each other.

Both Hitler and Goering surely wanted to invade Poland. Goering says, "Great, we'll attack from the east." Hitler screams "No, no! The north, you dummy!" See what I mean? They may agree with the overall goal but the conflict comes from how-to-get-there.

Norman Lear believes that "the best scenes are 'why are these two people arguing and why are *both* right?' " Remember the wonderful moments with Archie Bunker and Meathead? My fellow UCLA screenwriting professor Richard Walter, on this same subject, proclaims, "Nobody wants to see a story about the Village of the Happy People."

Mark Twain insisted that "The secret source of humor is not joy but pain." And pain is *always* the result of conflict. "My wife is leaving me." "I have cancer." "My lover came back." "It's harder to rob banks nowadays." "I want to go home." All of these are classic personal conflicts that have become wonderful drama *and* comedy.

2. Will Your Idea Go the Distance?

The Bibles of the performance writing-arts are Aristotle's *Poetics* and Lajos Egri's *The Art of Dramatic Writing.* Now is the time to begin talking about Aristotle's two-thousand-year-old "beginning-middle-end" structure. Aristotle was the first to put the storyteller's trade tricks down on paper. The beginning-middle-end concept is in Plato's *Republic,* but the elaboration of this insight you will find in Aristotle's *Poetics.* For more demystification, buy that slim volume, read it twice, then pick it up every three or four years and read it during your screenwriting career. Those are the few rules we have and need.

Contemporary playwrights and screenwriters use the "three-act structure" phrase as shorthand for their beginnings, middles, and ends. As you know, plays today are generally two acts in actual length. Shakespeare's *Julius Caesar, Macbeth, Romeo and Juliet,* and many other of his dramas have five acts. Don't get caught up in the literalization of the three-act structure.

Get caught up in the reality that the contemporary Act One, the beginning, is *the situation.* The idea. Why you call people to their neighborhood multiplex. Act Two, the middle, is *the complications.* The plot must thicken. Cause and effect. Push and shove. The third act, the end, is *the conclusion.* The climax. The catharsis. The wrap-up.

The scripts you release to the outside world should run between 100 and 110 pages. So, though you're not writing the script yet, you should have a good idea that promises to reveal itself completely around page 17 in estimated page count. That's your Act One. Act Two should take you from page 17 to approximately page 85. In this act, you develop the comedic or dramatic complications, the quicksand for most writers.

Generally we get Butch and Sundance to Bolivia, or E.T. on the way home, by approximately page 85 for the third act's unfolding. But the build from Act One to Act Three covers *so* much paper and thought. Let's see, page 17 to 85 or so is . . . gasp . . . at least sixty-eight pages! Therein lies the meaning of screenwriting life and the most necessary component in your accepting your own fabulous idea. Be forewarned. The second act is where many and even most movies get into their deepest trouble.

Pick an idea that promises lots of complications and ways to spin an audience into different emotions. You can't fill sixty-eight pages with a one-note story or one-joke comedy, so don't even try. Make sure your idea can carry the whole 100- to 110-page script. To repeat, *the idea is the most important.* The structure is second. Ironically, the script itself is least important. Of course it takes the most time. But a story and script can be "fixed." The idea can't.

3. Nothing in the Mind, Please

Don't pick ideas where most of the drama or comedy happens in the mind. Artists, writers, actors, architects are generally boring heroes because their inner conflicts are not easily dramatized, verbalized, or visualized.

A writer once came to me at Disney to present an idea. He had this story about a box that talked, walked, had arms and legs of a sort, and wore a gray fedora. Emotionally, the box had totally human characteristics. The box came to live with a shy young man and they bonded in an "odd couple" relationship. The box would go out and party while the young bachelor went to libraries. The box tried to get the young human into the life of life without success. The box's climactic adventure caused him to be captured by a governmental bureau (à la the FBI) who decided to destroy the carefree, troublemaking, lovable, and ergo clearly subversive box. "They" put him on a junkyard conveyor belt to be crushed at the belt's conclusion. The machines throughout the metropolis rebelled. Stoplights, jackhammers, hair driers, Mixmasters, and washing machines all went berserk in human-like rebellion for their box-friend. The young man then surpassed his previously exhibited abilities to heroically save his swinging roommate box for a funny and emotional third act.

I thought this tale could be marvelous for Disney, but none of the staff producers responded with equivalent glee. I finally went to producer/writer Bill Walsh, their peer of peers. I explained my dilemma, along with the story I suspect he had already seen. Bill patiently and kindly listened. When I finally concluded, he took a draw on his cigar, wriggled his mustache, and simply said: "Yeah, it's kind of funny, Lew. But have you thought about how that box would play up on screen?"

The sun burst through with rays of knowledge! This is a story idea that plays beautifully in the mind but when you get to the rectangular screen, it will be a box talking to a human and vice versa. It *will not* "play"! The audience has a prior knowledge about boxes. They are square or rectangular. Period. Remember the infamous George Lucas movie *Howard the Duck?* Because we all know what a duck looks like, Lucas could not get an audience to suspend their belief that Howard was a little person in a duck suit. It was a good duck suit but that's all it was and because of that, the thin strand of credibility that exists between seat and screen was irreparably snapped. On the other hand, we truly don't know what an alien creature looks like. This lack of knowledge allowed us to suspend our disbelief with E.T.

4. And No "Talking Head" Pictures

Always pick stories that scream for visualization. Talking heads are for the stage. You are writing screenplays, where the world is your oyster *and* your canvas. The world is yours; use it grandly.

I am almost angry that *My Dinner With André* was ever made. I feel that dinner scenes are among the biggest bores in the world: talk, talk, talk, talk. Yet, *André* was a lovely "small" movie that I would be proud to have in my filmography because of the beautifully written inner conflict and tension between two vulnerable men.

André prompts me to make my customary 434 disclaimer: I'm *always* talking generalities when I make encompassing statements in this opus. There will constantly be exceptions to my pronouncements. But please, please don't invalidate a general filmmaking rule by single or minor exceptions.

What I'm trying to convey are the basic rules. Not Lew Hunter's rules but the rules of screen history stretching back to the American invention of motion pictures by Thomas Edison. I vigorously tell my 434 gatherings it is wildly important to first learn the rules, before you start bending or breaking them.

So, as a rule, stay away from premises that promise drama in the mind or talking-head movies.

5. Sex and Violence

A painter has three primary colors on his palette: red, blue, and yellow. Everything else has kinship to those colors. As a screenwriter, you have two primary *emotional* colors: *sex* and *violence.*

When I first taught, one of the most sensitive students confessed to being actually angry at me for stressing this sex-violence concept. He thought I was talking about the Roger Corman-Brian DePalma ice pick in the eye-slasher garbage.

I drew out the plot lines of such classics as *Medea, Oedipus Rex, Hamlet, King Lear,* Ibsen's works, and anything by Tennessee Williams to buttress the case I apparently hadn't sufficiently built in his 434 class. Greek theater, Shakespeare, and actually everything of quality known to Western persons has a significant undertow of sex or violence or a combination thereof. To deny it is insane and even worse, wrong.

Freud insisted that sexuality is part of our every waking and non-waking thought. Remember your high school or college Psych 101 equivalent? Look at the movie ads in your local newspaper this very second. Easily eight out of ten ads will appeal to at least one of those basic human emotions. Not prurient, basic.

Rather than using the strong words "sex" and "violence," you may be more comfortable with the terms "sensuality" and "dramatic action." This does not mean blood and gore and naked bodies. Sometimes the most extreme form of violence is psychological violence. Excruciating sexual tension can occur in a scene where not one article of clothing is removed from a body. Tennessee Williams runs those sorts of dramatic bases brilliantly. Consider his *Streetcar Named Desire* or *Cat on a Hot Tin Roof.* Or Bergman and his *Wild Strawberries*. Eugene O'Neill and *Mourning Becomes Electra.*

John Wilder, who was the executive producer to my supervising producership on "The Yellow Rose" (an NBC television series), used to insist on "passion and tension" in every scene. That was his way of saying "sex and violence." The writing staff used to say, "Oh, no, we've got to put more P and T in for John." Of course, we all knew it was really for the audience, but John was the drill sergeant and making him happy was our initial hurdle. Passion and tension. Sensuality and dramatic action. It all simply comes down to S-E-X and V-I-O-L-E-N-C-E.

Actually I best like the semantics of sensuality and dramatic action. If you don't have sensuality or dramatic action in the Shakespearean or Greek theater sense of the word, you will likely have to pass out caffeine-laced popcorn to your audience. It will most certainly be "Village of the Happy People" time.

Did I sense your thought that *The Sound of Music* didn't fit the mold? Nonsense! The Nazis were the overall threat; the feelings between Maria and the children's father were sensual as hell. The life and death of the little alien threaten in *E.T.* The emotional violence between Hannibal Lecter and Clarice Starling in *The Silence of the Lambs*. The sexual tension and frustration between Archie and Edith Bunker. The list goes on and on.

The bottom line is, make sure your idea has the potential for sex and/or violence. You're then also halfway over the fence as far as your idea goes for second-act story stamina. Most importantly, your idea will now cause an audience to tilt forward in their seats with anticipation.

GETTING YOUR IDEA

In my beginnings as a writer, I had an "idea file" to which I contributed notions every now and then. Scraps like "Judge Parker's hangman." "A man cannot go beneath a certain longitude plane or he will die." "Update *Hunchback of Notre Dame.*" The notion of an idea file might be an account as valuable to you as any traditional bank savings account.

There are simply hordes of places for ideas. Places for you to see and go, internally *and* literally.

1. The Library

It sounds obvious but sometimes the most obvious is the most neglected. Set your writer's body in your favorite library section. Maybe it's music *(Amadeus)*. Or science fiction *(2001)*. Or sociology *(Fallen Angel)*. How about Americana *(Billy The Kid/Young Guns)?* Travel *(If It's Tuesday, This Must Be Belgium)*. Sports *(Field of Dreams)*. Classic literature *(Romeo and Juliet)*.

All of these screenplays could have been inspired by such a trip to your library. Of course *Field of Dreams* (based on the book *Shoeless Joe Jackson*) was literally in the fiction section, also fertile soil for screenplays. Many, many excellent books are yet to be mined from library's stacks. Getting rights to adapt the book into a screenplay is something you can accomplish if you contact the publisher and negotiate an approval. Remember though, that often means money. Unless you find something in the public domain (but check that with the publisher, too).

I purposely do not have a section emphasizing adapting books. After adapting many and working with book adaptations as an executive, I strongly believe the problems and opportunities are the same as in developing an original screenplay. The collection of facts is the only difference. Theoretically, the story and the necessary research information are already in the book. Often that is not the case, so you then resort to original research and original story development.

2. Magazines

Urban Cowboy and *Panic in Needle Park* had their genesis in magazine articles. As with books, money is likely to be required for the story, often paid to the original writer of the article. My sometime producing partner, Terry Keegan, saw a *People* magazine piece on the famous Tucker family in Kentucky, who adopted and raised a horde of children. He tracked the Tuckers down through a series of phone calls and negotiated the rights for the upcoming movie of their lives. It's that simple. Often zero money is needed up front to acquire rights. Dollars can be agreed upon when you've made a sale to a studio, network, or producer. This procedure is called the "Free Option" time. That most often includes your right to work with the story exclusively for an agreed-upon period (six months to two years is the norm). Such an agreement should include prearranged dollars or a percentage of profits for publication, merchandising, and worldwide rights. Have your lawyer get all the rights possible, which simultaneously gives you flexibility to relinquish some possible profits for the final "deal" structure. Sometimes all of these direct and ancillary rights are very hard to get. Sometimes they're easy to get. Ask, maybe ye shall receive. Do not trust dated book information. Seek a good entertainment attorney.

3. Newspapers

Pick up this morning's paper. Look at the front page. There'll be around ten stories. I guarantee you that six have the material for marvelous screenplays.

Maybe you'll read about a plane disaster *(Flight 409)* or the TWA purser who had to use her Shell credit card to pay for a hijacked plane's gas on the tarmac in 1985 Algiers. Perhaps Midwestern farms are going under *(Country* or *Bitter Harvest)*. A mass murderer *(Badlands)*. Aliens spotted *(Close Encounters of the Third Kind)*. A person who is perceived to be retarded but is in fact a savant *(Rain Man)*. A woman who studies wild animals *(Gorillas in the Mist)*. Are these rights available? Sometimes yes. Are they in public domain because they're in the newspaper? Often yes. Consult your nearest lawyer for rooting out the exact rights information if you're nervous. It may cost you a bit but your peace of mind will be worth the expenditure. You can call the newspaper and they will often point you to the people in the story. That will save lawyer legwork dollars. But eventually, you're going to need permissions via the law.

4. Biographies

You've always been fascinated or obsessed by Gandhi, Churchill, Mozart, Louis Pasteur, Alexander Graham Bell, Amelia Earhart, Howard Hughes, Hugh Hefner, Hugh Walpole, Groucho, Carry Nation, Adolf Hitler, or any one of thousands of alive/dead famous people? They're fair and good game. Sometimes you can glean enough material through newspapers and personal interviews. Often a book saves you such research and its dramatization rights are available. However you secure permission, you should finally check with your lawyer and tell him/her whom you want to write about and how you're getting the information so the proper permissions can be collected. If the subject has been dead at least sixty years, less approvals will be required. If they've recently gone to their reward or are still alive, you'll need various approvals and possible dollars to invest in your passion.

And then there are the internationally obscure personalities who have great story potential. Maybe the local basketball coach who challenged a group of losers to win *(Hoosiers)*. The high school teacher who inspired his math class *(Stand and Deliver)*. Or even your Aunt Minnie or Cousin Elmo or friend Fred. Everyone thinks they have a fabulous story. I'm talking about the one person you've come across who truly *did* have a fantastic story. Go for them. All can be strong grist for your screenwriting mill. When in legal doubt on anything, you really should work it out through a lawyer. Richard Walter's book *Screenwriting*, Cynthia Whitcomb's *Selling Your Screenplay*, and Michael Hauge's *Writing Screenplays That Sell* have legal and "option" pages that can prepare you for that eventual lawyer.

5. Classics

The French say it best. Pay "homage." Americans say "rip off." How inelegant. I'll say "appropriate" the plot of a classic novel or play and dress it with the clothes of whatever period you like.

Red River's plot was taken from *Mutiny on the Bounty:* Cowboys rebelling on a cattle drive instead of sailors on the high seas. *West Side Story* was *Romeo and Juliet* in a New York gang-infested neighborhood. *The Magnificent Seven* from *The Seven Samurai.* Ray Bradbury wrote a famous radio play, *Leviathan '99,* which he referred to as "a tip of the hat to Herman Melville." It's about a mad spaceship captain after a great white comet, *Moby Dick.* Joseph Conrad's *Heart of Darkness* begat Francis Coppola's and John Milius's *Apocalypse Now,* etc.

My first "out of the writing closet" screenplay came not from "homage" but from a desperate need to get a story line that could most effectively illuminate what happened to the Japanese-Americans before, during, and after Pearl Harbor. Everything I originally developed was far too preachy, reflecting my personal outrage for the persecuted. Messages really are for Western Union, as the old show biz saw goes.

Then I bought a ticket for Franco Zeffirelli's film of Shakespeare's *Romeo and Juliet.* Click, the light bulb switched on. The Caucasians could be the Capulets, the Issei and Nisei the Montagues. My Juliet would be Caucasian, and Romeo a Nisei. The exact historical and classical parallels kept developing from that conceptual point. It became an ABC motion picture for television in 1971. *If Tomorrow Comes* starred Patty Duke, James Whitmore, Anne Baxter, Mako, and Pat Hingle.

It worked out quite well, thank you, Bill S. All's fair in love, war, and developing story lines from public domain books or stage classics.

6. Conversations You've Had

In my *If Tomorrow Comes* case, the original idea came from history and from a conversation with my Long Beach uncle in 1959. He casually said all the "Japanese were put in relocation camps after Pearl Harbor for their own safety." I said, "Wait a minute! That never made the schoolbooks in Nebraska education. You mean over one hundred thousand people, mostly Americans, were put behind barbed wire in America within the last thirty years?" I was stunned. "Internment story" went into my idea file to be retrieved ten years later and developed into a remunerative ABC screenplay.

7. Overheard Conversations

Neil Simon's brother Danny was living with a buddy and future agent Roy Gerber when the two men were getting their first divorces. Neil overheard Roy say to Danny: "Wait a minute, Danny! We don't need to be faithful to our wives anymore. Let's do something Saturday night. I'll get some girls. Have them over, you'll cook. Why not?" Danny's eyes squinted. "What time Saturday night, Roy?" "Oh, hell, you know, Danny. Six, seven, maybe eight." To which Danny verily screamed, "What do you mean six, seven, *maybe* eight?! What about my roast!" From that overheard conversation, *The Odd Couple* was welcome to the world.

Just as you need the eye to see, you also need the ear to hear and overhear. One screenwriter friend periodically comes out of his Bel Air cave and rides city buses without any geographic destination. His creative destination is to overhear "real people" talk for dialogue, stories, and scenes. Erich Segal and Martin Scorcese were also reported to have received the ideas for *Love Story* and *The Baby Maker* through overheard conversations at bars.

F. Scott Fitzgerald was famous for his always-present pencil and journal, to his friends' constant irritation. He was always noting bits of heard and overheard conversations. Around Hollywood's then infamous Garden of Allah Hotel, Robert Benchley was forever threatening to stick Fitzgerald's writing gear where the sun, moon, *and* stars don't shine. Despite such threats, Fitzgerald managed to come up with some pretty good stories.

You're concerned about the morality of writing about conversations direct or overheard, as F. Scott Fitzgerald wasn't? I offer a William Faulkner quote: "An artist is a creature driven by demons. He doesn't know why they choose him and he's usually too busy to wonder why. He is completely amoral in that he will rob, borrow, beg, or steal from anybody and everybody to get the work done."

A famous story around Hollywood for years has been about Stirling

Silliphant *(In the Heat of the Night, Route 66, Naked City)*. Stirling's twenty-year-old son was tragically killed by someone who broke into his apartment and gunned him down. Stirling was explaining the view of the boy's room and body in the aftermath over the phone to a writer friend. As his passion and anguish grew, the writer friend interrupted. "Uh, uh, Stirling, could you talk a little slower?" *The son of a bitch had been taking it down.*

So maybe Fitzgerald, Faulkner, or Silliphant's friend can help you with the morality of taking from life, death, heard and overheard conversations. If not, not. Exorcise them from your mind, then you without writer's sin, cast the first stone.

8. Experience

As Tolstoy put it so eloquently, "One ought to write only when one leaves a piece of one's flesh in the inkpot each time one dips one's pen."

Your experience in the flesh is not only the best place to get ideas but those are the ideas that you will write best about. Some of them may be too painful or too immediate, but with the perspective of time you'll get a script out of it.

Check out Hemingway, Cather, Fitzgerald, Hellman, Faulkner, and on and on. Read *What Makes Sammy Run?*, *Huckleberry Finn, Moby Dick, Cannery Row,* and on and on. All authors who wrote from exact experiences, all novels written from exact experiences.

Willa Cather said, "I became an artist when I stopped admiring and started remembering."

9. Arenas

Arenas are an excellent place for ideas. I do not mean setting or locale but an entire self-contained physical and human world. Let's say you're interested in the world of the lumberjack. It's got sociological scope, visuals for the screen, and most importantly, *humans in stress.*

After your idea, you must enter into that lumberjack arena through experience or research and learn everything possible to develop an exceptional story. *Sometimes a Great Notion* (about an actual lumber family), *Jaws, D. C. Cab, Carwash, Diner, Mystic Pizza, Network, Wall Street,*

Talk Radio, Urban Cowboy, Platoon, and *Backdraft* were all movies initiated by writers who had an inordinate interest in the arenas of those stories, which served as a canvas for *humans in stress.* As Hemingway put it, you need an opportunity to have your hero/heroine demonstrate "grace under pressure."

Not only must you have knowledge of the arena; the arena itself should have something special for the audience to *see.* While they used to be called "Talkies," *now* they're movies and movies have to move. Yet the arena does not have to be a physical place. An arena can be spectacularly mental. For my *Fallen Angel,* I was initially interested in the arena of child pornography. It seemed fresh and dramatic. An arena of the mind for characters *and* audience.

10. Issues

My idea for *Desperate Lives* sprang from my obsession with the issue of drugs destroying our teenagers. Long before "just say no," I saw myself as a contemporary Paul Revere, warning "the drugs are coming, the drugs are coming." *If Tomorrow Comes* was born from the issue of Japanese-American internment. A constellation of television movies have been appropriated from "60 Minutes" issues.

Consider issues that particularly interest or inflame you. They're always in the news and always all about you if you in your personal *see* and *feel.*

11. History

Beyond your own experience, history is probably the most fertile field for ideas and probably the least sellable. Oh yes, a few historical pieces are shown on television and a minuscule few get through the theatrical movie system, but unless the incident has some contemporary relevance, it's a very hard sell. But no matter. If you get something in your writing teeth you have *got* to do, *do it.*

Forget about the marketplace. Follow your obsession. Obsession makes the best screen*play* character drive for screenplays, and obsession makes the best screen*writer* drive for you. Bill Goldman wrote a full *Butch and Sundance* screenplay on his own (without a paycheck). For Goldman and the screenplay, the gamble turned into a jackpot.

Most historical TV- or movie-movies have someone behind them with a stove-hot obsession. An "I'm-going-to-write-this-story" obsession. The dramatic dynamics of that passion, coupled with your historical subject matter, *can* collide to create a simply wonderful script.

12. Fantasies

Do you want to be someone you're not? I want to be in love with Pearl Hart, a woman outlaw in the Old West. Since I'm a Western freak, being any of the old gunfighters would be just excellent.

Maybe your fantasy is to be the toughest cop on any beat. Or a modern Amelia Earhart. Or a woman president. Or to go to Oz. Or into *The Abyss*. Or deep space. Or to be more James Bond than James Bond.

Fantasies are important for your ideas. Lucas and Spielberg certainly tapped into their fantasies when they created Indiana Jones, and I urge you to tap into your fantasies in everything that's even remotely connected to your screenwriting self. If we believe people in the mental health profession, your fantasies are bonded to your subconscious and that's where the creative juices of your screenwriting abilities lie. Wake up your fantasies whenever and wherever you can.

In our personal lives, we often find our fantasies are far more rewarding than reality. That's why you wanted to be a writer. It's like being a child again playing "make believe," but your mother doesn't call you in for supper. As you will get ideas from reality and pain, you may also find the equivalent mother lode in fantasy.

13. Fears

When stuck for an idea, another wellspring can be your own fears.

The most obvious creator who taps into his own fears, and simultaneously ours, is Steven Spielberg. Sharks, snakes, spiders, outer space, Nazis. In *Jaws, Raiders of the Lost Ark, Close Encounters of the Third Kind.* Stephen King, Edgar Allan Poe, Alfred Hitchcock all use fear to an electric effect.

Courtroom, prison, and medical dramas function at this primal level. For both creator and audience. None of us wants to be on trial, or in a cell, or in an operating room. Such fear can merge with your personal paranoia to create an idea that plugs into basic audience emotions. This connection can become a full screenplay of powerful writing.

14. What If . . . ?

The word "tricks" is unfortunately pejorative. As are "gimmicks," "devices," "tools," "contrivance," "formulas," and "craft." I fiercely maintain there can be *good* tricks, gimmicks, devices, tools, contrivance, formulas, and craft. Here is one method of idea discovery that is a positive trick: The "what if . . ." trick.

What if your daughter was led into child pornography? What if a shark went on a killing rampage? A cuddly outer space alien was left behind on earth? What if a woman went to live with gorillas? What if you discovered your son was a homosexual? Your wife a hooker? What if an earthquake hit Los Angeles? All were very successful TV or theatrical movies.

"What if" can be an excellent gauge for your budding idea but be careful the "what if" doesn't get too complicated. Remember though, many ideas are predominantly dependent upon execution. *Citizen Kane* and *Casablanca* would not be wonderful "what if" notions, as you've got to explain too much, but their scripts and execution were magnificent.

15. Love Stories

When you're considering an idea for a love story, always remember there *must* be an exceptional obstacle.

Love itself was the obstacle for the Arthur-Guinevere-Lancelot troika. And the *Casablanca* three. William Faulkner always felt the way to a best-seller was to put a woman between two men.

In our contemporary world, the traditional obstacles of race, color, creed, social, and economic barriers don't work as well as they once did. Yes, they are certainly present, but the audience doesn't now accept them to be overwhelming problems as we have seen them dealt with in many, many screen stories. Even mixing the genders, using Faulkner's formula, has become clichéd.

This is why most of our contemporary love stories are about "the halt, the lame, and the blind." For instance, *Dying Young, Children of a*

Lesser God, Longtime Companion. Physical disabilities continue to be real and somewhat new, as ailments and diseases are constantly being discovered.

If you find a fairly fresh obstacle, grab it, because we're all suckers for love stories. Ergo, you would also be well to always have a love story inside your principal plot. Romance of any degree gives an identifiable and vicarious overlay to your basic idea. Sometimes it's the glue that holds the various plot and character elements together. The cement that fills in the dramatic or comedic cracks. But whether you use love as cement, glue, or meringue, it's consistently a win-win emotion for your screenplays.

16. Revenge as Idea Stimulus

One writer friend was angry with a producer who had badly filmed one of his "love children" scripts. He chose to exorcise his rage through writing a violent, hard Western. Thumbing through his gunfighter books, he discovered Ben Thompson, the most feared gunfighter in his bloody era. Most who have read the script believe it's his best extant work. He's not sure about that, but he does know how cathartic it felt to write.

Bern Slade created many successful television comedies in the sixties and seventies. He wrote a series for NBC called "The Girl with Something Extra," starring Sally Field as a woman with ESP. Well, Bern felt NBC gave him a very difficult time with that series. After its eventual death, he vowed to write a stage play that would become an American little theater staple because it would not only be funny but cheap to produce. He would then never have to depend upon television for table bread. From that revenge stimulus, *Same Time, Next Year* was written. No doubt it was also cathartic to write.

So maybe there's that boss, or ex-husband, or job you'd like to take and "shove it." Do it in a script. Something good for the screen and for you could well happen.

17. Ideas from Concepts

Ideas are often more fragmentary than concepts. Ideas suggest your story's beginning. Concepts have both the beginning, a promise of the end, and often the second act, the middle. As a joke, Mort Sahl's capital punishment line, "If you don't kill them, how else are they going to learn" would be a concept that doesn't have an apparent second act. The same may be said for Callie Khouri when she had the concept of "two women on a crime spree" which pushed her to write *Thelma & Louise.*

A strong concept is the most important ingredient of exceptional music videos, commercials, or trailers that bally upcoming movies or series. A concept can be said briefly and everyone gets it, as opposed to the aforementioned *Casablanca* and *Citizen Kane.*

Director Rob Reiner gave screenwriter Nora Ephron the concept of a man and woman who become best friends. "Both are afraid of screwing up their friendship by screwing. And they do." *When Harry Met Sally* . . . was thusly created.

Producer Brian Grazier was driving along the Malibu coastline. He wondered what would happen if a beautiful woman washed on shore, came up to him, and said "I love you." No other motivation but love. No "hidden agenda," as they say in shrinkage. Simply pure, selfless love. Voilà, *Splash.*

My movie on child pornography, *Fallen Angel,* evolved from a concept. I could understand adults trespassing on the sexual innocence of children but I couldn't understand why children let them. Most youngsters twist their faces and "yuk" at the first glimmer of a mere kiss. After research, I developed the concept that in America, children are in one isolated population grouping, adults in the middle, and senior citizens at the farthest end of our national human spectrum. Each group does not relate to the other. Hence, pornographers and pedophiles have an open field, as they can and want to relate to our neglected children, their prey. From such concepts come characters; from characters, story.

So if you come up with an idea from life or your thought process that's beyond newspapers, biographies, history, etc., I'd call that a concept. Concepts are often the most dimensional beginnings for your screenplay structures.

SELECTING THE IDEA

Now consider your ideas, then pick something you *want to write.* Let it come from fascination, obsession, or emotional desire. All of your reasons to write screenplays should initiate from any one or a combination of these three needs. Forget writing for money, which means trying to second guess what the marketplace wants. By the time you write the screenplay, the marketplace will generally have gone on to another fad. Buyers of screenplays will most likely change their wants many times after you click out "fade in" on your keyboard.

A 434-ite of yesteryear submitted an idea he was embarrassed to present. Scott Rosenberg felt the notion was *too* commercial. It was about a girl who wanted to ride in Elvis Presley's Cadillac. The class knew Scott had an unnatural fascination with Elvis, Graceland, etc., so we all screamed in near unison, "Do it!" Greg Nava *(El Norte)* was visiting our workshop and suggested a thought you should often remember. "Sometimes ideas are commercial because they are good." Have we put too negative a connotation on "commercial"? Shakespeare would say "yes." Even if screenplays seem "commercial," write something of worth that you want to write, that you can see, *and* that you are capable of writing.

1. Researching Your Idea

If you haven't lived an idea, should you write it? In a word, yes. In a second word, research. For you *can* research your ideas so thoroughly that the information *almost* gives you the pain of life. Or joy. Or both.

Stephen Crane was nineteen when he wrote *The Red Badge Of Courage,* his tale of a young soldier living the horror of the American Civil War. Crane was never in *any* war. This delicate, sensitive teenager experienced that scathing hell through *research.* Research *became* his experience.

I visited all the relocation concentration camps that in 1942 imprisoned our fellow Americans for *If Tomorrow Comes.* I read everything available on that national scar, talked to hundreds of people who were incarcerated, and went to many functions in which I bore the only non-Asian face.

Six months after I began, I started to tell an ancient, first generation Issei details about what had happened at his camp. I suddenly realized that I, by then, knew more overall than most people who had been catapulted into that tragedy of American history. It was time to stop researching and start writing. Too much research can be the disguise of procrastination or fear. Beware of those possibilities.

Lee Levinson, my fellow executive producer on *Playing With Fire* (an NBC movie about juvenile arson) called one day in 1984. He asked if I would be interested in doing a movie about Vietnam vets and their post-traumatic years after the conclusion of that *particular horror*. We'd call it *Welcome Home*.

I missed the Vietnam War, being in the throes of establishing a show business career. But the Vietnam War caught up with me. My *Welcome Home* research became intensive and obsessive, because of my own guilt for having paid so little attention to the war *and* the incredible stories from the men and women who shared its obscenities. I would wake in the middle of nights sweating and crying. My darling Pamela would hold and rock me to pull me down from nightmares bound into what I was hearing and seeing by day. Vicarious pain.

The L.A. Hall of Justice basement contains the confiscated child pornography evidence accumulated by the Sexual Abuse Unit of the Los Angeles Police Department. I was allowed to scour this zone for my researching of *Fallen Angel*. Reading about what people sexually do to children, going even back to the very second of birth, was the most emotional purgatory I have ever experienced. Vicarious horror.

My knowledge of child pornography, of Vietnam, and half of the movie scripts I've written started at ground zero. For better as a writer, and often worse as a human, I'm now considered to be an expert in those areas. All from research.

Research: the word does not signify magic, but work. Yet research can be a personal and professional enrichment, even when you're the repository for tragic pain and shock.

If you are reading this in concert with a screenwriting class, you will just not have the time to research *and* write over a semester's or quarter's time span. Research in the summer something you're obsessed to do during the academic year. If you don't have sufficient research time, choose comedy or drama ripped from your own life.

2. You Must Be Able to Write the Idea

What do you do with the ideas when you get them? If you've researched or lived the idea, chances are you'll know what to write. Research and/or experience should force you to spread your psychological guts out before you and deal with the truth as you see, feel, and sort through it. From such truth comes the best quality for your ideas that metamorphize into full stories.

It matters not a whit what, where, or how you've learned about your idea. It does matter immensely that you've learned. For your idea's sake. "But what about imagination in writing out ideas?" you ask. I say imagination is far better utilized to move your ideas beyond acknowledged truth. Hemingway said, "Truth is best served through fiction."

The truth in whatever you write about will be blended, condensed, arranged, and ultimately bloom inside your imagination. Truth will generally be even better as a transplant, than the initial flower itself.

Truth plus imagination equals brilliant screenplays. Each element needs the other. Each alone becomes screenplay writing that is false or boring. *Fallen Angel* is my strongest personal example. A true idea inside a fictitious story involving a twelve-year-old girl and her family and a pedophile.

That famous Russian teacher Constantin Stanislavsky lives in the acting craft through his teachings and 1948 book *An Actor Prepares*. So should he exist in your writing tool kit. Stanislavsky tells actors to take a similar emotion and transfer it to the emotion that is to be acted on stages. Such as it was with my transferring my love of children to the love of children by a man who steps them over the sexual boundary line.

Or, maybe your mother has yet to die and your character is in abject grief over a mother's suicide. Did you have a friend commit suicide? Did you feel shock and sorrow? Since a mother's similar death would surely have an even greater impact, double your protagonist's response dramatically in dialogue and action, in gesture and grieving.

The Stanislavsky method works as well for screenwriters as for actors. Know it, use it.

Speaking of Stanislavsky, if you haven't taken acting lessons or done any acting, DO IT! Act. It is absolutely necessary. How can you be a wonderful writer if you haven't personally experienced the moments that make your audience laugh or cry and all the good and even bad things in between? Feeling audience reaction as a spectator is important but *nothing* is like being before them.

A possible exception can be made for those of you who wish to write comedy. Most comedy writers have been entertaining their families since the doctor's slap on their flanks. You chosen few likely already know your audience. Still, acting opportunities wouldn't hurt.

For the rest of you, get some acting experience to lay on top of those furrowed brows. It'll be gold for you. Actors can make wonderful writers. Robert Towne, Paul Mazursky, Elaine May, Paddy Chayefsky, Woody Allen, and on and on. At the beginning of their careers, all did some acting which significantly carried over to their ultimate writing successes. Shakespeare himself is of course the crown jewel in this celestial fedora of actor/writers.

3. Movie or TV Idea?

"To be or not to be" is far less of a puzzle than what is or isn't a theatrical movie. The feature movie divisions of most major studios are now run by people that initially came from the television world. Yet one of the most damning comments that can come from these companies about your script is, "It's TV."

Large budget movies could not be done for television dollars. As production people will point out, you use wide full shots in features, corners of buildings for TV. "Battlestar Galactica," as a TV series, followed *Star Wars. Star Trek* swings from television to features and back to TV, as does *Batman.* The Vietnam War is "shot" for *Apocalypse Now* and "China Beach."

So budget is a sometime criteria for whether a script is a movie for TV or for theaters. More often a movie's initial showing relates to the "Robert" factor. If it's a movie movie, it stars Robert Redford. If it's a TV movie, Robert Conrad.

Could not *Rain Man, Witness, Parenthood,* and on and on have been made with TV stars instead of Dustin Hoffman, Harrison Ford, Steve Martin, and on and on? Absolutely.

It's often easier to get headline or social event pictures done as television movies. You see them weekly: the latest disease, tragedy, or urban malady. That's because from idea to air can be accomplished in a six-month period of time. Theatrical movies take two years plus from idea to your neighborhood Bijou.

Sometimes the story's "heat" will dictate its exhibition venue. *Gorillas in the Mist* started in television development but was instantly a theatrical film when Dian Fossey was murdered. You can't have control over those sorts of events, so worry not.

Worry instead about selecting the idea you must care for and know. Don't censor yourself in emotions, sexuality, violence, language, or budget initially. Go for truth in your stories. It's easier to pull back on emotions, sex, violence, language, or budget when any of those elements seem to prevent your film from being made for TV. You want that problem.

4. The Decision

And now . . . *the* decision. For this moment and your example, I'm going to select an idea that will fit my emotional desire and one that holds enormous fascination for me. Madness.

Yes, madness. I consider the people in a stadium crowd. Each of their faces takes up a near ten-by-seven-inch aggregate of flesh space. And every configuration is different. Most of the faces are sane. Some are insane. Who is who? Madness and how it becomes human is fascinating to me.

I believe it's equally fascinating to a significant audience. My audience and your audience. It's a subject matter very closely related to our fears. Remember picking ideas that relate to our fears? Is there anyone among us who does not fear our insanity potential? Who is not frightened of being "committed"?

Former NBC president Herb Schlosser used to field "one line" premises of series ideas that had been pitched to the program department the previous week. Herb would dismiss nearly everything by a wave of his right hand and a "who cares?" Nothing more was said. We'd go right on to the next idea. I thought at the time "who cares" was especially callous. I have since come to believe that "who cares" is key to reaching an audience. *People have to care* to come to the screen. I now think "who cares" is a test you should give every idea before you get deep into its development. I believe an audience will care about madness.

During *the* decision, ask yourself, "Do I know what I'm writing about?"

I can write about madness as I worked at the mental institution in Beatrice, Nebraska, during my undergraduate days. Remember, being fascinated and wanting to is not enough. Beyond experience, particularly when one deals with complex arenas, I'll buttress that knowledge by reading all that I can about madness. Such comprehensive knowledge is responsible, moral, and right. On madness and *any* subject.

Now for my emotional desire. I also want to write a love story.

Audiences love love stories, and *I can write* a love story. Two people in love with madness as the obstacle. That's also a story I want to write.

5. Hasn't It Been Done Before?

But wait, say you or anyone, haven't love stories in madhouses been done before?

Ecclesiastes 1:9–10. "The thing that hath been, it is that which shall be; and that which is done is that which shall be done; and *there is no new thing under the sun.* Is there anything whereof it may be said, see, this is new? It hath been already of old time, which was before us."

Everything's been done before. Forget *Lilith, David and Lisa, One Flew Over the Cuckoo's Nest,* and a number of other "madness" plots and subplots already forgotten.

The second 434 rule (after the first rule, "you will turn in a draft in nine weeks") is, "you will *never* tell yourself or anyone that it's been done." We don't give a rodent's behind that someone else has done it before because they could not have done it the way you will. Always remember, individualism is what makes screenplays great, not their uniqueness.

It's *not what* you do *but how* you do. That is the razor's edge. No one can speak to madness in the context of a love story the way I can. Or you can.

6. Is the Idea Good for You to Write?

Now, your next to last idea selection question should be, "Is the idea good for me to write?" This may itself prompt a gaggle of career questions for the professional writer and the new writer.

When you're a new writer you must ask yourself if the idea will significantly help you develop your potential: 1. Can you best learn from this script? 2. Will it show people what a good writer you are? A "calling card" script, if you will. 3. Can you possibly get it sold somewhere downstream? Still, while you can keep this thought in mind, don't get caught up in the selling process. Leave that for your future days as a card-carrying WGA member.

Focus on the best development of your potential. Will your idea serve that necessary end? You need a resounding "yes" reply.

For me, I want the idea to be something that's psychologically right for me to write. Are my head, my heart, and my soul in an alignment that will produce my optimum work? The right answer must always be the same for you and the 434 student. "Yes, this is good for me to write."

As for the "Will it be a good calling card script for me?" question, I have written over fifty screenplays. Three scripts back I got a wonderful agent from a screenplay about literacy in the ghetto. It enabled her to see my current ability. Other scripts I have written have prompted people to meet with me to talk about my ideas for future scripts. Even if the topic is different, the calling card script can be submitted to show someone that you can write their project or idea. So for the new *and* professional screenwriter, yes, you want a good calling card script.

And now, for the easiest question to answer, of course you want to get it sold. Not downstream, immediately. In fact, yesterday. However, if you do sell, you do. If you don't you've created another "property" for your inventory. Notice the word is "inventory" and not "trunk"? Trunk is so totally negative. Inventory sounds like the Sears catalog or even better, Tiffany's. Somebody is looking for a Western? You've got it. A historical piece? You're covered. In the script I'm writing for this book, I'll have a love story, the one you are about to see developed.

Even if this "love story in a madhouse" or any of your scripts you write "on speculation" *never* sell, you must *love the process.* That should be more important to you than acceptance or sale. Make your principal reward the very act of writing. That will keep you psychologically afloat and able to handle those difficult and numerous rejections. "The journey is all, the end is nothing," said André Gide. Yes, this idea can be good for me to write. The journey can be all.

7. The Worth of Your Idea

Now I've done my research and I'll add in what I've experienced over the years. Some will be applicable, some not, but it'll all go in the gestation swamp. I think I'll make the lovers young, but not too young. Somewhere between the ages of nineteen and twenty-two, as I don't want the audience to think my hero and heroine are in puppy love.

Their love must have the potential to be real and forever. That'll heighten the jeopardy. Raise the stakes.

And I don't want both of them to be insane. That was done nicely in *David and Lisa.* It's good to know the films that have gone before so you can learn what "not to do" and also stay away from the identical beats. Though everything has been done before, one wants to be smart and individual and not *too* similar.

I'll call it "Love Story in a Madhouse" as a working title for now. I want the audience to identify with the sane lover, and he or she can carry us into this exotic world. In my experience as a writer and as a human, I've found troubled women are seen as sympathetic and insane men aren't. In other words, we would feel sad that a woman has been incarcerated. If it were a man, we'd probably feel that he did something to deserve to be put there. So I'll make the sane one my young man.

Good. That's fine. That's the idea *I want to do*. That's the idea *I can do*. That's the idea I believe is *worth doing*. Want, can, worth. The three round holes into which you must fit your three round "idea" pegs.

Your last question to be answered should be, "Does my idea promise quality?" Before and after "want, can, and worth," demand for yourself *quality*. Forget making a living, being famous, or getting rich. If you're targeted on any of these goals, you'll fail yourself, your society, and your world. My mother kept insisting, "We were put on this earth to do something more than take up space." She was right.

Finally, let's for a moment hear those who claim that ideas are worthless. Didn't I clearly say, "The idea is the most important part of the screenwriting process"?

I did and do say exactly that. Yet I want to also proclaim that *it is a process.* As producer, and my vice president boss when I was at NBC, Stanley Robertson repeated again and again: "My grandmother has ideas but she can't write her way out of a paper bag. Probably even our dogs have ideas. It's how you *execute* the idea that separates the professionals from the amateurs, the grandmothers, and the dogs."

And so it shall be with you. And me. But we need that great idea to start writing our way out of that paper bag. To start the process. To write the script. Oscar-winning actress Shirley Booth once said, "If it ain't on the page, it ain't on the stage." With ideas in hand and mind, we are now equipped to move onward, to get it on the page.

Chapter 2

THE TWO-MINUTE MOVIE

Now comes the most precarious screenwriting cliff to climb: the story. Writer/professor Stanley Ralph Ross (TV's "Batman," "That's My Mama," "All in the Family") claimed to his class, during my guest-speaking turn, that I have been involved with the development of more stories in my guises as writer, executive, producer, and screenwriting professor than anyone else in the world. I did a whiplash double take. We took a moment to tally. My God, over thirty years in the business of show, over five thousand stories. Sigh and whew. I emphatically don't want to be pompous or claim oracle status, but I have, as we say in the Midwest, "been to town." So let's go to town and talk story.

Remember, at midpoint in the preceding chapter I said the idea is most important, the story the most difficult, and the script the easiest? Scripts are the most time-consuming, but they are simply the stories played out on paper. If the story is badly developed, that will *always* be reflected in the script. If the story works and the script is not wonderful, the script will need rewriting, but those hours are not nearly as terrorizing to a professional as major restructuring.

Why terror? Principally because it was such painstaking work to get the outline well structured enough to get to the script stage. A nearly equal reason is that the most simple "suggestion" must be minutely examined to see how its inclusion affects the story as a whole. That takes time and concentration. If you slip up even once, you will feel the boob.

Some writers abjectly shrink in humility when it comes to story development. Because of this lack of self-confidence, they make themselves prey for the many piranhas posing as executives, producers, and agents who seem to have little or no sense of story apprehension. Surely you've heard, "Fools rush in where angels fear to tread"? Actors also love to play with their lines, little realizing what they are rewriting can throw much of the story out of its careful, often delicate construction. For instance, an actor can't decide to let the character be unable to swim in the page 23 scene that is being shot today, when in two weeks page 74 will be filmed and the same character must save someone from drowning.

Most professional writers who hate or fear the story development part of the process are those not grounded in the fundamentals of Aristotle's *Poetics* and Lajos Egri's *The Art of Dramatic Writing.* Many start writing by the seat of their inspired pants, use their good instincts, and begin selling very early in their careers. They didn't start out with the basics, 434 or its equivalent. Some finally enroll in classes and they often come away much relieved. The most common reaction is, "Oh, that's what I've been doing."

You won't have the shrinking writer problem. If you comprehend these basics and read Aristotle and Egri, you'll have a firm grounding in story before, on, and after this page. Don't stop.

In the 434 classes, at this point, you should write a two-page, double-spaced, two-minute movie. Maybe you'll find it easier to take your wonderful idea and roll it around in your mind to the shape of a two-minute joke, clean or scatological. Both "dirty" jokes and clean jokes must have a structure to work. You must have a structure.

> As for the story, whether the poet takes it ready made or constructs it for himself, he should first sketch its general outline, and then fill in the episodes and amplify in detail. —Aristotle

When you're starting to build your story, begin by thinking about your three acts.

The best jokes have three laughs. Remember the Chaplin-Keaton-Lloyd silent movies? Comedy surprise after surprise and generally one, two, three before the next laugh sequence. Or the Jack Benny radio show when a thief accosted Benny in an alley and growled to the world's stingiest man: "Your money or your life." Laugh. "Your money or your life!!" Laugh #2. "Your money or your life!!!" Whereupon Benny screamed in reply, "I'm thinking, I'm thinking!!" Laugh #3 went on for over two minutes. The longest in radio history.

Oral or written stories are also told in three parts. More commonly called "Three acts." Or, to be Aristotelian, beginning, middle, and end.

The beginning, Act One, is *the situation.* The middle, Act Two, *the complications.* The end, Act Three, *the conclusion.* Moss Hart, George M. Cohan, and George Abbott, all Broadway playwrights of yesteryear, have separately been given credit for this apt three-act construction definition: "In the first act you get your hero up a tree. The second act, you throw rocks at him. For the third act you let him down."

Sol Saks's excellent *Funny Business: The Craft of Comedy Writing* book wrote:

> Every humorous anecdote, every two-line joke, is a story and follows the three-act construction—situation, development, resolution.
>
> Take Henny Youngman.
>
> "Take my wife . . . please." This joke may be eligible for the Guiness Book of Records for having three acts in four words. "Take my wife," establishes that he has a wife and is going to talk about her, for the first act. "Please" may set another record for having two acts in one word. It is the second act in that it tells us that he cannot tolerate his wife. It then simultaneously becomes the third act by changing the meaning of the first, surprising and delighting us in the process by the deft word legerdemain.

Sol's "take my wife" example cuts it to the barest bone. You'll notice he's on my "situation, complications, conclusion" wavelength with "situation, development, and resolution." They're exactly the same. Both interpretations of Aristotle, the king of performance art simplicity.

Milos Forman *(Amadeus, One Flew Over the Cuckoo's Nest)* once said: "Radio didn't kill theater and records didn't kill live concerts. I think it will always be exciting to go and see a good movie on a big screen. It's not the technique which is going to attract the people to movies; it will always be the story." Hear, hear. And from a director no less.

F. Scott Fitzgerald believed "good stories write themselves. Bad ones have to be written." You can be a bit cynical with that "the story writes itself" concept. Put a pencil on top of a writing pad and watch. Flick on your computer and stare at the phosphorus screen. Roll a sheet of erasable bond into your typewriter and carefully contemplate the paper.

Nothing. Absolutely nothing. Someone has to activate the pencil, typewriter, and computer. MIT scientists admit that even the most advanced robot tells a lousy story. This is where you and I come in. We humans have to tell the story. The pencil will not move otherwise. Keyboards will not be depressed without our fingers. If we chose to be writers, it's all on us.

TRICKS OF THE STORY TRADE

There are certain screenwriting litmus tests a writer applies to ideas during the story development stage. They are generally applied instinctively by the pros. Beginning writers must learn these tests and consciously utilize them until they become second, third, and fourth nature.

I want you also to be able to talk the talk as soon as possible and be able to at least give the impression of being a screenwriter. Illusion is equally helpful to your own writing reality. Then after paying your dues, you will truly become a screenwriter. For those of you who have yet to hurdle the dues barrier, "trade" phrases will aid your screenwriter illusion for you and others.

1. Vertical and Linear Stories

The words "vertical" or "linear" sound academic and geographic, but they are frequently used in real-life film story conferences. Character or plot stories is another correct way to put it. In the fundamental texts earlier mentioned, Aristotle emphasizes plot, Egri champions character. Author Paddy Chayefsky used to claim character stories as his forte. Though there is some exceptional plotting in his famous movies, *Hospital* and *Network*, his plots are beautifully overwhelmed by his character development.

Patton, Citizen Kane, Butch Cassidy and the Sundance Kid, Fallen Angel, and *Dog Day Afternoon* are further examples of character (or vertical) stories. *Casablanca, E.T., The Godfather, Gone with the Wind, Doctor Zhivago,* and

The Wizard of Oz are stronger in plot, making them linear stories. The characters in all of these movies are predominantly whipsawed and affected by external events. In the more vertical character stories, the protagonists affect the events. Humans control their own destiny. Destiny more significantly controls humans in the horizontal plot stories.

You will always have a mixture of character and plot, but in nearly 100 percent of your screenplays either story or character will dominate. And that's all right, but you should be aware of it so you can better skew your story to character or plot for strength. Also, this clear knowledge can prompt you to add good plot to your character stories and good characters to your plot stories. Aristotle and Egri are both right about plot and characters. Chickens come before eggs, and eggs before chickens.

2. Drama or Melodrama?

Another Checkpoint Charlie for your idea. Melodrama is most simply a story where guns are available to solve character's problems. Drama is more realistic. If not truly honest, the dramatic stories give us an illusion of honesty.

Contemporary drama came to full blossom with Henrik Ibsen. In Ibsen's twentieth-century "every person" flower field of drama, playwrights Eugene O'Neill, Clifford Odets, Arthur Miller, and Sam Shepard bloom full and stand tall. These dramatists are going for the drama of honesty, and generally they succeed. Melodramas nearly always have chase sequences in their running screen time. Dramas tend to have lots of wrinkled foreheads instead.

3. Realistic and Nonrealistic Comedy

We can, as often, find exact writing parallels when comparing dramas and comedies. Neil Simon's comedy is as realistic as Ibsen and his contemporary disciples. As is "Cheers," anything by Larry Gelbart, and often Woody Allen. Many of the landmark television series are grounded in the nonrealistic melo-comedy turf: "I Love Lucy," "Laverne and Shirley," "Get Smart." Most contemporary series have a stronger bond with fantasized or idealized reality. "The Cosby Show," "Roseanne," "Murphy Brown."

The "broader" screen comedies, from Chaplin to *Ghostbusters* to *Batman,* have nonrealistic spines with sporadic inclusions of reality to keep the audience grounded.

4. Combining Drama, Melodrama, Comedy, Realism, and Non-Realism

Can you successfully combine reality and nonreality or melodrama and drama? A resounding yes! *Casablanca, Dog Day Afternoon, Butch and Sundance* are towering "for instances." But beware, it can be the hardest form of writing.

One minute you're telling the audience this is real, as in the case of *Butch and Sundance* and *Dog Day* where the event really happened. In another minute, the audience is asked to go along with "bigger than life" extensions of that reality. And in a select few films, we do. When such a blending of drama and melodrama or realistic and nonrealistic comedy works 100 percent, it generally results in a blockbuster film. When it fails, it's called a "yo-yo picture." It goes from the distributor to the audience and back to the distributor as quickly as a yo-yo goes from a hand to its full extension and back again to the hand.

5. Believable Unbelievability

Yet it is all an illusion. An illusion of believability, even from Shakespeare to Molière to mindless sit-com or cop-and-robber TV episodes. All strive to convince an audience who psychologically insists on believability, even in the unbelievable. Whether it's drama or melodrama, comedy or science fiction. We've been injected with fantasy since the first day our parents told us a fat man in a red suit was going to come down our chimney and leave us presents. We still want to believe.

Screenwriter Bill Walsh *(Mary Poppins, The Absent-Minded Professor, The Shaggy Dog, The Love Bug)* once said: "An audience must believe in and care about your lead characters over the unspooling of the first reel (ten minutes) of the movie. If they truly believe, you can take them anywhere in fantasy. They can believe in nannies who fly with the aid of their umbrellas. They'll believe in little VW bugs with human characteristics, a boy who turns into a shaggy dog, even a magical substance called 'Flubber.' "

This can even be applied to a wild and wonderful comedy like Robert Klane's *Where's Poppa?* that begins with the reality of a man (played by George Segal) waking up. With this man, we go through our own morning ritual. One eye opening. The other. Stretching, brushing teeth, shaving, combing hair. Then, on a head and shoulder shot, the man's hands rise above, out of frame. He adjusts something, pulls over his head . . . a gorilla mask. We, the audience, laugh in nervous apprehension. The scene cuts to a hallway where the man, now in a full gorilla suit, is stalking toward some unknown destination. We are then cut inside a bedroom. Someone is sleeping. The man in the gorilla suit bursts into the room and leaps on the bed. The sleeping figure bolts awake and kicks the gorilla-suited man directly in his testicles. As he screams in agony, eighty-plus-year-old Ruth Gordon admonishes him for waking her so early.

From there on, the story gets even madder, but it started in reality. Though the filmmakers and screenwriter didn't wait Bill's full reel before they got bizarre, the audience did identify with the man's waking routine for its initial character grounding reference.

There's a thin, invisible strand between the audience and the screen. It's called believability. That strand gets stronger and stronger as the picture progresses. It can be easily snapped if you start out being too crazy or unbelievable.

When that believability thread is not established, audiences are often thrown by the first few scenes and they say, consciously or unconsciously, "This is ______" (fill in words that translate to unbelievable). You have to make the audience care about your on-screen people and their dilemmas, and when that occurs you've created *believable unbelievability.* Audiences will just not get with a film that starts with what they perceive as unbelievable unbelievability.

Movies *are* unbelievable. You have to help the audience believe its unbelief. Remember the Bible phrase, "Oh Lord, I believe. Help me in my unbelief." That's your job as a screenwriter.

Melodrama stretches, bends, or breaks realism. As Olivier once said, "Drama would have you believe what you are seeing is burningly real."

6. Audience Caring

An audience must also "care" about your characters. You've got to develop your story so your viewers start caring about your on-screen people as soon as possible and keep that "caring" foot in the dramatic flame until the film's fade out.

Producer Irwin Allen *(Voyage to the Bottom of the Sea, Poseidon Adventure, Towering Inferno)* once said: "When I was a young man, I wanted to shoot a movie called *The Big Circus*. I was summoned before Harry Cohn, then head of Columbia Pictures. This mogul threw the script at me as I sat in his spotlighted visitor's chair. He said, 'This is a piece of shit, Allen.' I swallowed and said, 'What seems to be the problem, Mr. Cohn?' Harry Cohn said, 'You know that asshole who walks on that tightrope across Niagara Falls on page 19?' I said, 'Yes.' Cohn barked, 'Put him on page 49, you got a deal.' "

This change may seem simple, but the one line suggestion will dramatically affect the audience reaction. You see, we don't care if the tightrope walker falls in the water on page 19! By page 49 we will know him, care about him and identify with him. We, the audience, will by then be the man walking across Niagara Falls on the tightrope.

7. Open or Closed Stories

Along with determining whether your idea is best told through character or plot, melodrama or drama, you must consider the option of having your story open or closed.

An "open" story is one where the audience knows what's going on. We know "whodunnit." We know the villain. We know what's going on between the Joker and Batman. The Sheriff and Robin Hood. Or Ilsa and Rick. Butch and Sundance. With Columbo and his heavy of the episode.

In a "closed" story, the audience learns about the antagonist as the protagonist learns. Probably ninety-nine percent of all TV cop or disguised cop shows are closed stories.

Generally the audience will be more moved by closed stories, as they can most easily identify with the hero or heroine. This identification gives them the psychological illusion that they are the characters. "Open" or "closed" is a very real choice you will have to make if your idea is in the mystery genre.

8. Fourth Walls and Flashbacks

The aforementioned audience identification with your characters is the main reason why flashbacks, flashforwards, and narration are generally undesirable as storytelling devices today. These devices call the audience's attention to the fact that they are watching a movie, when they should lose themselves so much in the story and the character developments that they forget their audience status. They are *on* that spaceship. *In* that room. *Riding* that horse. *Kissing* Mel Gibson, Clark Gable, Marilyn Monroe, or Julia Roberts. They *are* the fourth wall of the location/set.

9. Red Herrings

When you want the audience to believe the butler did it when the benign librarian *really* did it, the butler is referred to as a "red herring." Magicians call it "mis-direction." Dramatists often refer to such a device as "setting something up on one page, paying it off on another." It is a means of surprising the audience and is a term nearly always used in murder mysteries.

10. Time Locks

If possible, another element to not only consider but to add to the story development of your idea is a "time lock."

The train is rolling in with the bad guys at noon *(High Noon)*. The bomb goes off in eight hours (any dramatic TV series). We only have an hour's worth of air in this submarine *(Run Silent, Run Deep)*. Tomorrow morning everyone either goes off to college or stays here *(American Graffiti)*. We'll make you or break you in six weeks *(An Officer and a Gentleman)*. Your lover has so many days to live (*Love Story* and every disease-of-the-month TV movie). Ilsa's plane out of Casablanca leaves tomorrow night. And on and gloriously on.

Glorious because the result can be just that if you can put a time lock in your story.

Forget the negative connotation of the words "trick" or "formula." Make them positive words. A time lock is an honest tool of your screenwriting trade. Plumbers have different-sized wrenches; we have time locks, red herrings, et al. By using this wrench, AKA time lock, you inject an urgency into your story that can give it additional drive to heighten audience involvement and anxiety.

Keep in mind that sometimes a time lock might feel artificial. Remember the audience's slender thread of believability? Don't break it. To bend it is fine, even desirable. Just don't shoehorn this piece of time-lock craft into your idea development if it will cause too many in the audience to discover the time lock "trick." That's only for you to know. Maybe a few other creators, but *never the audience*. We want them to be innocent and go along happily on our magical movie ride.

11. Telescoping Time

You have to make a choice about the physical time span of your story. Compression is generally the most desirable choice. The best example of screen time compression is the successful 1949 movie *Rope,* which played out its story in actual running time. Why this hasn't been a more staple tool of the screen trade is beyond logic. The audience is apparently so used to the Charles Dickens–like scene-to-scene narrative, everyone's afraid to reinvent the "running time" technique.

At the other extreme of the screenwriting time spectrum would be David Lean–directed epics like *Passage to India* and *Doctor Zhivago,* from novels by E. M. Forster and Boris Pasternak, respectively. These cover generations and are often magnificent in their historical panorama.

Either extreme will probably not work for the development of your story idea. Your tale will surely best be told somewhere between generation spans and running time. And when you make your choice, compress the story time as much as logically and emotionally possible for your audience.

If the story can take place over a summer instead of a year, do it. A week instead of a summer, do it. A day instead of a week, do it. Your characters should have only so much time to accomplish whatever you've foreshadowed they need to accomplish in your opening scenes. Truncating this time is a legitimate and desirable way of giving your audience a sense of urgency and energy. Less is more is a credo that is also applicable here.

12. Storytelling Is Exaggeration

Israel's renowned novelist Yigal Mosingohn once said: "Without exaggeration, we writers are *nothing!*" Exaggeration *is* our game. Our racket. Our art. Our territory. And as Harold Hill said in *The Music Man*, "You gotta know the territory."

Make your characters the heaviest heavies, the best good guys, or the nerdiest nerds. Go for the extremes.

We, the audience, identify with the *best* lawyer, cop, caped crusader. Not the ones who are just OK. We are also best threatened by the strongest antagonists, from Jack Nicholson's Joker to Captain Nemo, to Goldfinger, Long John Silver, the Nazis, the Sheriff of Nottingham, even the Devil. From these extremes come the best drama and melodrama. Past and present 434 crowds are always exhorted to "push it." Push the extremes. Pull out the stops. Arte Julian ("F Troop," "Amen") turned in his rewrite of *Boatniks* to the then Disney studio head Ron Miller. Miller called Arte in for a meeting, thumbed the script, and informed Arte it was "too funny." Arte instantly assured him, "Don't worry, Ron. I know with your help we can dull it down."

There will always be somebody to help you dull it down. To keep you from going over the edge. Most writers collapse before the edge. Try hard to fall *beyond* the edge in your scripts and in the development of your ideas.

When you honestly can, exaggerate your characters and your story elements. Be extreme. Not only will someone be around to help you dull whatever it is down, you probably will catch your dramatic overstatement with your personal, as Hemingway says, "bullshit detector." Then you utilize one of the most important writer tools. The wastebasket.

13. Writers Write

Forgo writing exercises when you're learning to write screenplays. Read the books by Bill Froug, Richard Walter, Bill Goldman, Syd Field, Linda Seger, Whitcomb, Hauge, Dorthea Brande, and Sol Saks for instruction. Read screenplays for form. Get into workshops, then write full, original screenplays. Learn to swim in the deepest part of the pool.

I once asked John Steinbeck how I could best learn to write. Steinbeck glowered through his bushy eyebrows and over his imposing facial foliage growled one simple word. "Write."

Mr. Steinbeck was relating to prose writing. In screenwriting, you do have to learn the craft but from that point on . . . write. Get out the pages.

If you must have an exercise, find a nearby child and tell him or her a story. But don't use the favorite children's books. Use the child's and your imagination. Tell the child to give you two characters. You'll decide which of the two will be the bad guy and which the good guy. You'd be surprised how many times my children heard about a savage squirrel or quail or rabbit. And conversely, a friendly octopus, snake, or bat. From those two characters, protagonist and antagonist, spin them a story without a book.

You'll be the most popular storyteller on your block. More importantly, you'll develop abilities you never knew you had and learn things about your mind you never knew you knew. You'll also have a wonderful time, with no criticism. The kid will love it and for you it'll be excellent training with homage to screenwriting's oral tradition.

PLOTTING OUT THE TWO-MINUTE MOVIE

The idea can come to you on the freeway or while you washing under the left instead of the usual right armpit on any morning. But the story that emerges from your idea needs intense logical and emotional development. Now write out your two-minute movie, two pages double-spaced.

Not three pages or one page. Three will force you to be too specific and intrude upon your later step outline process. One page will not be specific enough, which may give you an unwitting opportunity to con others or far worse, yourself.

When you lack the detail in one page, you may not discern the flaws in the story structure. The flaw most often glossed over is lack of substance. The idea just isn't strong enough to sustain 100 pages. And you might not see it. With three pages double-spaced you can clearly see if you have enough story, but it will be so detailed you may not be genuinely open to additional thought. This is a common problem after you've made the beat-by-beat story moves. So two pages. No more, no less.

Then tell about or show your two pages to carefully chosen friends. They may be quite helpful with both pleasure and input. When you are developing scripts, affirming feedback can be often helpful. You may well get notions to be immediately discarded, but you may also get wonderful inspirations. It's worth the ego risk.

Be careful to make sure the feedback person has a quality thought and feeling process. Often fledglings with good drafts go off for a minor rewrite and as often return proudly announcing a rewrite that begins at page one. I just tremble at this information. With the turning of every page, the subsequent reader would sink deeper into despair. The writers had come into contact with some well-meaning idiot who knew even less than themselves about screenwriting and influenced the writing for the worse.

One new writer wrote an especially moving script about teenage suicide. Just a few minor shadings to adjust in rewriting and she would have been home free. After conversations with friends, she did a "page one" rewrite resulting in a typical "who's got the underpants" script. She even took out the suicide, which was the unique reason to do the movie. Sigh.

Beware of such "friends." Yes, you need feedback because the isolation can be debilitating. Just make very sure it's good feedback from an intelligent, feeling fellow human. And don't ever get involved with anyone who wants credit for co-writing. A thank you, a bottle of Thunder Ripple, or some promise of future reciprocation will be exactly right. Bottom line, don't let *anyone* cash in on your insecurities. That's the game that's often played.

The two-page, double-spaced story, I feel, is the best way to first consciously develop your idea. Again, in this and the entire process, don't forget the wastebasket, or the equally important rubber snout at the end of your pencil.

Conversely, don't be quick to discard your first impression of anything. As mentioned, first impressions originate from your subconscious, the bedrock of your creativity. When logic takes over from that initial instinct, beware. Logic can lead you to "dull" quicker than those eager to help you "dull it down."

Let's start getting down to it. Writing our two-minute movie. I have an idea for this moment in time with you. A love story in a madhouse. I will assume you are concurrently developing your idea. From now on, I will develop my idea and expect you to be in step or not too far ahead. These screenwriting steps are taken by all professional writers with their slight variations. From the idea, to the general story layout (herein called the "two-minute movie"), to the step outline, to the script. Is this simple enough? I'll try not to complex it up.

1. The Characters

OK, the couple will be young. Late teens, early twenties. They'll seem more vulnerable and innocent, although the girl should be a tough, city girl. Yes, even from Omaha. That's a tough and forebidding town for any farm boy from Guide Rock, Nebraska, population 344. Opposites mean conflict.

My boy. What should I call him? When I was producing a series called "The Mississippi," in New Orleans, I saw my executive producer, John Wilder, stuffing a local telephone directory in his suitcase. John lowered my raised eyebrows when he explained he wanted the large book for southern character names.

Marty Ritt (director of *Hud, Norma Rae*) once said the best way to cast was to choose actors who personally were what they were to play. "Ninety percent of your actor directing is over before the camera has even rolled." Paul Newman was Hud. Sally Field, Norma Rae. Serpico, Al Pacino. Alvy Singer, Woody Allen.

I'm like that in screenwriting. I'll line out the general boundaries of the character, then mentally check through my friends, relatives, strangers, and especially enemies for a man or woman who has many of the needed traits in his or her real life. I have a cousin who claimed he could only stay in Lincoln, Nebraska, six days. "That's about as long as I can stand *ce*-ment under my boots." This seems to be a seminal attitude for my country mouse in this story. My cousin's name is Cliff, so Cliff's the name. I generally flip through my own family for last names. MacPherson seems good because I like the sound of the innocent's being a Scot. Stubborn, proud, wry, all of that. Cliff MacPherson.

When I was a flower child in the sixties, I remember picking my way through a "crash house" and seeing a wasted young man in a corner, repeating, "Susie, Susie, Susie," again and again. Even today I wonder about the complexities of a woman that put him in such a state. So I'll name my city mouse Susan (Susie is too little girlish). Every Susan I've ever known has been complex. Lots of snakes under their beds. The last name? Garber, from the Garber twins I knew as a child in Nebraska. Twins are complex. So is Susan. Garber also seems like a punctuation mark after Susan instead of a dominating last name. Susan Garber is fine. All the other names will come later, as they must serve the lovers' story as well as the lovers. They should not be so powerful as to dominate.

Everything must serve your major characters and story. Locale, vocations, automobiles, shaving lotion, perfume, pets . . . *everything.* Even above that, everything and everybody must serve the *"thou shalt not be dull"* commandment.

The name for my antagonist? Madness. Antagonists do not *have* to be human beings. Love stories need an obstacle. Madness is my obstacle, also the antagonist. Class, race, pride are other examples of formidable antagonists. In *Butch and Sundance,* wasn't time even more of an antagonist than the persistent man in the white hat? That man was a symbol of time's getting closer and closer to these outlaws, who were by then living out of their own time frame. *Citizen Kane* is a unique and splendid example of a protagonist who was also his own antagonist.

In my story, we've got some of that, as Susan will surely be Cliff's antagonist for a while, but she'll more surely be the "mouthpiece" for the real and most menacing villain, madness.

2. The Location

Now, while your characters are forming, is the best time to think about the beginning, middle, and end in the broadest parameters.

Let's start with location. In every American state, there is a town known more for its housing a mental institution than for the qualities of the town itself.

"Write what you know," I say again and again. I know Nebraska. I know the town that hosts the state mental facility. In Nebraska, the older generation would literally be frightened of "going to Midvale." The contemporary Nebraskan would be less concerned, as Nebraska is one of the most progressive states in ministering to the mentally ill. But, remember, we screenwriters work in extremes at all levels. Cliff will be frightened at the idea of being sent to Midvale.

3. The Beginning

Cliff and Susan should get to Midvale for totally separate reasons. Why? Because it will make it easier to create conflict. The cliché that opposites attract may not be true in real life, but in movies, opposites translate into comic and dramatic conflict in every aspect of your lead characters' lives. As Cliff is "country" and Susan is "city," I want to have Susan committed by someone who feels she is mentally ill. But how? I remember the true story of a mass murderer of years back, Charlie Starkweather, who killed thirteen people in and around Lincoln, Nebraska. His girlfriend, Carol Fugate, reportedly "egged him on," encouraging him to shoot victims again and again. A film, *Badlands,* starring Martin Sheen and Sissy Spacek, "paid homage" to the real-life story that got Starkweather the electric chair and Carol Fugate assigned to Midvale.

That's a way to get Susan to Midvale. They say if you take from one source, you're stealing, but two or more sources is research. Past news headlines and *Badlands* allow me to plead research.

Cliff's getting there will be tougher. But I remember reading something. I make it a practice to read six daily papers, ten monthly magazines, books and books and scripts and scripts and scripts. If I'm at breakfast, I'll read the printing on cereal boxes if I have nothing else.

So should it be with you. From such reading will come bits of information you may later utilize. I suddenly remember from some past reading that some states allow conscientious objectors to serve their alternative military service as orderlies in mental institutions in addition to the medical orderly or forest ranger aide options. I check and, yes, Nebraska is one of those states.

That's what I'll do. Cliff will "refuse to go off and kill people" in the Vietnam War. That can cause the strongest possible conflict between Cliff and his parents and the conservative Guide Rock environment. Susan's inherently got enough conflict, so I'm fine there.

All of this should give me an excellent beginning.

4. The Middle

Since I define "the middle," or the second act, to be "the complications," I shouldn't be in serious trouble. I've got the actions and reactions of Susan's parents to work with. I sense they should be tight, controlling, materialistic, and they live for other people's approval.

Cliff's parents would be simple, strong, too hard—farm people who look at everything as black or white. Gray is too confusing and never in their vision.

The institution's program director will be positioned between Cliff and Susan. Susan will be an important case study, so he shouldn't be one of the lesser staff therapists. He has a daily war with mental illness. His early recognition of the couple's growing love can give him a unique strategy to fight Susan's psychotic behavior. His own obstacle will be that as a mental health professional, he shouldn't use such a strategy, giving him a moral dilemma. That's drama, folks. Somebody going against the grain. Against the law. Against the norm. Against society. Against themselves. Against God, even.

Later, at the step outline level, we'll include more characters as you would throw logs in someone's path if you wanted to stop or impede their progress. Remember!? Conflict!

5. The End

Now, we deal with the end, known as the third act by screenwriters. When I first came to the entertainment world and asked a writer how he or she was, I would often get a head shake and a "I haven't got a third act" response. I rarely hear that phrase today. Writers just aren't infused with the need for the classic third-act climax, which is to the detriment of many nearly wonderful movies. Names? You want names?

Three movies could have been classics if it weren't for their third acts. *Hope and Glory* was a splendid recounting of John Boorman's childhood days in World War II London with the daily fear and jeopardy of Hitler's bombs laying much of the city to waste. But instead of reaching a climactic ending, the film just stopped. Boorman had all of the dramatic ducks in order for the best possible Aristotelian catharsis, but nothing. The story didn't end. It just faded out and end credits rolled. We were cheated.

A more successful film in box office dollar terms, *Broadcast News,* did exactly the same thing. Writer James Brooks ("The Mary Tyler Moore Show," *Terms of Endearment*) had a splendid cast, Acts One and Two, but no third act. The audience was poised to be powerfully moved by these mortals who deliver the daily television news to us. But again, the story stopped without an ending.

A spectacularly successful film, *Rain Man,* also similarly fell short. Had the third act followed through, the audience would have flooded every theater in the world with tears at final scene in the station. But Dustin Hoffman just leaves on the train, and Tom Cruise just blankly looks at his brother going off. No ending.

I assure you every one of the creators involved in these three films would probably violently disagree, but I'd bet they haven't read their *Poetics* lately. Those were not third acts. They were merely endings . . . actually stoppings. Let's you and I keep better in touch with Aristotle's third act principles. Also, have the third act in mind as very soon after the idea as possible.

In my "love story in a madhouse" premise, Act Three should be a happy or sad ending. Not sort of happy or sort of sad, but extremely happy or extremely sad. One or the other.

Extremes are the best choices we all have. Love or greed are the best motivational choices for your hero or villain; happy or sad are always best emotional choices for your endings. Oh yes, we'd like to also be profound, but let's work on that after we get the act ending down. The three mentioned non–third act movies were quite profound in body. Their endings unfortunately produced more bafflement than emotion. You want emotion. Emotion is the real gold at the end of the movie rainbow.

If Susan's cured, we're happy. If she's not only not cured but drags Cliff into her sickness, we're sad. If she's cured, Cliff, our protagonist and viewfinder into this exotic world, should be actively involved.

No, we can't have him taking on the functions of a mental health expert. That would be wrong and unconscionable to the world of mental health. Screenwriters should have responsibilities to everybody and, most particularly, to the field in which we've set our stories. That's my hang-up, some would say, and blessing, I would say. It should be both hang-up and blessing to you, too. This morality and conscience will be strongly reflected in the overall patina of your work and what gets on the screen. A patina called "honesty." You'll get applause.

So of the choices for the third act, I'll take happy. Let's have the audience leave the movie filled with positive feelings about the mental health care in our world. We'll also fill them with the catharsis of a wonderful love story, so they'll rush to tell their neighbors about this must-see film.

A profound sad ending may fail to achieve all of these objectives. Let's try for an audience-fulfilling ending. We want everyone identifying with the emotional landscape as chameleons identify with their geographic landscape. Let's try for maximum audience impact.

WRITING THE TWO-MINUTE MOVIE

Drum roll. Let's do it.

We have the beginning, the middle, sort of, and we know emotionally how we want it to end. Oh, wait. If we're not going to have Cliff function as a mental health expert, what can he do to impact the ending? At the conclusion of the Frank Capra/Robert Riskin pictures, the Jimmy Stewart hero would take over the film with his "common man" instincts and abilities. Up to the third act, things generally happened *to* him. Those films could be a beacon.

Cliff could break Susan out of the asylum. This will bring him into the ending and get the action-loving audience involved. Maybe I can show his driving ability at the front of the story, setting up the action payoff with highway patrol cars, planes, and whatever. Good. That's the specific third act.

1. Wait, Is the Research In?

One final caution for those of you who need to research inordinately. You'll probably get so much wonderful material for story and scenes, you'll eagerly start to work up the outline before you finish your research, but you shouldn't. One danger is, you'll have to do extra work as even more wonderful possibilities can roll into your notebook. The highest danger is that mentally you'll be closed down to those possibilities because you're so deep into formulating your beginning, middle, and end.

Wait until the research is *all* in, and then start building your story. It's sometimes very hard, but use your self-control. That's simultaneously a major need and pitfall for impetuous writers.

2. Titles

I need a title. I keep using "country and city mouse" as nicknames for Cliff and Susan. "The Country Mouse" seems all right, maybe good. Most people are afraid of mice so that might work. Today, the word "country" is at once strong and vulnerable. Many are familiar with the Aesop fable about the country mouse who was warned not to go to the city, so it's sufficiently metaphorical.

Neil Simon believes using titles already in our national lexicon is a plus. *The Odd Couple* and *They're Playing Our Song* would indicate he practices his preaching. That was my reasoning with *Fallen Angel.* Since *Grapes of Wrath* and the best, *Of Human Bondage,* have been taken, my new script will be the "The Country Mouse." For the moment.

3. Act One (Beginning)

Cliff MacPherson steps off a Farmall tractor and informs his waiting father he "ain't gonna kill no one." The farmer father is further shocked when his son says he's filing to be a conscientious objector. The mother looks at her two men. Stoic, silent, worried.

Susan Garber rebelliously screams, "I made him do it! Fry me! I'm as responsible as Bobby for killing those people!" Her black boyfriend (shocking for Nebraska. Remember, extremes?), on trial for a murder rampage, sits in gathering comprehension of his electric chair sentence. The Omaha courtroom violently reacts to Susan's hysterics. She is remanded to Beatrice, the state mental institution. As the jury foreman says: "By reason of insanity. We thought it only right considerin' you're a girl and all."

Cliff pleads to serve his two years with the Forestry Service in the Idaho wilderness. Cliff's draft board decides he ought to be in the state to help his paraplegic father with the crops. Cliff will be an orderly "in Beatrice." Cliff and his parents are stunned.

4. Act Two (Middle)

Cliff is told to take a pail of water to the Ward A bathroom. Cliff starts washing off "Fuck the World!"—written in defecation on the walls.

Around the tub is a shower curtain. Cliff pulls it back to find a catatonic Susan, author of the words.

Cliff's country simplicity and caring overwhelms the tough, angry Omaha girl. The farmboy takes care of her like "you'd bottle-feed a new calf that lost its mom." Susan emotionally moves from cynically berating Cliff, to appreciation, then adoration, and finally dependence.

Cliff responds to all the wounded birds in his daily chores around the mental facility. A loved stranger in the strangest land.

After his first kiss with Susan, Cliff is transferred to the most disturbed ward, F. Susan slashes her wrists with the sharpened edge of his belt buckle. It works. Susan is admitted to Cliff's Ward F.

Cliff's deepening love and care gets Susan stronger and seemingly well. The institution's director is troubled, even angry at the possibility of sending Susan home. "We get them well, then return them to the very environment that made them sick." A traumatic meeting with her parents. Susan dramatically regresses. Cliff separately comes to the same conclusion as the director. The city mouse is doomed to her psychosis forever.

5. Act Three (End)

A warning buzzer shrieks. It's Harriet in Ward D with her monthly escape attempt. Cliff wants to run with Susan in the other direction. No. She wants to get well and love him in the security of Midvale. "This is no place for two people who love each other," demurs Cliff as he tenderly puts her in his pickup.

The fugitive lovers are chased by state trooper cars and planes. Their most sophisticated communications gear against the wily country mouse. Cliff and Susan fake their deaths by plunging his pickup in the nearby churning, deadly Missouri River. As the bottom is dragged, the lovers steal a motorcycle, ride off to the Western sun, marriage, and their dream. The wilderness of Idaho.

GETTING IT RIGHT

Well, those are my two pages. How are yours?

Here are my notes: Still not thrilled with my title. As you can see, I choose to make Cliff's father a paraplegic. I know that special word because my father was a paraplegic. I know that special world. I also loved the scene with Jack Nicholson's character talking to his mute, stroke-stricken father in *Five Easy Pieces*. Cliff's father will talk, though.

Notice I instinctively used that old screenwriting teaching cliché "what do the characters want?" Cliff catching Susan up in his Idaho wilderness dream seemed right. "Where the deer come right up to you 'cause they never seen man. And fish don't know about hooks." I'll work those Eden lines in for my characters and for the audience, who have their own identifiable dream of paradise on earth.

Reaching for more extremes, I felt a teenaged girl with a black boyfriend, even today, would be a most extreme choice for a Midwest daughter. I'm not going for a big racial emphasis because that's not my story. I'll just have it there. Lawyers use a Latin phrase in the courtroom, "Res ipsa loquitur." That translates, "The thing speaks for itself." That's good for screenwriting, too.

More extremes. Writing "fuck the world" in her own fecal matter. Maybe Cliff should say, "Holy shit" when he sees it. The sound behind the shower curtain will be a giggle, and her first words to him could be, "I thought mine went to the pie factory," or better, "the Vatican."

When this scene was read by producer Billy Sackheim, his face knotted in disgust. I immediately tried to mollify. "Oh, you don't like the shit. Wait. Better idea. She'll be on her period and write 'fuck the world' over the wall with the blood waste in her Tampax." Billy screamed in accelerated disgust. I was actually serious. I tell this to illustrate my earnest obsession to push the drama. Push the effect. Go too far. There'll be plenty around to help you "dull it down."

Notice in the middle, three lines of pure writer tap-dancing. 1. "Susan emotionally moves from cynically berating Cliff, to appreciation, then adoration, and finally dependence." 2. "Cliff responds to all the wounded birds in his daily chores around the mental facility." And 3. "Cliff's deepening love and care gets Susan stronger and seemingly well."

Those three lines will probably comprise fifty pages of Act Two. Half the script. You see, I don't have the scenes *yet.* Remember, this is two-page-itis. For this story phase, I just want to get the broad beginning, middle, and end down to see what I've got.

Those three sweeping sentences are pointed out so you can be sure to catch yourself or others in such Fred Astaire routines. It's all right for news but don't be self-deceived.

Act Two ends with what Professor Richard Walter classically described "The Big Gloom": "That moment, occurring almost inevitably just before the beginning of the end, approximately eighty minutes into the film, where the protagonist is furthest from achieving his goal." And so it is with Cliff and Susan. "The city mouse is doomed to her psychosis forever."

The ending is an audience-fulfilling, rooting, rousing chase with twists to be put in at step outline or script level. Don't ask me now but it will come.

Getting the movie right at this two-minute development stage is wildly important. It sometimes takes more work than the detailed step outline. If your two-minute overview is good, your upcoming step outline will likely be even better.

1. Questions and Answers for Your Story and Characters

Here's where you can most easily hear suggestions from others or yourself: Should they be rich? Maybe one of the characters can have a physical handicap. Happy or sad ending? Is the hero in the right profession? Does he or she have a dream? A personality flaw? Something at stake, for instance.

Question your story. Question your characters. Think about Aristotle's plot emphasis, then the character emphasis of Egri, back to Aristotle, then Egri one more time. Push, prod, and poke your two pages. Everything will be much, much easier to change now than after you've committed to outline, and any problems not caught will quadruple in magnitude when you're writing the script.

"The Country Mouse" seems to work. We've got the elements for many audiences. The love story audience is most evident, then the action audience and the drama audience. Hopefully, there'll be enough *honest* smiles or laughs in it for the comedy audience. Obviously, it will appeal to a young audience by the virtue of the lovers' age. Finally, an adult, more cerebral audience would like to see the boundaries of madness explored.

2. Check Your Golden Buddha

But know the difference between *il*lusion and *de*lusion. Sid Sheinberg, the president and chief operating officer of MCA/Universal, has a splendid theory about illusion. "You find a pile of horseshit. You say, 'That's an interesting pile of horseshit. I think I'll make a Buddha out of the horseshit.' So you mold and shape and form a wonderful, even beautiful Buddha. 'I think I'll put gold paint on it and make my Buddha even more wonderful.' And so you do. There sits before you a beautiful, golden Buddha. Now it may be beautiful. And the world may also think your golden Buddha is beautiful. But you, you must *always* know that under that golden Buddha is horseshit."

And so it is with your stories. You must always know their weaknesses as well as their strengths. You don't have to tell anyone else. But you'll be far better prepared for rebuttal when the hour comes that someone points the perceived flaws out. Know your illusions. Destruct your delusions. Know what's underneath your Golden Buddha story.

3. Is Comfortable Dull?

I will consciously try for story twists and turns under my own Golden Buddha. But since madness is unnerving enough, I won't be too bizarre because the audience shouldn't be frightened by this movie. Maybe they should even be comfortable.

Comfortable? Isn't our job as dramatists to constantly surprise the audience? Yes *and* no. The most effective movies, in acceptance and quality terms, are those with a simple A-to-Z story line. From *E.T.*, *Butch and Sundance*, *Fallen Angel*, to less conventional yet equally successful movies like *2001* and *Star Wars* or the art house *Four Hundred Blows* and *He Who Must Die*.

Put an A on a blackboard, then a Z to the right, higher up and away from the A. Draw a straight line from the A to the Z. The audience wants their stories to utilize Egri's rising conflict theory in a simple, direct A-to-Z rising story spine like on your blackboard. The originality comes in with the zigzags when you crisscross back and forth along the A-to-Z straight line.

If the zigs and zags that represent scenes do not have a connective link to the simple A-to-Z story line, either throw out the scenes or make the link. Have a simple, dramatically ascending story line. Yet create fresh, surprising twists and turns along that comfortable straight story line.

UCLA alum Harve Bennett (producer of *Star Trek* sequels, "Rich Man, Poor Man," "The Six Million Dollar Man") was once informed by a set of series producers that they wanted to tell the first half of an episode through the deranged eyes of a psychotic criminal. The second half would have the same events as the first half, but seen through the cops' eyes. Fresh? Innovative? Surprising? Yes, but.

Harve was the West Coast ABC program head at the time. Harve said "no." To explain his adamant posture, he told them: "The audience is like a boy in his room waiting for his father to tell him a bedtime story. The father enters, slaps his palms together and says. 'Tonight, son, you're going to hear a new story. "The Emperor's New Clothes." ' The son immediately cries, 'I don't *want* "The Emperor's New Clothes." I *want* "Peter Rabbit." ' The exasperated father says, 'Son, I've told "Peter Rabbit" at least five hundred times. No, no, no. "The Emperor's New Clothes." 'No, Daddy, I *want* "Peter Rabbit." ' The father, not wishing to get his boy more distraught at bedtime, capitulates. 'All right son, "Peter Rabbit." Peter is in the cabbage patch . . .' The son interrupts instantly with, 'No, no, Daddy. *Mr. MacGregor* is in the cabbage patch, Peter comes down later.' "

That bedtime boy is your audience. They want the comfortable. They will actually be ahead of you in many of the most effective stories. And that's all right. That's the way they want it.

4. What's It Really About

After most new writers talk about their ideas and stories, the magic question is "what's it about?" Too often surface responses follow. "Two people fall in love in an impossible world." Or "a variation on a mother deer who is separated from her baby by a hunter's bullet and the baby must grow up to be a man deer." "Commitment" is another common response. After a polite blink, try asking, "Yes, but what's it *really* about?" You'll generally get blank looks.

"What it's *really* about" *is* the key question. Paul Schrader would ask about the movie's "theme": "All movies have themes. In an American Film Institute brochure, it says the three most important elements of screenwriting are story, characterization, and structure. Well, that's not true. The four most important elements are *theme,* story, characterization, and structure. You have to know in some way what you are about to do. Even if that theme gets rerouted or ends up in subtext, somehow there has to be some sense of why you are doing this other than to make money or meet girls."

Egri talks about "premise" in a more didactic manner but it all means the same. What's it about? And don't give yourself surface platitudes. You have to be able to answer truthfully. Make your Golden Buddha proud.

Like the crowd in that magic moment with Christ and the harlot, I can't cast the first stone. I wrote a television movie about medical malpractice. My director, Robert Lewis, said: "My God, this is wonderful. Do you know what you've done?" Toeing the rug, I feigned shyness and responded, "Oh yes, I've written a movie about a couple who lose their four-year-old boy. When they learn medical malpractice was involved, the mother decides to take on the system." Robert screamed: "Bullshit! You've written a wonderful story about how we all can come to a huge bump in the road, get over it, and go on with life!"

Robert was doing as all good creators should. Thinking of the audience. Realizing how right he was, I instantly adjusted the script in a relatively minor rewrite to subtly suggest that infinitely more universal "theme." My pal and fellow UCLA professor Howard Suber says in his superlative film structure class: "What the film's about is not the plot."

Francis Ford Coppola *(Godfather, Apocalypse Now)* once said: "Sometimes you never really quite understand what the movie's about until you go into a matinee screening at the Oriental Theater on a Thursday afternoon." The Oriental was a decrepit, 1970s, rancid-buttered-popcorn movie theater on Sunset Boulevard that showed movies in the last gasp of their initial release. Hopefully you'll discover what your movie is about much before the film is released. Preferably in this two-minute movie gestation period.

But don't let your "what it's about" be waved like a flag for all to see. Egri says "blend." "Neither the premise nor any other part of a play has a separate life of its own. All must blend into a harmonious whole." In other and final words, make your universal "what's it about" decipherable, but don't whack the audience over the head with it.

5. Second Title Thoughts

I'm still not crazy about my title. What about "Fire and Rain"? Does the James Taylor song preclude anyone else's using that title? I should get legal counsel if I wish to use "Fire and Rain."

After the fact, I learned *Fallen Angel* was the title for a 1945 Fox movie. Since it's a phrase in the American language lexicon, and since the 1945 movie was not a seminal success, the Columbia lawyer said it was OK to use.

The Bible is a good source. I love Ecclesiastes. Maybe I can find something there. Hemingway appropriated *The Sun Also Rises* from those pages. I remember Willa Cather read Ecclesiastes and other Old Testament books to warm up for her day's writing. OK. Here's the last Ecclesiastes verse. "For God shall bring every work into judgment, with every secret thing, whether it be good, or whether it be evil." "Every Secret Thing"? "Every Secret Thing." Sounds sensuous. Maybe even risqué.

Wait. My first movie was called *If Tomorrow Comes*. No, not the Sidney Sheldon book/mini-series of twenty years later (maybe the *Fallen Angel* lawyer worked on both titles).

My original title for that movie was "The Glass Hammer." I had a line where I was paying homage to an old Russian proverb. In the movie the Pat Hingle sheriff said to the Nisei boy: "Son, like my old daddy used to say, hammers can make steel . . . or break glass." I thought, by using lingual calisthenics, "The Glass Hammer" would look good on a marquee. Fragile strength, implied violence. I liked it.

ABC didn't. They changed the title. What about "The Glass Hammer" now? For "The Country Mouse"? I'll have someone give that anonymous Russian proverb to Cliff in dialogue and I can finally use, what *I* think is an excellent title. *The Glass Hammer* it is.

6. What's *The Glass Hammer* About?

Meanwhile, back to the magic query. "What's it about?" Often that 434 question is answered by, "oh, a lot of things." *The Glass Hammer* is certainly about madness. And commitment. And love. And certainly bumps in life's road. Those are too scattered and superficial. Perhaps

I should ask myself and you, as you're writing your idea out alongside me, what's it really *really* about?

Now my back is against the wall. I think . . . I think . . . it's really *really* about the daily battle between the simple and the complex. Say, not bad. Will it result in Egri's "unity of opposites"? Won't the complex win every time? I'll call one of my human sounding boards who has a right to his own opinion, screenwriter Jack Sowards (*Star Trek II*, "Bonanza"). He's a country boy at heart.

Well, Jack says, "Tennessee Williams did all right with that notion." Of course, *Streetcar*. Stanley Kowalski *did* win. The simple won over the complex. Thank you, Jack.

But is simple trivial? Here's Thorton Wilder: "I see myself making an effort to find the dignity in the trivial of our daily life, against those preposterous stretches which seem to rob it of any such dignity; and the validity of each individual's emotion." Simple is important. Stanley Kowalski is important. Cliff will be important.

I'm deeply concerned about our contemporary complex life overwhelming the simple, the pure, and most important, the love. Simple can reach into life's soul. And as important to me, my writing soul. And *your* writing soul. That's what your two-minute movie theme, your premise, your "what's it about," should accomplish. A reach into life's soul.

Figure it out, sooner if you can, but later if you must. You can shift your "what it's about" as you develop. But what your movie's about is the vein of gold you *must* eventually strike in your story. That's "why" the story should be. Hopefully you'll find that gold at this two-minute movie level. At least try. Hard.

Chapter 3

BUILDING YOUR CHARACTERS

Now you're getting to what screenwriting's really all about: *character.* Yes, you need both a wonderful idea and a story frame, but fine screenwriting comes down to the characters inside your two-minute movie idea. People "pushing the river." People trying to be better or worse than they are. People loving. People hating.

Be sure to read the Lajos Egri pages on character. That's as good as it gets. I do want to give you supplemental character thoughts I offer in 434. Adjunct thinking to put a contemporary skew on the Egrian character commandments.

The seminal movies in American society have one thing in common. Not genre. Not budgets. Not even good stories in some instances. CHARACTER. They *all* have memorable *characters,* that have become part of American culture. Scarlett, Sleeping Beauty, Rick. *Characters* played by Chaplin, Marilyn Monroe, John Wayne, Clint Eastwood, Jane Fonda, Clark Gable, James Dean, and on and on.

John Mitchell was the guiding light of Screen Gems, an early television subsidiary of Columbia Studios. He and an NBC executive were struggling over the money problems of a series. John said he had noticed, after the success of "Bewitched," "I Dream of Jeannie," and "The Flying Nun," that money spent for production didn't really make the difference. "The audience will watch the series if they like the *characters.* You could put them in a cave and they will tune in to see the show because of the *characters.*" John eventually took himself literally, as Screen Gems was the distributor of "The Flintstones."

A writing professor once said, "You must know everything about your characters, even to the change in their pockets." Many writers go on about character minutiae, but do not go on about character.

Initially, you push the perimeters of the story that comes out of your wonderful idea. But you must hunker down right away and *deeply develop* the character of your characters. Knowing the exact amount of change in their pockets isn't needful. *Knowing their soul is paramount.* Now is the time to build that soul and let that soul be part of your writing soul.

In story conferences, professionals often remind each other to "show, don't tell." So instead of talking about character, I will show you.

Here are exceptional character sketches from two exceptional 434 students of recent yesteryear. First, the souls of characters Mrs. Nielson and Mrs. Judson from Bob Manganelli.

> MRS. NIELSON, at age sixty-four is slightly plump and uncomfortable. If she sits too long she swells. If she stands too long she urinates. A widow of ten years, she lives on the ground floor of her daughter's tenement house. Memories of the Park Street house in New York, Judy's first steps, John's promotion, remind Mom how quickly time passes. Each Sunday however, she thanks the Lord for these memories. It's been one year since her cancer operation and she faces "THE ILLNESS" with dignity, concealing it from others and fighting for optimism. But GOD what she'd give to feel well again. She hates all the fuss her daughter goes through. JUDY helps, though; when depression sets in, she brings Mom to exercise class and they shop together. The illness has given Mom a certain wisdom, an insight that shows in her eyes. She understands the importance of a good family life and is proud of Judy, a symbol of her successful upbringing.
>
> MRS. JUDSUN, a thin, wrinkled, divorced forty-eight-year-old schoolteacher, knows damn well what problems are. She hates haircuts; they're always too short. She believes her bleached blonde hair and base makeup make her appear covergirlesque. Still rolling in her sleep, thinking how she never should have been cut from her high school cheering squad, she knows everything and nothing is right. She blames her doctor

for her problems. Ever since her last pap smear she's been discharging and she's convinced that her low voice is the result of the hormones he's been giving her. Trying desperately to busy herself, she feels there's not enough time in a day and always butts into the ten items or less line when she shops for the week. Growing up, Mom and Dad always paid more attention to her older sister Sara. She was the captain of her girls gymnastic team. She was the one who married the doctor. Daddy never touched Sara in her sleep.

Aren't those spectacular characters? Not Lawrence of Arabia in scope but Tennessee Williams spectacular in depth. These two character sketches would be a glorious story start.

Here's ex-student Donna Kuyper and her glorious start.

There's a look young girls get before they marry. I've seen it in the hundred-dollar face framed by Swiss lace in Beverly Hills and in the painted, tattooed face almost covered by muslin in an Indian village. You could call it fear or sadness but I trace it to a desperate sense of loss. A goodbye to youth and maidenhood, independent of technical virginity. This has been true from the beginning of time. No matter how happy the bride seems, if you look deep enough, you'll see the look in her eyes. Under the makeup, she knows. It is over.

You have to die to be reborn.

Darianne has that look. On the outside, mid-twenties. On the inside, a dreamy little girl. It started the night her father told her a fairy tale, then left to catch the red-eye express and never ever came back. That fairy tale stuck with her.

So she played the part of growing up, doing it quite well and delicately. When the boy next door grew up to be a doctor and asked her to marry him, she consented. And now she's got these two little wrinkles above her eyebrows. And her eyes drift off while you're waiting for her to decide whether she wants chocolate or fruitcake for the top tier of the cake.

"Is this all there is?" she said and you think she means she wants a bigger cake when in fact she wants a bigger piece of the cake. She thinks her fiancé is too predictable. Where's the man who's not afraid to orchestrate twenty people at a crowded matinee to stand up and move over one seat so we can sit together? Where's the surprise, like an instant picnic breakfast on Sunday morning on the roof of the telephone building? Where's the thrill—and yes, I mean sex.

She'll shake her head and straighten up and try to push all the questions to the back of her noisy brain. But the little wrinkles never go away. Is this a woman who's ready to be reborn?

You'd like to have Richard as your doctor. You can trust him. He double-checks his lab tests. He may not always make eye contact or remember your name, but he'll remember your disease. As a man he has to learn how to take risks. He's the kind who would never do anything on impulse. Nothing. Even if that cute golden retriever puppy was on sale. Even if he whined and whimpered and was going to the pound the next day. Even if he took his fat paw and spelled out Richard's name in the sawdust.

I won't say Richard's obsessive, but if we did a test and moved one item on Richard's coffee table two inches to the north, he'd notice. And move it back. He's never left home. He preferred to stay so his father wouldn't be alone. He's cute, even if his hair always looks like it was just cut. He's the kind of guy you just want to shake and mess up a bit and tell him to relax or get a massage and loosen up. Because underneath it all is a wild, wonderful, raw sort of energy that he's kept successfully buttoned-down, tied back, and pinned in all these twenty-nine years.

The 434 gatherings applaud exceptional student work when read aloud, and Bob and Donna got lovely ovations from their workshop mates. Those are character sketches that reach down beyond the change in pockets and into the deepest shadow of the character's souls. *You do the same* character workups before you start your step outline. It's like a boxer training for his fight.

HEAVIES AND HEROES

One can talk about archetypes and stereotypes and antagonists and protagonists but let's forego the academic dialogue. It gets down to heavies and heroes. Booing and cheering. From Greek theater to *Casablanca.* Shakespeare to *E.T.*

Don't make the villain too weak. If the antagonist is just a "Straw Man," it won't be much of an accomplishment for your hero to overcome him. Egri uses the term "unity of opposites" when he writes about heroes and heavies. John T. Kelley wrote, "If you use a villain, make him a beaut. Make him strong, sensible, persuasive. The more powerful the antagonist, the greater the victory for the protagonist."

Make both heavy and hero bright as you can. Ready and willing for battle. If possible, make them David and Goliath extremes. Or like Charles Foster Kane, who was at once a strong hero *and* heavy. A similar combined protagonist and antagonist is Travis Bickle in Paul Schrader's *Taxi Driver.*

If your story is "smaller," like Bob Manganelli's and Donna Kuyper's, go for extremes in paranoia or shyness or dreaminess or nerdiness.

1. Heavy Heavies

In the animal world, rabbits would be the heroes, and snakes the heavies. Yet, after gorillas, the most popular exhibit at zoos isn't the rabbit cage. It's the snake house. We love to see snakes, but only behind the safety of thick plate glass. So it is with our heavies. They're fascinating to watch. They're dangerous to watch. They're safe to watch. Audiences love to hate the heavy.

Actors much prefer to play heavies over heroes. There's far more for Nurse Ratched, Darth Vader, The Joker, or Captain Nemo to do in thespian calisthenics than their hero counterpoints. Richard Masur could hardly wait to play the child molester in *Fallen Angel.* Every quality actor quivers to do *Macbeth.*

You can apply the same logic even if the "heavy" is not human. Make the cancer the deadliest cancer your hero could have, or recorded history's most dangerous shark. Faceless like the FBI in *Running on Empty* or the "super posse" in *Butch and Sundance* are also extremely effective.

Whether the heavy is human, flood, disease, or beast, "Give me a good heavy, I'll give you a good picture."

You want to establish your heavy is a monster. For instance, a character is about to rob a bank. Have him, just before opening the bank door, shoot an old lady's dog. The audience will hate him. Ironically, probably much more so than if he had shot the old lady.

The most popular attraction in the zoo, the gorillas, are at once heavy and hero. Like King Kong. Like Charles Foster Kane, Willie Loman, Travis Bickle, or Macbeth. We love to love them and love to hate them simultaneously. If you find such a character in your world, your imagination, or in history, you can have a spectacular screenplay.

2. Flawed Heroes

Fellow teacher Mel Tolkin believes every major character should have a flaw. Mel was one of the original story editors on "All in the Family," and that show is a perfect example of his theory. Archie's prejudice, Edith's dingbatness, Meathead's liberalism, and Gloria's need for harmony are all vulnerable human flaws that were a part of their wonderful characters. Actors will just play the hell out of those flaws. No actor, no audience, wants to really be involved with a Dudley Do-Right character outside of "Bullwinkle" cartoons.

The best flaw is obsession. Your hero should want something so badly, he or she will battle any equally obsessed heavy to get it against all odds. That is the supreme conflict. Kane wanted to rule the world. Little Elliot wanted to get E.T. home. Rick risked his life for Ilsa. Butch and Sundance *had* to get to Bolivia. Obsession is the hallmark of every wonderful movie and every wonderful hero. Obsession. They don't "kind of" want the goal. Nothing but nothing is as important as that goal! Right, Scarlett?

The hero must have something at stake! Heroes must not be in a position where they can shrug their shoulders and walk away from the problem. They are going to see it through to the sweet or bitter end. The Richard Gere character in *An Officer and a Gentleman* had "nowhere else to go." He was locked into his obsession, therefore locked into the service. Nothing but nothing will be more important to burn in the wall above your keyboard.

3. Split Bananas, Not Heroes or Heavies

Writer Stanley Ralph Ross teaches, "One shark is worth two barracudas." So it is with heavies and heroes.

Two villainous characters cancel each other out, substantially reducing the power of your threat to the hero, and the power of your drama. Oh, your heavy can have henchmen do his dirty work, like Goldfinger's OddJob or Moriarty's men. But never have two equal antagonists. Pick one mean monster and make him, her, or it extremely formidable.

Conversely, we don't want two Ricks in *Casablanca,* two E.T.s, two Rhett Butlers, and so on. But wait, you say, "What about Butch and Sundance?" Butch really has the protagonist role while Sundance is a henchman, more reactive than active. Though he was not a subordinate in the film's title, or in casting, Sundance *is* the subordinate in the life of the story. In all "buddy" pictures starring two women or two men, one is always dominant.

The shark-barracuda theory is so valid on screen, it's worth another wall burn. *One heavy, one hero.*

4. Motivate, Motivate

Every classic human heavy has one of two motivations. Greed or power. Period. Don't look for more than greed or power. That's it. Villainy emanates from those two motives.

Every hero should have one consuming motivation. To overcome the obstacle. Be the obstacle emotional or forces of nature. Hence the hero is harder to act, to write, and to motivate. Heroes are at once more bland and more complex than heavies. But motivating your opposing forces is a *must* for a writer. To do that you *must* identify their wants and transform those wants into high comedy or drama.

Another John T. Kelley admonition was: "Motivate . . . motivate. Every character, no matter how evil or seemingly evil, is not without his good side and certainly not without a good reason for behaving as he does. Most murderers, unless they are maniacs, have logical, sensible, in a way almost sympathetic reasons, for having taken a life."

Bad men and women, though, need to have good reasons for their behavior. Reasons they feel are good, to rationalize their motivation for power and greed. The pedophile in *Fallen Angel* truly believed he was loving unloved children. It was his justification for wanting power over them. Hitler had his own horrid, passionate, and for him, logical reasons for killing Jews in his want for power. Captain Nemo wanted to rule the world by harvesting the sea to save the planet from itself. King Herod, Napoleon, the scientists in *E.T.*, Louis Gossett, Jr.'s character in *An Officer and a Gentleman,* all had very self-logical reasons for their want for power.

Antagonists who want the jewels, the drugs, the Rembrandt, the holdings in Fort Knox are generally less overtly convoluted characters, but they needn't be. That's between you and your writing muse.

5. Lousy Heroes and Heavies

Architects, painters, sculptors, actors, and especially writers make the lousiest heroes and heavies. Empathy is more important a characteristic than sympathy. We want to identify with our heroes and the audience does not identify with the artist. They have non-jobs. Most writers have had lay people seriously question, "yes, but what do you *really* do?" Refer to your parents for verification.

Another problem with artists is in the drama. Because so much of their work happens in the mind, gestating it is normally impossible to dramatize. The result may be visual or aural, but their creative genesis, the real magic, occurs in thought, and thought doesn't play on that screen.

Yes, there are examples of successful and even good movies that go against my edict. There are more exceptions to this general rule than most other precepts. But overall, be very sure you want your hero or heavy to be in an esoteric profession before you put him or her in vocational granite. The audience just won't identify with them as quickly as they'll identify with doctors, lawyers, blue collars, Indian chiefs, and even holy Ghandi-Christ-Buddha figures.

6. Exciting Heroes and Heavies

Putting your people in an exciting arena is very helpful to your dramatic or comedic agenda. Often the very story itself may dictate the professions of your major players. But when that's not the case, pick professions that have possibilities for interesting visuals and as well help the unfolding of your story: dock worker, shipping vice president, crop duster, bottled-water delivery man. They're all in your Yellow Pages.

I've used construction vice presidents a great deal. You can get an audience out in blue sky when he or she is working at a site. If you watch the sidewalks throughout your city, you'll notice people are fascinated with construction. In a script about bachelors, I thought and thought and rejected and rejected before I put them in a supermarket. I liked the John Denver character working at a supermarket in *Oh God* a lot. It's a more visual place than an insurance or general business office, and it's a locale audiences identify with because they are in a grocery store at least once a week. It hasn't been done to death like the lawyer and doctor worlds, where you would just have an office set no matter how ingenious your production designer might be. A grocery store certainly isn't the only world I could have set these men in, but a grocery store just felt right. And it's entertaining. When "right" and "entertaining" come together, generally you've made a choice that will be a major asset in building exciting heroes and heavies.

CHARACTER DIALOGUE

Set up your characters in conflict, not conversation. When you're tempted to write a "conversation," or "talk," or "visit," or anything similar, don't. Always remember Egri's "rising conflict." That's conflict between *characters*. Your characters.

Though John Wilder wanted "Yellow Rose" passion and tension, he as often didn't want "television conflict." Two people yelling at each other without any honest motivation. You don't have to have screaming scenes to exhibit conflict.

A scene in which a mother thinks the adult male coach she's talking to has seduced her twelve-year-old daughter—that's conflict. She wants to go crazy but the struggle within her is to hold it back as she may be wrong. That can be an electric scene, even though on the surface they're talking about the girl's batting average.

You shouldn't write the dialogue. Let your characters write the words. You will have, during the writing of your scripts, your own multiple personalities. That's great. That's fun. Your child personality will do the talking, as will your curmudgeon and erudite characters. And they'll all go through you. Don't block them.

1. On Being Too Brilliant

> Character and thought are merely obscured by a diction that is over-brilliant.
> —Aristotle

Be very careful of your intelligence. One of our most skilled screenwriters is a triple Phi Beta Kappa. His characters are so bright they snap, crackle, pop and even explode off the page and screen. Unfortunately, his janitors and filling station attendants also sound like Harvard graduates. Paddy Chayefsky had this same problem late in his career, as did G. B. Shaw and often Eugene O'Neill. *Let your characters be your characters.*

2. Snappy Sayings and Witty Patter

Writer Richard Alan Simmons *(Price of Tomatoes)* takes everything he loves out of his scripts. He reasons that the bits of dialogue or pieces of character business or descriptions writers most cherish, we like for reasons away from the story. Away from truth. Perhaps it might be a ground axe. A "message." A clever phrasing. They generally draw too much attention to themselves. And more damningly, attention to the writer. Take them out or put them in a file for slain "love children."

William Faulkner once said, "In writing, you must kill all your darlings."

A producer-writer once riddled his scripts with such self-conscious gems. Every time one of his episodes came in, we NBC executives held up the draft with two fingers, sighed, and observed, "More snappy sayings and witty patter." He really did have a clever way to twist words but this gift did not cover up his weak story lines, and the audience picked up on this. One year he premiered four series that were almost immediately cancelled. My own snappy saying reverberated throughout the industry when I referred to him as, "A man for one season."

3. Playing Dialogue vs. Reading Dialogue

You may be surprised at how well a script reads but doesn't play. Conversely, scripts that seem merely adequate on paper, periodically explode on screen.

Entertaining the reader of scripts is *not* our primary mission. Arte Julian was once summoned to the office of his "F Troop" producer Hugh Benson. Hugh told him he would have to rewrite a scene, because it just wasn't funny. Arte took the script and said, "Not funny, Hugh? Here, let me play it for you." At the end of Arte's acting out all the parts in the four-page scene, Hugh was literally screaming with laughter. Arte looked down and spread his hands. "Not funny, Hugh?"

The producer wiped tears from his eyes and replied, *"Well, if you're going to play it like that!"*

Arte is also an actor (you may have seen him in a running "Bewitched" role). He is another example of why you should develop your acting skills to help your writing skills. Very specifically, your *character*-writing skills.

4. Characters as Pearls

When you're trapped in the deepest story corner, rejoice. *That* is when wonderful things can happen. When you're in a corner, always look to your characters to lead you out. *They* will show the way.

To rejoice when you're in story trouble is also the oyster-pearl metaphor. A grain of sand, a life-threatening irritant, gets in the oyster's shell. To protect itself from this threat, the oyster repeatedly envelops the sand with a milky substance, and a beautiful pearl is created. You can take story trouble and get from that a beautiful story pearl. Through character, the milky substance.

Good writers *always* look to their characters when they are in story trouble.

Frank Pierson was dramatically stymied while developing *Dog Day Afternoon* from a real-life incident of a bumbling bank robber who took hostages when confronted by police while his holdup was in progress. Frank struggled and struggled with the story of this small-time hood until the key came to him. The Al Pacino *character* lived for everyone but himself. His wife, his children, his homosexual lover. He even lived for his hostages. Like the scene where he demanded a pizza be sent in for a pregnant woman. "It's hot enough? If it's not hot enough I'll make 'em bring in some that's hot." Frank's *character* got him out of his story corner.

Pick the metaphorical thought that best works for you. I most often use "key." The key to the story. That key is always through character. *Your* consciously focusing on *character.*

THE COUNTRY AND CITY MICE

Character and plot must intertwine. Remember: "no *character* is an island." Like chickens and eggs. Like Egri and Aristotle. Both get equal billing. The plot must serve the character, the character must serve the plot.

With that caveat indelibly branded in the front of your brain, let's you and I do a half page or so on the major characters for our stories. But don't think length, or minutiae, think soul.

I'll go first. Cliff's fairly well defined in my mind. He's innocent of city life. His concept of solving someone's mental problems would be to grasp firmly that someone by the elbow and say in his best John Wayne manner, "Now you just straighten up here." Cliff is so much an anachronism, he would be considered a dinosaur even in the cornstalks. Remember, extremes? I'll make him the most innocent of innocents. Like my cousin Cliff, he'll be blond. Wry as hell, like his Scots MacPherson heritage. The Scots are pleased if you pick up on their humor, if not, that's fine too, aye. That's Cliff. He grew up with birth, life, and death, as his family's farm animals are always birthing and dying. His daily work has been dedicated to the quality of their lives.

Cliff fell in love with his first-grade country school teacher. He tried to wrestle Janet Moranville to the meadow grass while her sister Twila stood over their five-year-old twisting bodies, rubbing "shame-shame" forefingers together, then pointing them at Cliff. Even as an adult, Cliff falls in love with someone every spring. Every fall that someone is with someone else. Generally without even the slightest awareness of Cliff's full heart.

Cliff has had only one idol. Rich Mendenhall, the ex–All State quarterback for the Guide Rock Warriors. Rich is only six years older. God, does Cliff want to be like Rich. He'll feel that way when he's fifty-four. But not the Rich of sixty, the Rich of eighteen.

Cliff's father would not let him play football. Dad was stricken with a debilitating stroke when Cliff was twelve. He's had to work on the farm. Giving birth, life, and death to the animals. Cliff's ready for change.

Susan Garber hates her mother, her father, and most vehemently, herself. This rage is amplified every year. Every week. Every day. Some of those days, she feels like the top *is* off her head and everyone is vomiting down her neck.

Susan only loves rain. She hates the same rain when it lasts more than an hour, but during that hour, she's cleansed.

Last year at three o'clock one morning, Susan got out of bed and walked naked around her Omaha block. She said to the draining thunderclouds: "Pain . . . loneliness . . . contrast. A soul reaching into the marrow of hell that lives in the center of a teardrop. The lesser colors of a rainbow can bloom and buzz, cry and ache. The night dreams fade. The day grows to a specter that throws you out, up and backward, slipping in your own desperation. Your own liquid shriek. A life of promise smolders, sparks, smolders, flames."

No one ever knew about Susan's rain walk. Not even Susan.

Those are my character sketches. The specifics on Susan don't seem as important as the reality that she is mad, and getting madder. I'll find out her details in the step outline and script. Oh, I think her family should be wealthy. Maybe her father's an Omaha meat packer. It seems more dramatic than most other professions, and it's indigenous to the area. That's good, as Cliff is totally of his area.

NUDE IN THE RAIN

I often say in 434, "I want you to spread your story and your characters before you as if you were to lift your intestines from your stomach and arrange them on a table. *Your* guts, not anyone else's. Get inside of yourself. Pull things out. Don't be safe."

I can't ask you to forgive me when I get personal, because that's the way I teach. It's been repeatedly pointed out my ways are exceptionally self-revelatory, and because of that, fairly unique and effective. I once passionately cried to a 434 grouping, "I'll do and say *anything* to get you to write better scripts." And from the end of the long workshop table came the meek voice of Diane Saltzberg. "Yes, and sometimes you embarrass us *so* much, Lew."

I was down at a point prior to my darling Pamela. It rained. I walked around my block nude at 3:00 A.M. Came back and sat at my Remington typewriter. And wrote what is now Susan's rain walk.

I was drunk at the time. Not tipsy, or staggering, or inebriated. Drunk. I poured the garbage from my mind into my typewriter. In the morning, I looked at the pages and correctly concluded I was mad. Hopefully the catalyst was alcohol and not the real thing. But I had the sober intelligence not to throw it away. I thought I could perhaps use that moment in sordid time somewhere, somehow. Now, it seems right for Susan.

ANOTHER MOTTO FOR WRITERS

Never throw anything away! Even, or maybe particularly, drunken ravings. Also never give away your original. Originals are intimidating to people who read. Make copies and more copies!

Ernest Hemingway once lost an entire novel on a train to Paris. Perhaps he was walking nude in the rain on that train.

THE LITTLE PEOPLE

Time and again, student, novice, and bad writers write their secondary characters as afterthoughts or non-people. You see this when characters are given numbers instead of names. Hood #1, Cop #3, Man #1, or Woman #5. Often you will see Girl, Boy, Man, Woman, Cop, or Hood. To many, it suggests how little care and feeling the writer could have for human beings.

First off, they need names. They need characteristics. Dimension. Yes, even your love. The reader and the film audience should subconsciously feel the writer has thought through his or her people with the same sensitivity as vested in the major characters.

On a more practical level, imagine yourself on location. The director is almost ready to have you, the producer-writer, send the actors to the set. You look about and say, "OK, who's Cop #1? Good. Now we need Thug #3 over, oh, you're Thug #2. Good, you're Thug #3. Got it. Now over by the pine tree is Cop #2. Good, you're number . . . oh, sorry. You're #3." See how dehumanizing it is for the actors? *You* have the control to prevent this from happening.

A good time back, Walt Disney told me a story. He had just finished *Bambi* and he showed it to a few guests and his family. When he put Diane, his daughter, to bed that night, he could see she was very troubled. "What's the matter, honey?" asked the great man. "Bambi's mother died," responded Diane. She accompanied this baring of her heart with wracking sobs. Walt, in almost equal anguish said, "Honey, honey, it's only a movie." Diane Disney wasn't appeased, for quickly she responded, "But Daddy, you could have made her live." Walt never lost that moment, which affected every Disney story session when endings were discussed.

And so it is with you. You can make them live. Or die. Or have names instead of dehumanizing numbers.

People who can really matter in getting your script made may feel that your numbered characters are superficial, and hence that could carry over to the star roles. That determination will never be truly revealed to you. It'll be buried somewhere in the rejection speech. Numbered characters may not be the only reason, but could contribute to their decision.

Oh, maybe if a character has one line, you can get away with calling him or her OBESE COP, or NERVOUS NURSE. Giving them a character trait reveals *some* thought and caring. Even then don't *ever* call your heavies thugs, hoods, or any other condescending term. Make your bad guys bad. Don't trivialize them in *any* way.

A man who felt even background characters deserve histories and dignity was Jan Kadar, the extraordinary *Shop on Main Street* and *Lies My Father Told Me* director. Jan was directing *Escape From Hell,* an NBC movie localed in a real-life Montana institution. Jan was so concerned with dimension in everything, he persuaded the background people, commonly known as "extras," to come in on their day off, and helped them develop their characters. He didn't direct by saying "do something crazy" behind the star Alan Arkin during scenes. He worked out, with each person, their individual character traits. One talked into a shoe trying to contact his dead mother, while another juggled pink elephants, and another recited nursery rhymes.

Most directors, actors, and, even more sadly, writers just sluff the lesser roles off the back of their hands. You give these characters careful, creative thoughts and decisions. Over the stretch of your entire story, it'll lend your script a special glow.

NIXON, CATHER, AND TOLSTOY

Here are character thoughts from three wildly different, successful, and good writers. From Agnes Nixon, the acknowledged doyenne of daytime drama, who created "One Life to Live," "Search for Tomorrow," "All My Children," "Another World," "The Guiding Light," and "As the World Turns": "Situations change, human nature does not." Her fictional children may suffer from Vietnam flashbacks or AIDS but their real problems are born in the soul. "My secret? I always know who the character is before I start writing. My characters are characters who have a history."

Willa Cather was a drama critic for the *Lincoln Star* prior to her Pulitzer Prize–winning fiction career. She was talking about the actor but let's substitute "writer." "A writer's mind is his genius. It should be fed by whatever is best in science, letters, art. He should know, through imagination and research or experience, how it feels to be an Egyptian sunning himself on the marble steps of the temple of Elephantine. How it feels to go up to the Acropolis on a blue spring morning in Athens. How it feels to be a thirsty Bowery boy, hesitating between a free lunch of pork and beans or cornbread and cabbage. He should know how to ascend the steps of a throne and how a peasant scrapes the mud from his wooden shoes. Potentially he should know all manners, all people, all good, all evil."

A tall order? Not at all. "Through imagination *and* research or experience." All of that can be and should be yours *before* you start your script.

Take Agnes Nixon's secret of knowing your characters and Willa Cather's researching or experiencing your characters, then beam that combination through a Tolstoy filter: "We're all different, we're all alike. We are rivers. Broad, narrow, warm, cold, shallow, deep." The way you develop your characters and the characters themselves will be different for any given story situation. But the characters will *be.* And for them to be, you must have them broad, narrow, warm, cold, shallow, deep.

Chapter 4

THE OUTLINE FOR YOU AND "THEM"

Screenwriting life is a game show. We escalate from plateau to plateau, thinking and answering until the ecstatic conclusion.

From the idea to the multiplex and its fame and fortune handmaidens. But no, no. By now you're in this for quality. Remember? Do only your best work. From that effort, your chances will be infinitely higher than if you start out to consciously write a "commercial screenplay." Screenplays "they're" looking for today will cause "them" to stick fingers down "their" throats tomorrow. But everyone's looking for quality.

The strong majority of professional screenwriters tremble in fear at the story plateau in this game show of life they've chosen to play. Most writers lack the confidence you can gain from the study of structure. Study films. Study scripts. Read and re-read Egri and Aristotle. William Froug. Richard Walter. Linda Seger. Go to workshops and classes. Challenge. Experiment. Best of all, write. From all of this activity and energy comes confidence. With confidence, the dragons of fear and trembling can be vanquished.

Your script is obviously the most time consuming. But trained chimpanzees and sophisticated robots can turn out 100-plus pages.

So far you're doing fine. Just fine. You've read your reading. You've got a wonderful idea that you're able to do and that's worth doing.

You've got your beginning, middle, and end from your two-minute movie. You've got your characters.

The next step is to develop the story in detail, scene by scene.

Aristotle said: "Of all plots and actions, the episodic are the worst. I call a plot 'episodic' in which the episodes or acts succeed one another without probable or necessary sequence." An illustration of this can be found in those Christmas letters you get every year. The chronological recitation of the yearly events may initially be interesting, dramatic, or funny, but after the novelty wears off, each event becomes less captivating sentence by sentence until finally boredom attacks.

Sketches in variety shows can be entertaining for the three- to twelve-minute haul. They're built on one joke or insight. Performers try desperately to end the sketch prior to that old devil boredom. Why do sketches fail to go the feature film length distance? No character, no second acts.

They have beginnings, middles, and ends, but the second acts and the characters are never developed. This is where your outlining comes in. You need to develop the cause and effect, the push and pull, and the actions and reactions, as well as the characters. This is best done through outlines.

Outlining frees your creativity. When writing the screenplay, outlining allows you to focus your heart, mind, and imagination on the dramatic potentials within each scene, without being shackled by storytelling bonds. You've already told your story at the outline level. You have your idea, your basic story perimeters, your characters, and your scene-by-scene, often called "step," outline. Now you can soar. Invent. But *in control.*

Wonderful screenplays are not runaway trains. They are not "all over the map." They do not have everything thrown in. Wonderful screenplays are the beneficiaries of careful, premeditated structuring at the development level. From this structure comes a whole which you want to appear spontaneous, but is actually the result of a careful plan.

William Goldman is the contemporary guru on structure, because of one simple, clear, and constantly quoted line within *Adventures in The Screen Trade.* "Screenplays are structure." He elaborated,

> When I say that screenplay is structure, it's simply making the spine. And you must protect that spine. There can be wonderful scenes but if they're off the spine and you see them in a movie, they will simply die.

If screenplays are structure, "spine" is the soul of structure. The soul of the screenplay. That's the "what's-it *really*-about" concept.

You can put a novel aside and later return to the story, but movies keep moving. And even novels keep moving, per Thomas Wolfe: "What I had to face, the very bitter lesson that everyone who wants to write has got to learn, is that a thing may in itself be the finest piece of writing one has ever done and yet have absolutely no place in the manuscript one hopes to publish." "Protect your spine" is another motto to be branded in your mind at every outline step.

THE STRUCTURE OF STRUCTURE

In life, things happen one after the other. In structure one thing happens *because* of the other. Structure is that simple and that hard.

You need to develop the eye to distinguish wheat from chaff. That comes from experience and intellectual dissection. If either fail you, try a friend, but have your bull feces detector on at all times. Either cut the elements that have little or nothing to do with your story, or better, bind them into your story/structure/plot.

At all steps along the story way, make sure the scene you're in was caused by the scene that went before. And the following scene is there because of the one you're in. Keep that rhythm going and you'll have a damned good story.

1. Scene Cards or Step Outlines

Scene cards and step outlines are for your eyes only. Most professional writers write their scripts from a step outline.

Scene cards are a carry-over technique from the days when writers worked in warren-like buildings on studio lots, and would wander into each other's rooms and help with one another's story problems. The cards would often be thumbtacked to their office walls.

I started to use cards but spent too many minutes shuffling through them. They would too often get stuck together with condiments. After a number of lost time spans, I said nuts to it. I also have never understood the advocates who say you can put card C in card R's place and that can clear up your entire story. If that were so, card R shouldn't have been there in the first place.

A number of excellent writers still use scene cards. If scene cards are best for you, do it. An admired writer, Mayo Simon, once brought his step outline to my office. It was written in large script on six-foot strips of butcher paper that Mayo pinned to my burlap-textured wall at NBC. He made the sale. It worked and he works. So do what you will: scene cards, butcher paper, erasable bond. But do a step outline.

2. The Step Outline

The step outline, for you, is the scene-to-scene development of your story. Your two-minute movie. Scene to scene to scene. I am defining a step as something one script page or longer. Some steps will reflect one page, others eight to ten. Most will be four or less.

I was writing for Paul Newman. He squinted at one point and said, "I hate you television writers," one of which I was at the time. I asked, "Why, Paul? What did we do wrong?" He told me. "You guys only think in three-page scenes." He was then working on *Rachel, Rachel,* a marvelous movie with many scenes longer than three pages. I've never forgotten his insight. Years later, because of Paul, I look at scenes I'm writing or have written and constantly ask, "Is that all there is?" Have I sluiced all the dramatic gold in the scene?

An episode of "Moonlighting" had a scene when Maddy wanted David to take her to a wedding so she wouldn't have to hear the "when are *you* getting married" questions. That scene could have been three pages but it was fifteen. She was cagy. He was coy. She was direct. He was a "smart cracker." She was angry. He got angry. They hit each other. They cried. They laughed. It was all marvelous. The writers dug and dug to the soul of the story, then the characters, the soul of series television.

My 434 eight always hear me recapitulate *E.T.* when we get to step outlines. Sometimes a scene can be written in two-word bursts. Words that are iceberg tips:

1. Alien lands.
2. Alien-boy.

But that's too short for me. I would do:

1. An alien spaceship lands. E.T. is left behind.
2. E.T. goes to a suburban home. Little boy having a pizza party.
3. E.T. connects with the boy.
4. Boy smuggles E.T. into his suburban home.

3. Breaking It Down

Musicians often believe math is much more applicable to music than it would seem. This is also true of the craft of screenwriting.

Formula is a pejorative word but there are *good* formulas. Screenplay outlines are, in the positive sense of the word, a formula used since the feature film was born.

At UCLA, our core screenwriting course is the original theatrical motion picture, 434. We believe all forms of screenwriting, from the fifteen-second commercial to the longest mini-series, share the same qualities. All require the same Aristotelian narrative structure and must meet the same criteria: "to *not* be boring!"

Ergo, the step outline formula can be applicable to any length screenplay. Here's what I teach for TV and feature movies.

You'll have between thirty and forty-five steps. Remember a step is anything one page or longer. Someone driving up to a house and going in to confront their significant other would constitute one step but two scenes. The drive-up is not a step.

You see what you're additionally trying to accomplish via this type of structuring is a way to keep a first draft from being too short or too long.

4. The "Little" Scenes

Don't at all devalue the importance of quarter- or half-page scenes. Let's say a woman drives up to a house, goes inside, and shoots her husband. No dialogue. That could be almost half a page. Let's not tell but show.

CUT TO:

EXT.—SUBURBAN STREET—NIGHT

Betty MacKelvey wheels into the driveway of her home. She thinks, then backs out of the driveway and parallel parks in front of the house. She gets out and moves in a somnambulant way to her porch steps. Her Ferrari idling. A shotgun at her Yves St. Laurent side.

CUT TO:

INT.—MACKELVEY LIVING ROOM—NIGHT

John MacKelvey is absorbing "Monday Night Football" on their large screen TV. Betty opens the front door. Frank, as usual, ignores his wife's entrance. Betty lifts the Winchester pump. She blows away the large screen TV. She blows away John.

That's an important story occurrence. But in production manager parlance, that's a third of a page which encompasses two scenes. Even less can be a following scene:

CUT TO:

EXT.—7-ELEVEN STORE—NIGHT

Betty comes out of the advertising-festooned doorway and stops. The Ferrari idles before her. A Big Gulp in her right hand. She studies the car, the Big Gulp, then angrily heaves the cherry confection over the cherry-red vehicle. Betty collapses. Sobbing, then laughing, then as suddenly, Betty is silent.

You *can* make that living room confrontation a multi-page scene. Certainly not the Big Gulp scene. Yet that "little" scene could be the most dramatic scene in the entire movie. For many that was the Tom Cruise/Dustin Hoffman moment in *Rain Man* where the two brothers danced to Muzak in the elevator. Another scene under a page.

5. The Thirty-Step Outline

But for the purposes of your step outline rhythms, *and* coming in with a 100- to 110-page, "on-time" script, count the steps as scenes with one page or more and include the shorter scenes with the before or after step. Or when you're writing the script, if a "7-Eleven" type scene comes to you.

If you use this technique and have an Arthur Miller-Eugene O'Neill textured story, you'll need around thirty steps. People will have lots of passion and tension to get out. A number of your scenes will be five to eight or nine pages. Another number will be one or two, most will be three or four. Let's average it out to three pages for each step.

If you have thirty steps at three pages a step, that's ninety pages. Your screenplays should be between 100 and 110 pages, so at ninety pages, you're almost there. Since most screenplays are too convoluted, it's usually easier to add ten pages than cut ten.

Anything under 100 pages doesn't appear to be a real script. It also seems amateur. Anything over 110, excessive. Over 130, obscene. Usually 110 pages is 110 minutes (the rule of everybody's thumb in single-camera production is one minute to one page). So 110 pages is quite enough for most movies.

6. The Forty-Five Step Outline

If you have a comedy or action/adventure story, you'll be closer to forty-five steps in your outline. The very pacing of the piece will give you fewer scenes over five pages and more one- and two-pagers.

Approximately thirty steps for drama, around forty-five for comedy or action/adventure. These gauges will keep you from over- or underwriting close to all the time. A large student pitfall is overwriting. Their outlines will come in at sixty-plus steps. They always plead, "But they're short scenes. They'll go quickly." Some weeks later, I end up getting panicked phone calls. "I'm on page eighty with half the step outline to go!"

Did you say "maybe fifty-five?" No. *Forty-five!* Maybe, just maybe, one or two more. Not ten.

THE STEP OUTLINE AND THE THREE ACTS

You need to know about the three-act page count structure *now*. At the step outline level. Not when you're "into script."

1. Page 17

Remember the first-act end as "the situation"? This is when E.T. meets Elliot. When Rick gets the transit letters that can get two people out of Casablanca. When the reporter's "Rosebud" obsession flashes us back to Charles Foster Kane's separation from his Colorado parents. When little Jennifer is initially approached by pedophile Howie in *Fallen Angel.* When Butch talks to Sundance about going to Bolivia.

When I was discussing this page 17 reality with UCLA alum Greg Nava, he immediately went to his award winning *El Norte* script. There it was. The Nava/Thomas heroine decides to go north on . . . page 17. The staggering majority of quality scripts land Act One, the situation, either side of 17. Hence, the not-so-arbitrary page 17 edict to 434 and you.

The audience doesn't want to wait to, say, page 30 to find out what they're watching. It's similar to business meetings. In the initial banter, the reason for the meeting is foreshadowed. The participants also use the time to get to know each other. The talk is a bit revealing, as someone will have a small story about their spouses or the cute thing a child did that morning. Somewhere into minute eight of an hour-long meeting, someone will speak the reason everyone's been assembled.

Like a movie's Act One. The foreshadowing of the situation, the character revelation, then the total unveiling.

From my floating page 17 concept, let's turn to more mathematical equations. Three into seventeen is almost six. Approximately six scenes at an average of three pages each for Act One. In *The Glass Hammer* step outline developed concurrently with these pages, Cliff enters the mental institution in scene six. The script shouldn't be far from page 17. Some scripts I've used ten scenes to page 17, others four. That *always* relates to the genre of the story. Comedy and action-adventure will be closer to ten scenes.

2. Page 85, Maybe

Now Act Two. The complications. Time for the plot to thicken. The end of Act Two is less exact, as it is so dependent on the twists the story must take to get to a wonderful Act Three.

Page 85 is most often the norm. But the third act could take only five pages and you'll end Act Two at around page 100. Conversely, your story may dictate a long or complex Act Three which can start at page 70.

In *The Glass Hammer,* the escape from Beatrice is the third act. That should take about five or six scenes. They'll be mostly chase scenes which can be complicated, so I'll stay on the three page average. I'll guess it will take six scenes. Another seventeen or eighteen pages. That's pretty close to page 85. Let's see, six scenes in the back, six in the front. I've got a dramatic story here so I should have close to thirty scenes. Six and six is twelve, twelve from thirty is eighteen.

That shouldn't be a guess far off the eventual mark. Eighteen steps or so for Act Two.

3. To 100–110

As you see in my *Glass Hammer* case, the Act Three scene and page count length is well estimated during the deliberations for Act Two. But only the floating page 17 is firm. Don't lock yourself into page 85 or anything else. Acts Two and Three page numbers are totally dependent upon your story.

4. Like A, B, and C

For step outline and page count information, it's A, B, C simple. Don't get too mathematical, too complex, or too soulless.

The audience subconsciously knows what it wants. Your job is to give it to them. Without the seams showing. Your step outlines, act ends, and analytical thinking should all be *completely disguised.* In some movies and episodes you can almost see the script conference chatter running alongside the story line. Don't get caught up too far beyond the three-act structure and page 17. The rest of the process should be as organic as possible. Your soul talking to the audience's soul.

SCENE DO'S AND DON'TS

There are many "do's" but only a few "don'ts" when considering scenes for your outline.

Your primary goal with scenes is to progress the characters and story, keeping the audience from boredom. That means giving the actors and director scenes they can play. Scenes that are dramatic or comedic. Scenes that have the potential to be staged so everyone will be interested or entertained. The primary responsibility lies with you, the screenwriter.

Here are the major caveats for the scenes you put in your outline.

1. Sitting Down Scenes

Beware of: Bar scenes, sometimes called "swizzle stick" scenes. Coffee scenes. Eating scenes. Sitting down scenes.

Of course there are wonderful exceptions, in which the setting psychologically contributes to the passion and tension inside the scene: the *Tom Jones* eating orgy; *The Thomas Crown Affair* chess game; Sally demonstrating to Harry, in a crowded deli, how women fake orgasms; the sexless breakfast montage in *Citizen Kane;* the swizzle stick scenes in *Casablanca;* the two families blending at lunch in *A Man and a Woman;* and the aforementioned *My Dinner With André.*

Beyond lack of imagination, a major reason you see so many eating scenes on TV and so few in theatrical films is that old devil budget. Most TV movies and episodes have less money and need to shoot between six and nine pages a day, and it's much quicker to film a five-page sitting scene without actors or cameras moving. *But most sitting down scenes are boring.* Have as few as possible in your step outlines.

Don't get caught up in dollar fretting when you're a beginning writer. Save that for the budget rewrite. You'll be surprised at how little some apparently costly scenes can be shot for and vice versa. For now, at the "spec" script level, write the best you can write. *Spend all the money you want.*

2. Surprises

Because the audience has been barraged by so many TV and feature stories in their collective lives, you can almost see lips move along with the dialogue. The story turns are *so* predictable, and the surprises *so* few.

Surprise was the cornerstone of director Howard Hawks's career.

One of his wonderful writers, Leigh Brackett, said Hawks deliberately and constantly pushed her for surprises and more surprises. He liked to set up the audience to expect one thing, then deliver another.

All of Hawks's 1940s screwball comedies, all of Chaplin, Keaton, Lloyd, layer surprise upon surprise. Every screen story that ranks in your top twenty has surprises or it wouldn't have been so memorable. These are the things you tell your back-fence neighbor when you're talking to them about the film.

3. Foreshadowing

As jokes need to be set up in comedian monologues, so you need setups for comedy and drama.

If someone's dog dies in your story, you want to foreshadow the dog, and its vulnerability to eating something that might be dangerous or to chasing cars. Then the audience anticipates. When the death finally comes by something the dog ate or by vehicle, it will have much more impact when you've "set up" the dog's habits.

Anticipation is often as wonderful, or as suspenseful, as the realization of the end result. Anticipation is the ancillary best of foreshadowing. Put a gun in a drawer and you'll have the audience leaning forward every time a character goes near the drawer. The cutting back and forth between Frankenstein and the approaching crowd is so memorable. Roy Huggins ("Maverick," "The Rockford Files") has a wonderful example. In our 434 gatherings, we call it the "bear on the beach."

A couple are kissing in a convertible on an oceanside cliff. It would certainly be an audience shock if a bear attacked the preoccupied lovers. But think of all the attenuated, excruciating suspense you can add to the situation when you show the lovers, then cut to show the bear on the beach. Back to the lovers, then to the bear noticing them. Back to the lovers, then the bear climbing up the cliff. Again to the lovers, then the bear approaching the convertible. See? That sequence can be drawn out and out, giving an audience three or four minutes of the highest identifiable anticipation.

The protagonist can be also effectively foreshadowed for the audience. Audiences could hardly wait for Batman to come on screen. You anticipate the foreshadowed Citizen Kane's coming on screen throughout the entire movie. Ingrid Bergman's Ilsa is foreshadowed with the

"As Time Goes By" tension when Rick's piano player starts the melody. We wait and wait for The Godfather. When the "Columbo" pilot was shot, twenty-five minutes of foreshadowing was written and filmed before Peter Falk, as Columbo, came on screen.

4. In Painted Corners

Look to your characters to show you the way out when you've painted yourself into a story corner. Again and again, at this level of script development, this simple credo will rescue you. It's *the* major trick of this trade.

You're in that same story corner. You're thinking "character." What would he or she do? At this crossroads, think of the obvious. Be it plot or character twists, what's the most obvious thing that could happen?

In one of the "Yellow Rose" stories, we had a moment where Sam Elliot's character and Cybill Shepherd's character were on the romantic precipice of a kiss. A kiss seemed too boring. I was in a corner. Then I recalled a Phil Saltzman thought I have used again and again before and since. "Take the obvious and turn it 180 degrees." Cybill pulled her fist back and smashed Sam full on his poised mouth. Sam's character was surprised. Most importantly, the audience was surprised. And delighted.

Sometimes the 180-degree turn is wrong for your character, so you'll discard that concept. But often it'll be a major trick worth turning.

When you've exhausted the 180-degree consideration, and others suggested, and some you've hopefully devised, you may say, "My God, I'm blocked!" Don't be. My mother used to mumble about things she didn't wish to deal with: "Pay no mind to that." When people ask me what do I do when I get blocked, I reply, "I don't." Do not acknowledge such an occasion.

John T. Kelley wrote: "No matter how little you feel like working, force your mind to continue thinking about the story or idea under consideration. Eventually the wheels will begin to turn. Usually it won't take more than five or ten minutes at the most." Jack London *(The Call of the Wild)* said: "You can't wait for inspiration. You have to go after it with a club."

5. Telling "Them"

In yesteryear, orating was a genuine art. William Jennings Bryan, Abraham Lincoln, Mark Twain, preachers. Communities turned out to hear their first-rate orations, speaking on any subject. The bible on speech-making is Sarett and Foster's *Basic Principles of Speech.* Their edict is the commandment for all fledgling orators. "Tell them what you're going to tell them. Tell them. Tell them what you've told them."

When you're developing your story, before, during, and after, give a thought to "telling them what you're going to tell them, telling them, then telling them what you've told them." Three thoughts for three acts. That circle can work powerfully. It is often like "la ronde" in poetry where the end is the beginning and the beginning the end. Rosebud at the beginning and end. The Lone Ranger riding into town, then back out. Bambi's birthing to his son's birthing.

YOUR STEP OUTLINE—ACT ONE—THE SITUATION

Elizabeth Barrett Browning wrote: "How do I love thee? Let me count the ways." New and experienced writers often don't count the ways available to begin their story. From Snoopy's, "It was a dark and stormy night and a shot rang out," to George Lucas', "Long ago, in a galaxy far, far away," to Citizen Kane dying. In every wonderful film opening, step one shares a single monolithic fact. It is not boring. Pick and start with the most passionate, exciting, funny, or tension-filled scene you can find in the uncounted ways.

Most often you're best to begin with an event. A spaceship landing. An outlaw trying to rob a bank. A man being killed in front of Rick's Place. A small abused girl slipping into hysteria.

1. Unpeeling Onions

After the first scene, begin to unpeel the onion. Strip away layers of story and character scene by scene. Don't blow out everything up front. Reveal more and more about your characters as your story unpeels. This technique adds mystery, tension, and suspense to melodrama, drama, or comedy. Movies too often tell the audience more than it wants, or needs, to know. The audience's "need to know" should always be in your story mind, but especially in Act One. *Withhold as long as you can.*

2. Pace Yourself

A young bull and an old bull crested a hill. They looked down into a verdant, lush valley. A herd of beautiful, sensuous cows grazed on the valley floor. The young bull excitedly exclaims to the old bull: "Hey, let's run down there and make love to some of those cows!" The old bull patiently replied: "No, my son. Let us *walk* down there and make love to them *all.*"

Thus it often is with young *and* old writers. We want to break into a dead run with our wonderful research, insight, and drama. We must pace ourselves. Be patient. Walk to the cows. Tease the audience with our backstory knowledge, revealing it gradually through our character's actions.

We often begin before the beginning. A frequent problem with new writers is their jamming much of their information up front in screenplays. Then the Act One ends at page 35 rather than 17. The audience reading your script will be asleep by then. They want to know the situation much earlier. If not they will stop reading.

YOUR STEP OUTLINE—ACT TWO—THE COMPLICATIONS

Now get into the information. The back story. The character mystery. Subplots. Action, reaction. Cause, effect. Complications.

This is where the majority of films and writers fall on their rumps. F. Scott Fitzgerald said American lives don't have second acts. He could have been as easily talking about most screenplays.

Second acts are especially needed today. In the thirties and forties, movies were approximately seventy-four minutes long. The exhibitors wanted them to be the top or bottom of double features, with a cartoon, a newsreel, and a short.

That's why so many of the best older pictures cause panic in your heart. You love the fantasy world in which the movie has placed you. Your wishes are fulfilled. You can feel it's going to end. You don't want it to end. Oh, no!! It's ending.

When was the last time you felt that way with a contemporary film? Even when you've enjoyed the make believe world, you don't have much of a twinge when you sense the approach of end credits.

At one hundred plus minutes, it's time to go. More is not more. The same narrative storytelling is still in effect, used in the days when the films were twenty-five minutes shorter. That means more second act. For the less satisfying movies, Act Two is either too complicated and boring or too thin and uncomplicated and also boring.

Occasionally plots are wildly complicated but the action or the comedy carries the picture, as in *Rambo* or *Lethal Weapon II.* The audience has such a good time they don't care about the Act Two twists and don't even demand to be able to follow them. It's the "dazzle-them-with-footwork" technique. You shouldn't rely on that gambit. Those films are generally structured that way because the scripts were too long. The first showing was far too many minutes and deep cuts had to be made in the movie, excising scenes that would have explained much of what seems puzzling. Most of the audience will not be that discerning or interested in the logic. They ride with the escalating emotion.

You will find that many of the entertainment industry's middle management people are very intelligent. Most will have law degrees or MBA's. Few will be steeped in creative ability, knowledge, or instinct. To contribute *and* earn their middle management salaries, they give "notes" on scripts. The notes are not from the soul but from the mind. They're logic notes.

Hence, when all the logic is put in a script and the film runs long, their editors, peers, and audience tests go for the emotion. That's the major reason many of the good movies you see have logic gaps, assuming you notice or care. The general audience won't.

Be most attentive to character development in your middles. Err on the side of being too thin in your plotting. It's easier to add twists. Consider the stories of the most entertaining or moving movies you've seen in the last year. They've either had great film footwork or powerful simplicity. The A to Z concept with zigzags back and forth across the straight Peter Rabbit–type story line. Think simple and profound.

1. Scenes without Words

Unfold your simple, profound second act through action as much as possible. Think of ballet.

The Black Stallion was best in the first half, when the story was told without words.

An Ernst Lubitsch–directed comedy of yesteryear had a colonel philandering with his general's wife. The colonel's in her boudoir when his general walks up the outside staircase. The colonel hides just as the general enters the bedroom for a romantic interval with his wife. Cut outside to see an air raid siren blasting. Cut inside to the staircase. The general charges from the boudoir, rushing for his post, pulling his pants up. He stops. Around the waist, the pants are significantly smaller. His face washes with the realization that his wife is philandering. There are no words in the scenes, just truly moving movie writing.

2. Scenes with Words

Yet, take much to heart Paul Newman's "you TV writers only think in three-page scenes" admonishment. There are times when you and your characters should let it out. Mine the dramatic bullion. Do the Maddy-David "Moonlighting" fifteen-pager.

William Bradford Huie's and Paddy Chayefsky's *The Americanization of Emily* has three five-minute scenes with James Garner and Julie Andrews that are just spectacular. Rent the movie. Find them. Get in touch with fine dialogue writing. It doesn't and shouldn't all be MTV quick cuts or M.O.S. (M.O.S. is a film industry term dating back to when German director Eric von Stroheim would tell his crew, "Ve'll shoot dis mid out sound.")

3. Obligatory Scenes

Whatever the Act One situation, somebody somewhere in the second act has to tell someone else E.T. wants to go home. That Butch and Sundance want to go back to a simpler life. Citizen Kane wants "Rosebud." That Jennifer will have to testify against the pedophile. Or play

"As Time Goes By." These "talk" scenes were written and shot with invention inside passion and tension.

Sadly, most obligatory scenes lie flat like pregnant buffalo. Talking heads going on and on to each other. Talking heads. There is very little invention, with few audience surprises and less pleasure.

Identify your obligatory scenes. Examine and reexamine their quality. With that study, you will likely push yourself to something much better than your first thought. This is the one point in screenplay writing where you can and must be extremely analytical. Fine obligatory scenes are difficult. However, you can add surprise and delight if you examine and reexamine what the audience expects. Then write with twists and invention, using unusual locales, dialogue, or contrapuntal tension. *Disguise your obligatory scenes.*

4. Disguising Exposition

In first, second, or even third acts, DISGUISE YOUR EXPOSITION. That will not often be done literally at the step outline level, but here is where you should notice the potential problem and put arguments, sexuality, car chases, or camels in the scene. Humphrey Bogart said, "Whenever I have to deliver exposition, I hope they put two camels behind me fucking so the audience'll have something interesting to look at."

Show, don't tell. You're writing movies. Make them move. John T. Kelley wrote: "Tell the story in terms of action as much as possible. Even false action which is only motion. Motion such as opening and closing doors, riding in cars, walking down halls is preferable to no action at all. Always better to let something take place before the audience's eyes or ears than to summarize it in expository dialogue. Try to sandwich it in with action, action, and more action."

5. Math One More Time

Let's calculate how many steps you'll need for your second act. Act One should be between six and ten steps. Depending on story. It's safe to say no more no less.

Act Three, the conclusion, generally uses between three and ten steps. Remember, screenplays should run between thirty and forty-five steps depending if you're doing Arthur Miller, James Bond, or Woody Allen.

That leaves between fifteen and thirty steps for Act Two, the middle. Steps with *profound* simplicity, steps without words, steps with words, disguised obligatory and expositional steps, steps with apparent dead ends, steps with action. Most of all, steps that never bore.

YOUR STEP OUTLINE—ACT THREE—THE CONCLUSION

Many call Act Three the climax, the resolution, or the catharsis. Conclusion includes all three and more. Conclusion also includes epilogues, a theater term. "Tags" in sitcoms. The scene that often comes after the final dramatic or comedic conflagration. The scene that will make people laugh or cry and then run from the theaters and television sets to tell everyone what a wonder they've just seen.

Aristotle defines the emotion that should be felt by your audience in the third act as the catharsis.

The S. H. Butcher *Poetics* notes on catharsis:

> The poets found out how the transport of human pity and human fear might, under the excitation of art, be dissolved in joy, and the pain, escape in the purified tide of human sympathy. In *Romeo and Juliet* the tragedy does not lie merely in the unhappy ending of a tale of true love. Certain other conditions, beyond those which contribute to give a dramatic interest, are required to produce the tragic effect. There is the feud of the two houses, whose high place in the commonwealth makes their enmity an affair of public concern. The lovers in their new-found rapture act in defiance of all external obligations. The elemental force and depth of their passion bring them into collision with the fabric of society to which they belong. Their tragic doom quickly closes in upon them. Yet even in death the consequences of their act extend beyond the sphere of the individual. Over the grave of their love, the two houses are reconciled.

That's what it's really about. The story beneath the story. The emotion from the regeneration of puppies crawling out from under the porch. E.T. in the sky, homeward bound. Butch and Sundance in the freeze frame of immortality, entering the cacophony of rifle fire. Rosebud on the burning sled. "Louie, I think this is the beginning of a beautiful friendship." Miss Jane Pittman taking a drink of water from the "whites only" fountain. Jennifer about to testify against the pedophile.

All moments to never forget. Moments in which "certain other conditions beyond those which contribute to give a dramatic interest are required to produce the tragic effect." Capstones to what has gone before. The climax of the climax.

> The end is the chief thing of all. —Aristotle

The last-act scenes that have gone before your end credits take three forms. Action, talk, or a combination thereof.

1. Action Act Three

The second act ends. The protagonist is going to take physical action. Here's where most famous film chase scenes are cued: the world seemingly racing after E.T. and the children, the car chase madness at the end of *The French Connection,* the gun battles that conclude *Butch and Sundance,* and the various *Rambos*.

2. The Talk Act Three

The second act ends. The protagonist is going to take verbal action, such as the destructive verbal action of Charles Foster Kane, the dialogue war between Shirley MacLaine and Anne Bancroft in *Turning Point,* or Paul Newman's summation in *The Verdict*'s court.

Going for a catharsis with talk is easily the most difficult. Writing skill must be at its zenith. Squealing tires, hoof beats, and blazing guns demand the equal skill of special effects and stunt persons. Using only words based on what has gone before is at once tricky and potentially rewarding. It is also cheap. Your production manager will love you.

3. The Talk and Action Act Three

You don't *have* to tie up every ribbon and bow at the end of Act Three.

A rough cut of *The French Connection* was shown to Richard Zanuck, then production head of Twentieth Century–Fox. The last scene in the movie showed Gene Hackman's detective chasing Frog, the French villain, into a building. The lights came up and Zanuck said, "Let's put a gunshot on the track." Those around wondered and why'd. Zanuck told them that would give the audience something to talk about on the way to the parking lot.

Far, far beyond the parking lot, we continue to talk about "Rosebud." Did Rick get away? Did Butch and Sundance really die after that freeze frame? Did the kids fly off with E.T. or come back? Did Annie Hall return to Alvy Singer? Alfred Hitchcock was once asked a "why" after showing one of his films. "Oh, that's for the icebox talk." Talk during the late night raid on the icebox. A technique he consciously used in his pictures.

This theory does not advocate obscurity or ambiguity, but you don't have to explain every action and reaction at the end. A UCLA professor of yesteryear, Hugh Gray, in his English accent, insisted that we "expect the audience to bring something to the seat besides their awwss."

PROMISE

Outlines need not be funny for comedy stories. Or exciting to read for adventure, nor fearful for drama. Outlines need to show the structure of the story and have the promise of maximum comedy, adventure, or drama. Promise is the magic outline word. The promise that will lead to an extraordinary script.

On a practical level, outlines give people, beyond your own sanctuary, a road map for the journey they are about to take and pay for.

We all have differing habits, abilities, desires, and dreams. I'll tell you the way I build my step outlines. You develop your own ways as time and experience compel.

My rhythm, as I previously stated, is to get the research in, gestate a few days, then sit in my home's most comfortable chair with a yellow Papermate throwaway pencil that never needs sharpening and a lined $8^1/_2 \times 11$ inch notebook pad.

I like to write my step outlines in longhand, because it allows me to erase and it keeps me in touch with the way writing began. The latter is fully an emotional reason. Probably because I'm so grateful God allowed me to become a writer, I constantly pay homage to my literary heritage.

William Mastrosimone *(Extremities):* "It's important to write quickly because creativity comes from the unconscious, which I think we all accept as truth. The unconscious mind perceives truth without compromise. The more time you allow to go by, the more your conscious mind will censor, edit, and distort."

Mastrosimone's thinking is most valid for us when we do step outlines.

I give it three days. That's my normal step outline time: a third, a third, and a third.

I'll write out the first third on day one. Reread and gestate until day two. Then I'll rise, read the first third, then flow into developing the middle third. I'll take a break, then reread and lightly polish it, just before bed. On day three, I read the first two-thirds, then again flow into the final third. On that day, or some days after, I'll reread. And generally be satisfied with what came out.

During those three developing days, I constantly refer to a single page I've compiled from research and thinking. On that page I've lined out three vertical columns. The first column gives me a list of scenes I feel, from research and instinct, should definitely be in the movie. Like an escape scene, a scrubbing defecation from walls scene, making love in the lobotomy room, et al.

In column two, I list bits of business that seem unique, dramatic, or funny. The towels orderlies wear on their belts to gently choke an out-of-control patient. A patient always scheming to "run." The "pack room" bedpan. Shock treatment, etc.

The final column is for pieces of dialogue I've picked up in verbal or written research that seem to be exceptional and should be included in the script.

I find this one page invaluable, as it continually gives me triggers of inspiration and also keeps me on the mark, Goldman's spine. I also don't have to go back, after I've finished the step outline, and include choice "have-to-be-included" scenes and bits of dialogue. It's practicality serving creativity, exactly the way it should be.

THE GLASS HAMMER STEP OUTLINE

1. Susan screaming at the courtroom verdict.
2. Father and son in barnyard conflict re son's decision to be a conscientious objector.
3. Susan's admittance-to-the-insane-asylum interview.
4. Cliff's draft board interview and their decision.
5. Going around Ward A, each patient giving their name, Susan meets her human future. Paula sleeps. All after a walk by Ward F, the most disturbed ward.
6. Saturday afternoon, Nebraska football game on radio, Cliff arrives and walks up the asylum steps. Passing Susan's mother. Cliff's dad and mom watch from a nearby pickup. Unnoticed by Cliff. The father rubs his eyes. A scream comes from Ward F.
7. Cliff meets Tom. A fellow orderly. A "born-again." They go to Ward A. Cliff sees the "deformed" people. The freaks. Learns about the use of towels.
8. Shock. Monster mask. The wards getting ready for Halloween. Cliff: "They don't appear crazy to me." He's shown stainless steel bathroom mirrors. Dents and scratches. Self-hate.
9. Cliff sent to Ward A to clean the walls.
10. He discovers feces. Meets Susan. "Why'd you do a thing like this?" She sees his brass cowboy belt buckle.
11. Christmas tree decoration scene. No sharp ornaments. Cliff and Susan attracted to each other. He gives her his belt buckle. The "born-again" goes off at someone putting a cross in the crèche manger. Cliff and Susan don't hear or notice.
12. Cliff and Susan play "fox and goose" in snow. Escape buzzer from Ward F. Harriet's making her monthly break. They're alone as everyone runs to Harriet's distraction. Cliff kisses Susan. She withdraws. (My rain-walk writing?) Runs. He chases but is stopped. "Help us get Harriet!" He reluctantly obeys. Susan goes to stainless steel Ward A bathroom mirror. Looks. Slashes her throat with his belt buckle. She's sharpened the brass edge.

13. Cliff in Medical Hospital to pick up Susan in asylum van. They've just put her to sleep. Cliff wheels her out on a gurney. Derisive comments about the "nuts" as he goes by "locals." Maybe a chase.
14. Cliff wheels her into Ward F. Puts her to bed. Inmates taunt the "conchy" (C.O.). Observing nurses comment on his request for a transfer to Ward F. They'll let him taste the action as the inmates take Susan's pillow and play keep-away with it. Feathers burst out. Cliff gets frantic. "You're getting me in Dutch!" It's broken up. He begs the nurses not to report the disturbance. Inmates overhear.
15. The director questions Cliff. No one volunteers for Ward F. Is Cliff one of them? Cliff is finally OK'd to transfer.
16. Ward F. Cliff goes to Susan's corner. Knees drawn to her chest. On the floor. Her birthday. Cliff lights candles on a cake. They talk. She starts to "go down" into her madness. He tries to stop her. The inmates pick up his panic. They attack Cliff. The struggle is broken up. Other orderlies drag Susan to "pack."
17. Cliff is in the "pack" room. Three other patients also packed. All like mummies. When she "comes up" the pack attendant calls the director. The attendant explains to Cliff how the others attacked him for his sanity. Director comes. Shock treatments for Susan. Cliff shouts "no." Director listens. He's got 400 patients. Would be nice to cure one. The director will use Cliff's feelings for her to bring Susan to sanity. OK? OK.
18. In the asylum chapel. Cliff pleads with Susan. Bullies. Fails. She remains catatonic.
19. Shock Room. Tom, the born-again, runs the machine. He explains. There is real hope if a convulsion occurs. If not, it's over. Only Jesus left.
20. Susan wakens. Cliff gives her warm milk and honey through a straw. She hates it but is lucid. "You sure are a sight for sore eyes."
21. Susan getting well montage. Loose association scene. End with her returning to Ward A.
22. Nebraska team in spring workouts. Susan and Cliff on asylum grounds. He went home for a furlough last weekend. Brought back an old junk pickup under the mulberry trees. Tension about her folks coming. Utilize selective inattention on a sane

level. They talk about kissing. Then do it. Again in the chapel. Everything's fine. She *is* getting better. Maybe make love. Joy, poetry. Born-again Tom interrupts. Angry, shouting, crazy.

23. Her birthday again. Cliff takes her to parents in the visiting area. They talk. Much tension. Susan gets tighter. Then, they tell her she's coming home. Susan numbly accepts the information. They cheek-kiss her and leave. Can't be late for Nebraska football.
24. Susan walks to the pack room, lies on the pack table. Submitting herself.
25. Later. Cliff by her side. She's wrapped à la mummy. More warm milk and honey through straw. She sputters. Is again lucid. Happiness from Cliff. He takes off her wrapping. Director comes in. He's going to keep her here. Sickness is her only solid ground. Director tortured. Exhausted and angry at curing people, then sending them back to the very world that made them sick. "Besides, Cliff, you'd be able to see her more." "But it's dangerous," says Cliff. "There are crazy people here."

    Buzzer sounds. Oh Jesus. Harriet again. It's that time of the month. The director takes off, expecting Cliff to follow. "Let's go," says Cliff. "Leave here. Escape. Harriet'll take up their time." Susan protests. Cliff's tired of pleading. Standing around. Waiting. He's going to do something. Right now. Cliff wants to marry her. They can get out. Have a sane life.
26. At the alarm. It's not Harriet! It's the sleeper, Paula.
27. At the junk pickup, Cliff and Susan escape. They put on "hippie" clothes and wigs. Cliff had secretly been planning their breakout.
28. On the highway, they're spotted by the patrol. As they are headed toward the Missouri River, the Missouri patrol are brought in from the opposite direction. A sheriff plane above.
29. Patrol plane and cars chase the pickup over the historic Brownsville Bridge. The pickup veers through the railing, into the deep river. All think the lovers are dead.
30. Cliff and Susan take off disguises downstream. Get on his old Harley motorcycle, previously in pickup truck bed.
31. Susan and Cliff ride into Idaho. His dreamland in America. "Deers eat out of your hand in some parts of Idaho. They just ain't seen man."

They get married in Ketchum with the Beatles V.O. singing "Can't Buy Me Love" on track.

Last shot. The lovers riding into Idaho's Sawtooth wilderness. A V of geese chase spring to the Canadian horizon.

THE END

That is a step outline for myself and most. Julius Epstein told me he does exactly this in longhand. If that's good enough for the co-writer of *Casablanca,* that's more than good enough for yours truly.

What we have here in my and all step outlines, like in the full outline for "them," is not great literature. What we want is a carefully thought out, researched, rising sequence of cause and effect events. Ice field story tips that promise potential for a passionate screenplay.

1. Vise and Revise

You'll like the practicality of physically laying the pages before you. Six in this *Glass Hammer* instance. There it is: your story. You can hover your sorcerer-like hand over it all and say: "Let's see, this is very strong here. Oh, oh. Listless here. My God, the ending isn't as action strong as my beginning. Here's a visually exciting scene here. But it's like a volcano in the Sahara. Got to build to that scene better. Better locales. Better tension in the talk scenes. That's it. They're just talk. I've got to get some passion in there or take them out." Vise and revise.

2. A Screenwriting Flow Chart

You can—and some do—rough out horizontal flow charts of your story to also pick up strengths and weaknesses. Describe a step with a word or two, then the next step and on and on to the end. Be honest. Look at the scenes by themselves and give them checks for impact. Impact would mean passion, tension, action, or just excellent drama or comedy. Four checks would be the ultimate, down to one check, which would indicate that the step just lies there. After evaluating and checking, this method would allow you to better spot traps. First try to eliminate the one checkers. Maybe by choosing a better locale or using a piece of information that inspires dramatic or comedic sparks. Or adding another person who gives the scene tension. You should help that step dramatically with such additions. Then try to turn two-check steps into three-checkers. Sometimes you can see a run of two-check steps and overtly try to break that monotony with stronger tension and passion. Break things. Yelling. Sex. Sometimes though, you should acknowledge an audience's need to rest after a run of high intensity scenes or one "drop dead" scene.

Many writers use similar flow charts to give them that sort of perspective. I no longer do. Passion and tension via teaching, writing, and living is such second nature to me, I find the "lie there" scenes don't even come into my head anymore. But at first, the chart was helpful.

For you? Maybe, maybe not. It's another tool at your disposal. Practicality again serving creativity.

THE REVISED STEP OUTLINE

Now you've done your step outline. Sometimes you'll step back from the pages a day or more for perspective and reread in horror. What a bucket of hog slop! More times, you'll say, "Not bad. Not bad at all." Occasionally, but rarely, you'll react in affirmed joy. Yours, *The Glass Hammer,* and most step outlines will fall in the "not bad at all" category. I'll give you typical thought processes for making *The Glass Hammer* better than "not bad."

1. Second Thoughts

The first concentration should be on the quality of drama or comedy.

I don't feel I'm in bad shape here. My writing den wall credos are quite well followed.

The hero has something at stake: madness is a hell of an antagonist. Every scene is there because of the other. That's the most difficult and important axiom. Here also is one heavy, one hero. And finally, conflict is in every scene.

2. Third Thoughts

But I'd like to do more with the love story. Maybe get some car action up front to show the audience Cliff is really expert behind steering wheels. Foreshadowing. Then, maybe a chase with the "locals" when he's bringing her home from the hospital. Could set that up with a race or something back in his own town, or in the country, perhaps in the first scene. Then both chases will be heightened. Use the audience's anticipation to lift the action drama higher. Yes, that'll do it. A "chicken" race right off.

The institution's director seems too functional. I'll make him a tortured Geppetto. He's playing God with these kids' lives and he's shot through with human guilt.

I'll be sure and make the parents more "heavy." More responsible for Susan's mental health, but not aware of it.

Like to get Cliff more involved with the physically deformed who have been dumped into the institution as some dump garbage in a swamp.

Among your second considerations should be the marketplace. Will it be attractive to those who buy? Can you sell it?

"Period" stories are harder to sell than contemporary, today pieces. This story *is* timeless. Also, try not to have slang in the dialogue or "flavor of the month" fads. I think I'll make it a current story. Forget Vietnam.

I want to add continuous references to Nebraska Cornhusker football. It's the state's obsession. And an excellent running metaphor for the story and those in the audience who search out metaphors, allegories, and life's meaning.

On a dramatic TV series, one character is a ward of the court in a social work setting. I checked with the Nebraska mental health administrators, and they occasionally use a ward of some court. Good. That'll be my contemporary shoehorn to get Cliff into the asylum.

An ancillary benefit just materialized. In talking to the Nebraska mental health experts, my "writer's responsibility" bell clanged. Nebraska is, in day-to-day fact, one of the most progressive states in mental health care. My research and experience reflects the fifties and sixties. I think I'll write the picture the way I want to and know, with shock treatments and "pack rooms," since they're very visual and terrifying. Then, prior to shooting, I'll consult a local expert to get me up to mental health date. I anticipate cutting some dramatic goodies, yet adding new and even better bits from reality. Also, *Hammer* may eventually shoot in a backward state or God knows where. The whole process can be much different. I'll just write this "spec" draft the best I can and adjust closer to the camera-roll day.

If I do shoot in Nebraska, I want to use a facility near Hastings. For the town, picturesque Superior in the middle south of the state. And on the Missouri River. So, to give an audience the optimum visuals, I'll pick a surrogate midwestern town name. Middale. Midvale. Midvale, that's it. Many of Walt Disney's mythical live-action towns were called Midvale. Homage to Walt is always appropriate.

FROM GOALS TO REALITY

Those are the goals I want to achieve in my step rewrite. Now I'll be specific and write in the changes.

Step 1 now has a Step 1-A. Step A will be a chicken race between a local hero and Cliff. Both in pickups. Cliff's does not have doors. Neither will veer. Head-on collision.

In step 2, Cliff decides and tells his father he will plead guilty to vehicular homicide. Father angrily objects.

Step 4: Cliff's judge chooses to send him to Midvale as a ward of the court.

I'll add a step 10-A. Short scenes with Cliff and the director. Then Cliff at the Dairy Queen to set up the later race.

Step 13-A: A race with the Dairy Queen locals.

Step 22-A: Susan's parents leave their affluent home. Want to play a scene with her mother and father interacting with each other *and* see the Garber home.

Step 25-A: Susan and Cliff plan escape. They choose their goal. Idaho. (Needed more of a build to the escape.)

Step 25-B: Cliff goes back to his own home to get the old pickup. (Wanted a last sad scene with his parents to see the love he's giving up for Susan. More hero pressure.)

Step 25-C: More Cliff and Susan planning.

Also, I'm adding a few research notations for Step 26. Here they escape. And they'll use a physically deformed patient to help them. Cliff will hurt at this.

That's my revision for now. Yes, much more can be and will be done in the context of writing the first draft. Remember, *you are not irrevocably married to your step outline!* Very close to it but not irrevocably. You'll make small changes. Take out scenes. Add scenes. But the overall story sweep will be this step outline road map.

YOUR STORY IS NOW TOLD

Your challenge, your opportunity, and your goal is to be creative with characters, dialogue, staging, locales, business, and "touches" when you write your script. With all of that, wouldn't it be purgatory to also simultaneously be telling your story?

It's exactly like Stephen Sondheim writing a love song: "If you told me to write a love song tonight, I'd have a lot of trouble. But if you tell me to write a love song about a girl with a red dress who goes into a bar and is on her fifth martini and is falling off her chair, that's a lot easier, and it makes me free to say anything I want."

The final "story" word to Aristotle: "As for the story, whether the writer takes it ready-made or constructs it, the writer should first sketch its general outline, and then fill in the episodes and amplify in detail."

OUTLINES AND TREATMENTS

The new screenwriter is often thrown for too long on the language of the craft. It's only important you understand the talk quickly and get on to writing matters less superficial.

Just get a screenplay that became a movie and copy the form. Do *not* use the accessible *Butch and Sundance* for a model. It certainly is entertaining to read and gets the story across but it's too off-putting a style for people reading you, a new writer. You should write in master scenes. Eliminate camera, editing, music, acting, casting, and directing instructions. And leave out the scene numbers. You may find those on a "shooting" script. Your production manager, assistant director, or a secretary, will add those when your script gets put into production. You just stick to the facts. But rest easy. You'll also see the correct form in this book when we get to *The Glass Hammer* pages.

By now, you understand that plot, structure, and story are really the same? The on-paper ways to express plot/structure/story, though, are mechanically different. Let's clear those up.

There's an outline you will do for a studio, producer, investor, network. But before that outline, there's an outline you will do for yourself.

The outline for "them" used to be called a "treatment," but is now simply called an outline. The scenes *can* be chronologically numbered as they tell the story for your proposed script. Generally the scenes are not numbered and briefly recount the tale in prose terms. It's a bastard form of writing. It's certainly not screenplay writing.

Most professionals won't submit outlines. They feel they've paid those dues when they were fledgling writers. You will probably have to do them early in your career. When pros do write outlines, they will probably submit something closer to the "step outline," with minimal description or adjectives. And that will often be a "talking paper" for a meeting.

Even if professionals do put something on paper, they will rarely accept a "cutoff," which is a clause in their contracts giving the buyer the right to "cut the writer off" at the outline stage. With that clause, a writer may never even get to write a "paid for" script. Generally, professional status and ego prompt the writer and agent to refuse a "cutoff." Emotionally, as well as practically, we feel we are script, not prose writers. If we're going to fail, we want to fail with the script.

Lastly, and most important, most don't want to risk blowing it all out in the outline. Professional screenwriters don't want to be restricted by the more specific boundaries needed in a twenty- to fifty-page outline. They want to create and invent within the general step outline, not the detailed prose story line.

OUTLINES FOR THE NEW WRITER

You'll likely have to write the hated prose outline when you are "hired" at the genesis of your screenwriting life.

If you are writing on "spec," write and let people read only a full and polished script. "Spec" means "speculation" writing. You're speculating someone will like your work. That's not only a commendable attitude, it's almost mandatory to start your career.

That's "spec" *screenplay,* not outline. Many times I've been confronted by new writers near tears because someone wants to buy an outline they had submitted. The buyer didn't want the writer, only the outline; their plan was to have an "experienced" writer "go" to script. My advice has always been to try and make a Writers' Guild minimum deal to write the script, with larger dollars to come if the writer is asked to do even one word of rewriting on that first draft. That ploy often works. You and my new writer friends want to be *script* writers. Not outline writers. You'll only get a touch closer to being a professional writer by selling outlines. So don't send out spec outlines, only spec scripts.

THE OUTLINE FORM

The full outline for "them," studios, producers, networks, financiers, is closer to short story prose than a script. You can have numbered steps or paragraphs, but most writers don't. This full "presentation" outline should be between twenty and forty-five pages; usually it's closer to twenty than forty-five.

Use only Pica or what you have that appears to be Pica typeface. If you use a typewriter, do *not* use elite, because your pages will eventually be typed up in a professional venue, and it will come out twenty percent longer.

I suspect though, most of you are happily computer literate and should be informed to use the Pica or Courier typeface of your printer. Do not use a dot matrix printer. The type is hard to read, and even though we use computers, we don't like scripts that look or read "computery." Contradictory, yes, but reality.

For producers, professors, readers of all sexes and ilk, *double-space.* Your material is much easier to read if it's double-spaced. Advertising copy chiefs believe the most valuable space in ads is the white space. That's the space that allows you to best read the typeface. Thus it's so with double-spacing. Also be sure to quadruple space between paragraphs for more valuable white space. And finally, give your reader comfortable margins at the top, bottom, and sides.

After "how do you get an agent," the second most asked question of writers is "what do you use to write?" Yes, I confess, I use a typewriter. In one of my jobs at ABC, I was the manager for their On-Air Promotion Department. I was dictating a letter to my secretary Marlene when I noticed her forty-year-old Remington and marveled. With appropriate awe, she told me it belonged to Ernie Kovacs when he had a classic TV series at ABC. I said, "You mean he could have been using this typewriter, got up from it, then drove from here in the rain, and wrapped himself around that telephone pole on Santa Monica Boulevard?" She felt that could have happened.

Six months later Marlene transferred to another department. I accidentally passed her vacated office during another overachieving evening. The room now had only a desk, a chair, and Ernie Kovacs' typewriter. Well, dear reader, I had never stolen anything since Captain Marvel comic books and Baby Ruth bars in C. M. Taylor's Guide Rock, Nebraska, drugstore, but I summarily put the typewriter in the trunk of my '56 Packard.

I drove by the ABC guard's gate office, shoulders crimped with guilt, staring forward in simulated creative thought. Convinced if I had eye contact with the uniformed man, he would immediately know, point, and scream, "Stop thief, come back with Ernie Kovacs' typewriter!"

To this day I expect C. M. Taylor and that guard to come for me, but I'm not giving up my Ernie Kovacs typewriter. In twenty years as a professional writer, every shekel I've earned has come from my mind, into Ernie's typewriter, and onto light blue, to-save-on-the-eyes, erasable bond. Thank you, Ernie. I'll keep the Remington flame ablaze. Perhaps, considering the writing quality of yesteryear, we writers *should* return to quills and inkwells.

Chapter 5

THE ACT ONE SCRIPT
(The Situation—to page 17)

House painters say preparation often takes longer than the literal house painting itself. Certainly when you factor in your research and life experience that went into the development of your story, you have spent significantly longer than the one or two months it should take you to write the actual script. So out the rollers, brushes, typewriters, word processors, quills, inkwells. But wait.

Did you just scream "One or two months!?!?" Rest easy but work hard; you can do it. If you're going to be a writer, train yourself to be good *and* fast. "Drama" is a Greek word that means "to do." Let's do. Let's do comedy. Let's do drama.

THE SCRIPT FORM

Script form is a boring subject for professionals. Terrifying for beginners. Rather than a diatribe on indentations and do's and don'ts, let's again "show not tell." The screenplay pages of *The Glass Hammer* should be example enough, but let's talk about some variations. They can be minor to experienced writers, but possibly major to you.

You'll occasionally see "continued" at the top left or bottom right of the script page. This is a designation that the scene indeed continues.

This is a production desire sometimes preferred by producers, production managers, first assistant directors. Don't put these "continued"'s in your "spec" script. They clutter.

Don't number your scenes. Yes, scenes are numbered in *shooting* scripts but for the "spec" script, forget it. At the "spec" level, scene numbers are also more clutter.

Your scene headings will be:

EXT.—LOCALE—DAY

or

INT.—LOCALE—NIGHT

or

EXT.—LOCALE—NIGHT

or

EXT.—LOCALE—DAY

EXT. or INT. are abbreviations for exterior or interior. LOCALE is self-explanatory. As is DAY or NIGHT. The latter is always manipulated incorrectly by beginners. Film only registers DAY or NIGHT. Think about it. When you show a sunrise, you have to add a soundtrack rooster crowing to convey the day's beginning to an audience. Without the rooster, the same shot can be a sunset. You see, film doesn't record DUSK, TWILIGHT, DAWN, EVENTIDE, SUNSET, MORNING, THE NEXT DAY, etc. It's only *DAY or NIGHT*. There's a lot of snobbery on this issue between the production people, known as "below the line," and the "above the line," so-called creative people.

A production-grounded person reading your script will consciously—or, as bad, subconsciously—consider you an amateur if he or she sees anything other than DAY or NIGHT after your locales. It's struggle enough to be a beginning writer without *looking* like a beginning writer.

ONLY WRITE IN MASTER SCENES. Some new, and even old, writers feel it's important to drop CLOSEUP, or ANGLE ON or

P.O.V. into their scripts. Let me put it to your logic. You're going to tell Coppola, Spielberg, Pollack, et al., where to put a CLOSEUP?

Some writers will capitalize anything relating to the sound track. For example, a car horn HONKS. A sparrow SINGS. This is your choice. Many do not capitalize sounds, but if one doesn't, it's not a problem.

Phone scenes often have subtle differences. Some intercut from one scene to the other. Others write INT. or EXT., the locale, DAY or NIGHT, then indicate INTERCUT AS NEEDED. Most cut back and forth.

If there is anything not mentioned or covered in *The Glass Hammer* pages, I guarantee your script won't be made or broken because of that possible "anything." Use your best graphic arts sense; then put "anything" in a way that might seem clearly presentable to a prospective buyer.

1. Looking Professional

What *will* break you right up front is sloppy script form. Anything that keeps your pages from looking professional, such as misspellings, typos, write-ins, bad grammar, can just kill you.

Most professionals who read, from studio presidents to story analysts and secretaries, have a horrendous amount of material to consider each week. A script that comes in with less than perfect form is practically always thrown on the return pile as soon as the readers see that lack of care. Get in the habit of presenting scripts with *perfect, professional form,* for their sake. If you give someone a sloppy script, you're likely communicating to that someone you don't respect them enough to give them a script with perfect form.

As importantly, sloppy scripts are generally a pain in their backside. When beginning writers ask people to read scripts, they are usually asking for a favor. You're requesting two hours of life, their personal life. Got it? The least you can do is give them a clean and perfectly formatted script.

You may not have the greatest control over your muse's creativity. You do have total control over script form. Ask your significant other, your Aunt Hazel, and at least one more person to read your scripts for flaws, even if you've gone to a professional typing service. They are less likely to make mistakes but still do. One of the typing service tricks is for their non-typing employees to proofread scripts by starting at the end, double-checking the pages, moving backward to page one. Then, the reader doesn't get caught up in the story. Yes, that isn't fair to Aunt Hazel.

2. Wrylies

Frank Pierson *(Cat Ballou, Dog Day Afternoon)* once confessed to writing more "wrylies" than he should. "You know, where you type in the character name, then underneath in parentheses, you put words like "wryly."

```
                    FRANK
                   (wryly)
        And then Frank speaks the line.
```

Oh, do we screen writers like to help our actors. We'll even break up a speech with "wrylies."

```
                    FRANK
                   (wryly)
        And then Frank speaks the line.
                    (beat)
        After he murders the six-toed cat.
```

We have the gall to tell actors to hold a beat after a dialogue sentence! Chutzpah of a high rank. Using "wrylies" is as bad as directing the director with camera angles and closeup indications. Don't.

DON'T DIRECT THE DIRECTOR

There's little directors hate more than to read a script that tells them how to shoot a movie. That's their job. They just don't want or need a writer to tell them when to use a closeup and when to use a long shot. What you do as a writer is *suggest* images they might react to inside the description.

Or professionals and you can lead the director or reader by capitalizing the name of the character, double-spacing, then writing out what he or she does in lowercase below the name. Here's how on a page of *The Glass Hammer.*

CUT TO:

CLIFF

is anxious to go as it's the women's bathroom. He swings the door open for Tom.

CLIFF
Things still make more sense for me here instead of that freak farm on the other side.

SUSAN

sees them leave by staring through a shower curtain tear at the dented metal mirror.

CUT TO:

EXT.—MIDVALE DAIRY QUEEN—NIGHT

A QUASIMOTO HEAD

licks a "Dairy Queen" cone.

CLIFF

smiles as he waits in line to be served. The Dairy Queen is surrounded by Trick-or-Treaters of all ages.

CUT TO:

See? That's directing the reader but in a style that doesn't rile directors.

DIALOGUE

Most people believe they can write good dialogue. At least that's what they say. Let's hope in your case good dialogue writing's a reality and not your illusion.

1. On-the-Nose Dialogue

F. Scott Fitzgerald desperately wanted to be a successful screenwriter. He could not write good dialogue. Ernest Hemingway and Willa Cather prose does not contain good performance dialogue.

Most bad movie dialogue and Fitzgerald/Cather/Hemingway prose dialogue is "on-the-nose." Dialogue that says the obvious, like "Oh look, here comes Jack." In movies, we see Jack coming. We let the audience's eyes supplant talk.

Disney tells their nature film writers, "Don't have the narrator say 'Oh, look, there is a beaver. He's getting out of the stream. He's going up to a tree. He's chewing it down.' " The audience sees that. Let the narrator inform about something like the ecological state of the valley and stream five million years ago. Narration that serves a complementary aural counterpoint to the visuals.

In the John Brady interview with Robert Towne, Towne talks about being in a Jeff Corey–San Fernando Valley acting class with Jack Nicholson. He said Jack gave him his best insight into dialogue writing. "Watching Jack improvise really had an effect. His improvisations were inventive. When he was given a situation, he would not improvise on the nose. He'd talk around the problem. And good writing is the same. It's not explicit. Take a very banal situation. A guy trying to seduce a girl. He talks about everything *but* seduction. Anything from a rubber duck he had as a child to the food on the table or whatever. But you know it's all oriented toward trying to fuck this girl. It's inventive and it teaches you something about writing."

Perhaps you've been on the giving or receiving end of "What's your sign?" or "Oh, you play tennis, too?" Pick any bar, roadhouse, TGIF club and listen. That's dialogue. And it's not on-the-nose.

Here's another wall credo. Put this one up in neon. GOOD DIALOGUE IS DIALOGUE THAT ILLUMINATES WHAT THE CHARACTERS ARE *NOT* SAYING. This pronouncement is right after the "less is more" motto. Harold Pinter forged a career from dialogue that masks smoldering character passion.

2. The 180-Degree Dialogue

Remember when you were developing your story, taking the obvious and turning it 180 degrees? That "trick," in the positive sense of "trick," can often help when writing or polishing dialogue.

Take the most obvious line a character can say, flip it upside down. If the person would say "black," let him say "white." Instead of "I love you," "I hate you." See where that takes the moment. Sometimes a concrete wall, sometimes Quivera, the goldfield. It's always worth a try when you struggle for that perfect line.

3. Less Is More Dialogue

If your character can say something in six words rather than seven, take out the extra word. *The reader* will appreciate it. Less to read. *The actors* will appreciate it, as there will be more to emotionally act because there's less dialogue to speak. *You* appreciate it because less dialogue will help you be as good as you want to be.

Sometimes it's "Ping-Pong" dialogue. Yes, you'll want your "I'm mad as hell and not going to take it anymore" speeches. But you'll want just as many scenes with back-and-forth repartee that illuminates *and* entertains.

4. I Remember ZZZZZZZ

Kill any dialogue that follows "I remember" or "when I was young." My daughter Eileen refers to it as "dwelling." She and her college pals like to get together and "dwell." That's fine for college reminiscences in real life. In movies, it's a bore, and a snore.

Your rule at work here is Aristotle's unity of action. "The play should be about only one thing, and that thing should be what the *hero is trying to get.*"

5. Reality Dialogue and Movie Dialogue

One of the gaping dialogue abysses a screenwriter can plunge down is "people talk like that." Your dialogue must give the *illusion* of reality, rather than reality itself. Reality in dialogue is often boring.

Listen to people. They interrupt themselves, they stutter, stammer or say uh-uh-uh all the time. And their words are often banal. Assuming you're not Oscar Wilde, listen to your own dialogue. Put it on tape. It may sparkle in real life but not on screen.

In the sixties, someone asked me to write a Mafia movie. They had twenty-two hours of tapes recorded from phone lines someone had tapped at a famous Mafia hideout in Appalachia. The idea of being able to pull a movie out of that kind of dialogue sounded like a plan.

For twenty-two hours, I listened to grown men playing make-believe. They all imitated Jimmy Cagney: the guttural growls, everything. "Yeah, we'll take da stoolie down to da riva and stuff a canary in his throat." "I got da poifect cement overshoes for da joik." It was life imitating the movies. Then and certainly today, such dialogue in a screenplay would be the recipient of verbal vegetables.

We want the "illusion" of reality in our movies and specifically our dialogue. A short few years later, Puzo and Coppola came along with the *Godfather* sagas. It wasn't reality but the audience bought it as a brilliant illusion of reality. Your screenwriting dialogue goal.

6. Obscure Dialogue

Never write dialogue only a few will understand. Those lines will always pull people away from your film and cause Elmo to nudge Harriet. "What's that mean, Harriet?" "I don't know, Elmo." You want your audience to be lost in what they're seeing, not having to admit to their seatmates that they don't know what was just said. Or worse, having to explain it.

Be simple but not simplistic. Like *E.T., Butch and Sundance, Casablanca,* and *every* popular movie of quality.

7. Let the Actors Act

So very often, writers will have superfluous dialogue skilled performers can communicate with a look or gesture; facial expressions can cut through so much talk. Don't be so subtle, though, that the script-reading audience won't "get it." Be just subtle enough so they will. Yet remember to have a discussion with your director before you shoot the scene. You may agree you don't need some words at all.

You see that is writing which allows the audience to write the lines, to participate in the actor's inner dialogue. It'll be far better than *anything* you can write.

8. Expositional Dialogue

Disguise exposition with comedy, chases, lovemaking, arguments, when someone has somebody frozen at the end of a Smith and Wesson, et al.

In the Sanders/Mock *Words into Image* video series, Paul Mazursky talks about exposition, less is more, and *not* being on-the-nose. "I don't think people speak expositionally in real life very often. They rarely say things like "You're a wonderful person. I'm having a great time. I really think highly of you and I'd like to marry you and then we'll have some children." I like the kind of dialogue that seems ordinary but filled with emotion underneath. You know, the putting the light out in bed, then saying "By the way, I'm leaving you." That's all Harold Pinter by way of Mazursky, by way of Ibsen, and back to the Neanderthal cave fires.

9. Dialects

See how silly writing out dialects can be.

HENRY

Now ywal come out to this here absobluomon-lutely skeeter-filled holler'n gitcher. . . .

Avoid dialects. Just give a hint of the flavor.

10. Comedy Dialogue

The best comedy comes from character and/or the situation. So does your comedy dialogue. In *Crimes and Misdemeanors,* Woody Allen's character has a screamingly funny observation. "I haven't been inside a woman since I went to the Statue of Liberty." It's a marvelous one-liner. The joke line is right for the movie because we know Woody's wife sexually shut him down a year ago and Mia Farrow's character keeps rejecting him. The line was just a "throwaway," too, which made it even more real. *Always* make sure lines like "I haven't been inside a woman since I went to the Statue of Liberty" come from character *and* situation.

In monologues, the comedian and band drummer often work together. When the jokemeister is nervous about a joke, he has the drummer put a rim shot, or a "barumpbump," as punctuation at the joke's conclusion. A variation on sticking one's elbow in someone's ribs. "Get it, huh, get it?"

Don't. Don't write one-liners that need rim shots for script dialogue. They're practically always surface writing, and they're often out of character. They always detract from the story.

DESCRIPTION

Ah yes, here's your chance to prove to the world you're an undiscovered Fitzgerald, Hemingway, or Cather. Right? WRONG!! Scripts are not the forum to impress anyone with your heretofore undiscovered literary genius.

Some writers go on and on, even describing the flocking design in wallpaper. Or tell us about the "azure sky glinting through the symmetrically splayed, bleak, winter birch branches." It's self-conscious, gratuitous, and often infuriating writing. Once again, less is more!

1. Shooting Adjectives

Novelist Frank Yerby says he "used to be adjective-happy. Now I cut them with so much severity I find I have to put a few back."

Willa Cather says: "I believe every young writer must write whole books of extravagant language to get it out. It is agony to be smothered in your own fluorescence, and to be forced to dump great carloads of your posies out in the road before you find one posy that will fit in the right place. But it must be done, just as a great singer must sacrifice so many lively lyrical things in herself to be a great interpreter."

F. Scott Fitzgerald turned a script in to his then-employer, MGM. Everyone at the studio thought the draft was the greatest creation since sliced apricots. But the wily old studio head, Louis B. Mayer, was not fooled. After he read the script, he had to pass by Fitzgerald's office door on his way to what they then called "rushes," now "dailies." L. B. opened F. Scott's door and as quickly closed it after his wise declaration: "Mr. Fitzgerald, we cannot shoot adjectives!"

Don't include adjectives and elements in the description we won't see in the movie. This includes extra backstory, unplayable attitudes, memories of a character, and references to outside events.

THE BEGINNING

The story starts at the point where nothing before is needed. Don't "set up" the action. Start with the story in motion. Lajos Egri's "rising conflict" theory should be emphatically present in scene one. The beginning. And that scene should foreshadow the story. Even the ending.

Recall "la ronde" in poetry. The end is the beginning. Alpha and Omega. Rosebud at the beginning and end of *Kane.* E.T. coming in, then going out. A plane at the beginning and end of *Casablanca.*

1. The First Page

Screenplays should snap, crackle, and pop on page one. We're in a fast-food world. Write that first page so brilliantly the words leap from the page and seize the reader. Exactly like that Paul O'Neil quote for prose. "Always grab the reader by the throat in the first paragraph, sink your thumbs into his windpipe in the second. . . ." Do just that in your screenplays.

Here's the *Fallen Angel* first page. It also shows you how to handle two blocks of simultaneous dialogue.

FALLEN ANGEL

An original screenplay by Lew Hunter

FADE IN:

EXT.—TWO-STORY HOUSE—DAY

A rental. It's an older house but well maintained. Its pleasant facade belies its interior. A CHILD's WAILS emanate from inside.

MICHELLE (O.S.)
No! You promised!

CUT TO:

INT.—HOUSE BEDROOM—DAY

Collapsed in a heap on the floor, MICHELLE, a thirteen-year-old girl, is near hysteria, clutching, almost mangling a stuffed kitten. HOWARD NICHOLS, 35, is at her side, offering a pill and an orange soda. Howard is a soothing, charming WASP. They stand in the dead center of the bedroom serving as a practical set with attending 16 mm camera, boom microphone, lights, etc. A cold, angry director waits with an embarrassed soundman and cameraman. Fourteen-year-old DAVID HARRIS, naked but for boxer shorts, stares in bewilderment from a nearby bed.

MICHELLE
(to Howard)
You said the zoo!

HOWARD
(calming)
Come on, Angel . . .
(offering pill)
. . . you'll feel real mellow. Like always.

Michelle shrieks and smashes both pill and beverage from Howard's hands with her cat toy.

MICHELLE

You promised!

Michelle starts tearing at the made bed, the drapes, etc. Howard recovers and finger-snaps to the doorway.

MICHELLE
(demolishing)
When I say "no," I don't mean "yes"!

HOWARD
(to David)
David, back in the other room, please. We're not quite ready.

The quaaluded youngster placidly obeys. The deadly cool director, DENNIS FALLON, 25, simultaneously moves to Howard.

HOWARD

This has never happened before. If I could just have a few days to work with her, she'll be better the next . . .

DENNIS
(interrupts)
You don't understand. For her that's it. Bring on the next one.

HOWARD
(almost whining)
You know you're awfully hard on her.

DENNIS
(firm)
Did I get her pregnant?

The *Butch and Sundance* first page is excellent and easy to come by, as is *Citizen Kane*. All of the screenplays in the Sam Thomas "Best American Screenplays" editions have esophagus-clutching capability. You can be sure a page about a spaceship landing and little innocent creatures tottering out would also fill any throat-grabbing bill.

Don't *ever* rely on the last half of your script being brilliant. Few will get to that section if the first five and ten pages don't happen and happen strong.

But be extra safe. Grab them, seize them, hook them *ON PAGE ONE!*

2. Tone

The first few scenes are the frame for your movie. Like an oil-painting frame. These scenes give the audience your story's perimeters and tone. Some movies fill only the smallest portion of that mythical silver rectangle. Others simply overflow their boundaries.

Science fiction is the most needful for the initial scenes to set up the film's perimeters. If you break those laws and rules later inside the picture, then you'll snap the audience's suspension of disbelief. Sundance cannot become a cowardly gunfighter after the first reel. E.T. cannot be a nuclear dump mutant. Rick could not loathe Ilsa and use the Casablanca letters for his own exit. The *2001* monolith cannot be a plant of the twentieth-century "Wheel of Fortune" gagsters.

3. Setups

Walk on the Wild Side started with main titles. They were brilliantly designed by Saul Bass and featured a black cat stalking a metropolis, fighting another cat, and further extraordinary night footage. That sequence was so extraordinary, nothing in the following drama did or probably could have followed the audience's high.

In story meetings, sometimes the choice is to *not* to do something with action, drama, or comedy because the picture would emotionally peak too soon and undercut the second or third act. That's rarely a problem but if it does come up, try first to strengthen the balance of the movie before you have the hero get AIDS, shoot his mother, or hang-glide off the Empire State Building in Acts One or Two. If you can't top your visual or dramatic action with what's coming up, you'd best drop or mute the contemplated scene.

Robert Altman and Ring Lardner, Jr., chose to start the *MASH* movie with helicopters flying in newly wounded from the Korean front. The first preview audience was stunned at the blood, movement, and reality. They didn't know they were watching a "comedy" after that first shocking scene.

The problem was solved not by adding slapstick but laying the song "Suicide Is Painless" over the scene. Though there weren't any laughs by the choppers coming in, the music and lyrics told the audience that laughter was approaching and when it arrives, go ahead and laugh. The second audience loved the film, and so did we.

4. Sepia Scenes

An Officer and a Gentlemen set up its audience with the hero as a young man, watching his womanizing father in dusky sepia tone prior to the colorized time the film chose for its present-day story start. That set the tone for drama and gave the audience the message they were about to see the story of a young man trying to define himself.

The same device was used for the comedy *Back to School,* starring Rodney Dangerfield. Rodney was shown as a small boy, again in sepia tone, telling his tailor father he was going to be exactly like him. The father informed the young son he was going to school. Then a montage showed Rodney's nonacademic success at "Tall and Fat" men's clothing shops and into the movie's story. The audience was given a glimpse of the film's premise while the comedy was given a realistic undertow that made the audience identify and care about Rodney's quest for college.

5. Pet the Dog

A story conference shorthand glossary would include "pet the dog."

That's the moment when you show your hero or heavy to be human underneath bluster or cynicism. Humphrey growling to the newly married *Casablanca* couple to "put it on 22," Howie telling Jennifer "My mother beat me, my father drank. Then my father beat me, and my mother drank," or Sundance *not* killing the gambler in the opening poker scene.

The best "pet the dog" scenes are in Bogart films. *The Treasure of the Sierra Madre, The African Queen, The Maltese Falcon,* all of them. It was an overt part of the Bogart formula. "Pet the dog" is shorthand for showing vulnerability. It's a personality trait that should be occasionally evident and always latent in your heroes and heavies. Most especially in the first act.

6. Runners

Start your runners in the first act. Show your audience characters who mooch cigarettes, love fast food, scratch their privates, speed, drink, or whatever character trait that gives them identifiable dimensions. Hopefully, that runner can be used in the plot development. In *Silkwood,* Meryl Streep/Karen Silkwood was always wrapping food leftovers in aluminum foil and jamming the little crumpled balls in her refrigerator. In the first act, her roommates teased her about this habit, saying something about mystery meat inside each wadded clump of foil. This was the setup, just like the setup in a joke. The writers then wisely let us forget this affectation until the third act. Men were trying to find incriminating evidence of radiation in her home and, bingo! It was in one of the aluminum foil packets she had left over from a work lunch.

We saw Jack Lemmon's bogus breasts dropping in *Some Like It Hot,* a runner used throughout one long scene. In the same movie, Tony Curtis' weakness for betting was used throughout the film. Remember Popeye's love for spinach?

A similar story conference glossary term is "playbacks." The audience mentally plays back information like the food in aluminum foil or the dropping breasts. Use runners and playbacks. They flatter the audience, who feels good by remembering the reference. Like monologuists' contemporary humor on politics and current fads is flattery humor. The audience flatters itself for being up on the latest to get the joke.

DISCIPLINE

Is discipline your middle name? If not, you probably won't make a living writing. To rewrite Thomas Edison: "Writing is ninety percent perspiration, ten percent inspiration." You *have to have discipline.* Somehow, some way. I'm always writing. Ask my beloved Pamela about my writing beside a daughter about to have her first baby. Or at football games. In paths of approaching tornadoes.

The idle mind is the writer's work-ground. If a fleck of boredom comes into your brain, write. Literally or mentally. James Thurber's wife once caught him, at the dinner table, staring into a ceiling corner. Her palm slammed the table, causing the silverware to jump. "Dammit, Thurber! Stop writing!"

Perhaps your motivation *is* guilt or passion or hunger. Find it, use it. Your creativity's the art of it all, your discipline, the anchor. Hemingway wrote twelve hundred words a day. When he knew he was going fishing the next day, he upped the output to twenty-four hundred so he wouldn't be guilty of not writing. Alexander Pope referred to that malady as "The Divine Guilt." Not writing when you know you should be.

> I don't make myself work. It's just the thing I want to do. To be completely alone in a room, to know there'll be no interruptions and I've got eight hours is exactly what I want. Yeah, just paradise.
>
> —William Burroughs

1. Rhythms

We've talked much about the rhythms in your stories but we need a strong word about your personal writing rhythms.

For my script rhythm, I try for ten pages a day, not 110.

In the morning, I polish the pages I wrote the preceding day, because: 1. I'm closer to the fever that caused them to be written. 2. They need polishing, since I don't let myself get stuck. 3. It's my warm-up for the day's original pages.

This process is not new. In 1837, English novelist Anthony Trollope told the literary world: "By reading what you have last written, just before you recommence your task, you catch the tone and spirit of what you are saying, and will avoid the fault of seeming to be unlike yourself."

I start my rereading and polishing at six or seven in the morning, but sometime before noon, I want to be into the new work. I then go after those fresh pages with as much focusing as I can accumulate.

The one thing extraordinary people in all jobs have in common is focus. When they are focused, they define the word. Focus. Then you can write by your daughter's birthing bed, your mother's funeral casket, inside of tornadoes, etc. It also helps cut off pain or boredom in your personal life. Turn off the phone, or better, let the answering machine pick it up, because it may be a job call. Schedule meetings late in the afternoon, *after* your page goal. Sometimes you may get beyond your page goal. That means you're either on a roll or want to finish a scene. Once in a while, I'll hit fourteen pages and consciously stop myself. I reason by that time, I'm at the shank end of my creativity and won't be as good as I can be. The best motivation of all to quit at page 14.

Ten pages is *my* rhythm. It can be yours. It doesn't have to be. You'll find your own, but two caveats. Anything under five pages is too little, anything over fifteen is obscene. Whatever the number, *you must get out the pages.* A writer has many sides but no two sides are more important than the selling side *and* the writing side. Both have to function if you're going to be a working writer.

> Write without pay until somebody offers pay. If nobody offers pay within three years, the candidate may look upon this circumstance with the most implicit confidence as the sign that sawing wood is what he was intended for.
> —Mark Twain

2. After Writing

Following dinner, or as we native Nebraskans say, supper, I polish the day's new pages. After that, I can be with the family, if they haven't gone with the winds. Sometimes, I'll read nonfiction. I never pick up fiction when I'm into a script. I'm afraid someone's writing creativity will get in my mental path. I don't wish to be intimidated. I also don't want to steal, borrow, or pay the author homage subconsciously. So when I'm into script I stick to nonfiction.

To conclude my day's rhythm, I've picked up some knowledge about sleep-teaching programs that play tapes while you slumber. Hence, I *again* rewrite or polish the new work, hoping creativity will continue throughout my somnolent night.

An important precept to get from my writing rhythm is the over and over again polishing. Three times prior to the next clutch of pages.

3. When to Write

Another set of three: morning, afternoon, night. Your choice of writing time depends on your individual mind, body, and life structure. Joseph Heller wrote *Catch 22* from four to seven each morning, before taking the train into New York for his 9-5 advertising job. Harlan Ellison won't even think about physically writing until after midnight. Novelist Bill Katz starts at two in the morning. Catherine O'Hara believes that "nighttime is really the best time to work. All the ideas are there to be yours because everyone else is asleep."

When you're into script, write whenever but write. Don't let nonsense pull you from your daily page count. Be ruthless on yourself and on others. They might not love you. But you've got to *write to be a writer!*

4. Where to Write

When I'm developing story, I like to use a pad and pencil so that process can occur in any invigorating place.

When I'm into script, I can write anywhere I happen to be. I used to need every grain of sand in place on the Mojave Desert before I could get down to writing. I then instructed my children, "When Daddy's writing, no one is to bother him unless they are on fire and can't beat out the flames with one hand."

My work on television series arrested this isolationist, dilettante posture. The pages had to be gotten to or written on the set. No time for the muse.

Mark Twain best liked to write in bed. Hemingway stood at a tall desk. Six-foot-five Thomas Wolfe also stood, writing on top of an icebox, then throwing the longhand pages into a pickle barrel for his secretary to collect and type. Some writers like to pace a large room. Dorothy Parker said all she needed "is room to lay my hat and a few friends." Oscar-winner Dalton Trumbo only wrote at night, in a filled bathtub with a board spanning the porcelain sides to support his manual typewriter.

Whether it's bathtubs, beds, bars, football fields, a sarcophagus, it makes zero difference. Wherever you are, wherever you can, write and write on!

5. What to Write With

Ancient typewriters, stubby pencils, sophisticated word processors, microcassette recorders, pens and inkwell, hammer, chisel and stone . . . again, zero difference. Get out the pages whether they're papyrus, parchment, or pulp.

6. Life Changes

The time, place, or method in which you write may change a little or a lot. That will depend upon your real-life status from year to year. That's all right.

Some stay in habits out of superstition or comfort and fret about getting stale. You shouldn't worry. Each script will be so much different from the others that your interest will be stimulated by the new world your story leads you to explore. One year it can be Vietnam nurses, Northern Ireland, and professional football. Another year it's condors, alcoholic housewives, and Goebbels. Subjects, not methods, create stimulation that keeps writers alive and vital. We are the chosen. If we try.

THE GLASS HAMMER FIRST ACT

Harlan Ellison says: "My imagination is like a swamp. I picture this still, watery expanse in my mind. Bloop, up comes something I might use to the surface. Bloop. Another. Bloop, there's another. Bloop. Bloop. Bloop. I then choose the useful things and the bloops I don't want or need resettle to the bottom of the swamp and once again the water is flat. Until the next moment I want to summon something from those depths."

I'm sometimes a "ceiling" writer. Other times "garden." Bloops come to my inspirational surface when I stare at the ceiling, or to my right, out the window, into my garden.

You've done your research, your story; now bring on the swamps, ceilings, gardens, and your special place. It's all paradise, yeah, William Burroughs. Let's do it.

THE GLASS HAMMER

An original screenplay by Lew Hunter

FADE IN:

EXT.—MEMORIAL COLISEUM, LINCOLN, NEBRASKA—DAY

Seventy-six thousand, one hundred and forty-three cheer the University of Nebraska football team fighting their way through adulating fans toward the dressing room.

SPORTS ANNOUNCER (V.O.)
Unbelievable! For seventeen consecutive years Nebraska wins its first football game of the year! And the seventeenth victim this year is none other than perennial football power . . .

CUT TO:

EXT.—REPUBLICAN RIVER ROAD—NIGHT

Two pickups. Nebraska teenagers in the truckbeds and cabs. Each vehicle also contains over a dozen watermelons. It's the September Saturday night before the University of Nebraska kids go and/or return to school. Some of the recent graduating classmates have chosen to work as waitresses in nearby farm towns, or on their fathers' farms, or are prematurely pregnant and will not be going to a so-called "higher education" experience. All are particularly buoyant as Nebraska has just won its first game of the season over Notre Dame. Threshold time for everyone and everything in the Cornhusker State.

Each pickup has a "plugged" watermelon with a dozen or so straws protruding from the fruit. This melon has been filled with vodka and allowed to set overnight.

Currently, the youngsters are quiet. The revving motors create a loud and only noise. A local "hot-rod" RICH MENDENHALL, 25, drives one pickup, a new Chevy. CLIFF MACPHERSON, slightly younger, handsome, is behind the wheel of one of his father's pickups, a '70 doorless Ford. Cliff, like many farm boys, took the family's farmyard junk vehicle, modified it, did some piston re-boring, and gave the engine an extra "turn." Now, it's very "hot."

All the teenage eyes are on a letter-sweatered huge FOOTBALL PLAYER in the back of Rich's truck, holding a watermelon above his head. The cars are paralleled on this sandy, dirt-bottom road. Lights shining. Ready to move. Now, the signal. The football player heaves the melon. It strikes the ground between and in front of the pickups. The cued vehicles leap forward, accompanied by the shrieks and laughter of entertained young men and women.

THE TWO PICKUPS

peel off, side by side. The football player has another melon above his head, taking a weaving aim on Cliff's truck.

CUT TO:

INT.—CLIFF'S CAB—NIGHT

Cliff is grim but enjoying. His best friend, RANDY, is nervous in the passenger seat, arm protectively thrown around his exhilarated girl, ARLENE.

CUT TO:

EXT.—ROAD—NIGHT

The football player dares . . .

FOOTBALL PLAYER
Clifford! Show us your hands! Catch!

He shotputs the large, striped watermelon.

CUT TO:

INT.—CLIFF'S TRUCK CAB—NIGHT

The melon impacts on the hood, spraying fruit, juice, and seeds over the windshield, obscuring visibility. Cliff drives blind.

CUT TO:

EXT.—ROAD—NIGHT

Cliff's vehicle whipsaws the road as he slows and fights for control.

CUT TO:

INT.—RICH'S PICKUP—NIGHT

Rich laughs with the two girls, HEATHER and HILARY, in his cab. The farthest girl, HILARY, reaches and honks the pickup's horn.

RICH

Gonna be like Nebraska whippin' Notre Dame's ass today!

CUT TO:

INT.—CLIFF'S PICKUP

RANDY

(plea)

Let's quit, Cliff. The air is clearing the windshield.

CLIFF

I'll get him! Fourth and long.

CUT TO:

EXT.—ROAD—NIGHT

The trucks APPROACH. Cliff is indeed "getting him." They pass by. The teenagers in the separate pickup beds throw watermelon rinds at each other. Laughing. Shrieking.

CUT TO:

INT.—CLIFF'S PICKUP—NIGHT

Through the splattered windshield, a near ninety-degree curve approaches. Cliff pulls even with Rich, looks to Randy and Arlene, winks, then attends the upcoming curve.

CUT TO:

EXT.—ON CURVE—NIGHT

Cliff has the inside of the road and simply doesn't negotiate the curve until the last second. This forces Rich to go straight, into a standing cornfield.

CUT TO:

INT.—RICH'S PICKUP—NIGHT

Bounces over furrow, knocks down cornstalks.

HILARY
You shoulda took him, asshole.

RICH
Your asshole. Cliffy boy's going to pay!

CUT TO:

INT.—CLIFF'S PICKUP—NIGHT

ARLENE
(looking back)
Rich is still coming.

RANDY
(to Cliff)
Let's go home.

CLIFF
I been workin' on a U-turn at seventy-two miles an hour. Old moonshiner trick. Hang onto your hat.

RANDY
(warning)
Cliff . . .

ARLENE
Okay . . . do it.

Cliff considers the rearview mirror.

CLIFF
Well . . .
(slows)
. . . we got time to be normal.

CUT TO:

EXT.—ROAD—NIGHT

Rich's pickup has regained the road. Cliff makes a conventional U-turn with his doorless truck and guns it toward the approaching vehicle.

CUT TO:

INT.—RICH'S PICKUP—NIGHT

HILARY
(excited; declarative)
Chicken!

RICH
I am going to nail Cliffy's shitface ass to his own barn!

CUT TO:

INT.—CLIFF'S TRUCK CAB—NIGHT

RANDY
(plea)
Come on, Cliff.

CLIFF

It'll turn out.

CUT TO:

EXT.—ROAD—NIGHT

The two pickups race to race to each other on a flat road that cleaves prairie hay flatland. The teenagers in each vehicle are now frozen. Waiting.

CUT TO:

INT.—RICH'S CAB—NIGHT

All three anticipate. Hen clucking comes from the teenagers in the truckbed.

HEATHER

(referring ahead)

He'll chicken, Rich.

HILARY

He was chicken in football.

CUT TO:

INT.—CLIFF'S DOORLESS TRUCK CAB—NIGHT

RANDY

He's crazy, Cliff.

CLIFF

You got that right, Randy. But so am I.

CUT TO:

INT.—RICH'S NEW CAB—NIGHT

Tension . . . tension . . . then . . .

CUT TO:

EXT.—REPUBLICAN RIVER ROAD—NIGHT

In SLOW MOTION, the killing pickups race to each other. The teenage passengers leap from the vehicles, rolling to each roadside ditch. Both drivers do not "chicken." The vehicles crash and destroy. Head-on.

CUT TO:

EXT.—OMAHA, NEBRASKA'S SUPERIOR COURT BUILDING—DAY

Above, a V of geese chase scudding clouds to the southern horizon.

JURY FOREMAN (V.O.)

. . . in the State of Nebraska versus Susan Ellen Garber . . .

CUT TO:

INT.—SUPERIOR COURT ROOM—DAY

Eleven MEN and a token WOMAN fill the jury box. A pudding-faced pharmacist is the only member standing. He plays the role of FOREMAN with extreme relish and is paternally proud of the decision. Other jurors are clearly impatient with his theatricality.

JURY FOREMAN

. . . we find her . . .

He dramatically pauses. The Judge's fingers drum.

SUSAN ELLEN GARBER is slumped at the defendant's table, seated next to COUNSEL. Her long, straight, blonde hair conceals even a partial view of her young face. Parents ROY and ELLEN GARBER are in the b.g. Roy owns the Nebraska Meat Packing Company. Ellen Garber is an aggressive, dominant woman with pheasant tail feathers in her fall headdress. Roy displays a red and white "Go Big Red" button on his expensive lapel.

JURY FOREMAN (CONT.)
(pleased, deliberate articulation)
. . . U-nanimously . . . not guilty . . .

THE COURTROOM PEOPLE

are pleased and reveal this in varied personal degrees. We now see caucasian Susan's black co-defendant, BOBBY BELL, 24, who smiles and shoots a "right on" fist at the still-bowed girl. The foreman tacks on the obligatory sentence completion.

JURY FOREMAN
(throwaway)
. . . by reason of *in*sanity.

Now he is more emphatic with his personal comment to Susan and everyone.

JURY FOREMAN (CONT.)
We thought it was only right, considerin' your folks and all.

SUSAN

is still immobile. Mrs. Garber ignores her husband's cheek peck and leans across the rail to victoriously pat Susan's arm. It is on this touch the girl erupts.

SUSAN
(screaming)
I'm guilty!

THE COURTROOM

lines overlap. Everyone consciously, even desperately tries to keep the girl from destroying herself.

SUSAN'S LAWYER
Please, Miss Garber.

JUDGE
(gaveling)
Order . . . uh . . . Mr. Granville, instruct your client . . . uh . . . dismissed.

MRS. GARBER
Susan, you don't mean that.

SUSAN
I killed those four people just as much as Bobby. You give him the chair! That's for me! Give me the chair!!

JUDGE
Take charge, Deputy.

SUSAN
I cheered him on. I . . . you're wrong . . . Jesus, you're wrong.

SUSAN'S LAWYER clamps his hand over her mouth as the DEPUTY SHERIFF arrives. They start to drag her away.

BOBBY BELL
Don't hurt the best cunt I ever had!

Mrs. Garber stands and stares at the hated man. Bobby makes a jeering wolf-man gesture to her. She startles in fear.

BOBBY BELL (CONT.)
If you're half as good, you're next, Big Momma.

A second DEPUTY starts to pull Bell away. Roy Garber is looking after their daughter. His wife points at Bobby Bell.

MRS. GARBER
Roy, do something!

MR. GARBER
(still looking to Susan)
Fuck him, Ellen.

ELLEN shocks in reaction as Roy moves to Susan, who bites her lawyer's finger and screams with a freed voice.

SUSAN
Can't you see?! I should be fried like Bobby. I . . .

The lawyer's uninjured hand aborts her continuation.

THE JURY

is immobile as this reaction uniquely affects their previously deliberated and solidified emotion. The sound trails off as the principals are violently torn from the courtroom. Then, silence. The foreman turns and looks at his still-seated peers, as their attending DEPUTY has had to help in the defendant removal. The twelve are without exit instructions so they wait . . . and deeply think. An old RETIRED FARMER hacks, spits in his handkerchief and speaks.

RETIRED FARMER
First the nigger, the murders, now this. Maybe she *is* bats.

The foreman, a Dale Carnegie graduate, tries to pull something positive from this bizarre moment.

JURY FOREMAN
Well, gentlemen, Excuse me again, Mrs. Craig.
(she nods wearily)
Let's be thankful we got out of that motel. Now we can go see The Big Red personally nail UCLA Saturday.

CUT TO:

EXT.—FARMYARD—DAY

MILT MACPHERSON, a fifty-year weathered Guide Rock, Nebraska, farmer, stares off. The Nebraska-UCLA game can be heard V.O.

CLIFF MACPHERSON rolls into the barnyard with their John Deere tractor. A 1978 Ford pickup, also with its doors off, rots by an equally rotting corncrib. Rhode Island Red chickens are laying eggs in the seat and load bed. A double-sickled haymower and a Scotch collie dog trail Cliff. The fertile Republican River Valley sweeps behind Cliff, who punches the tractor's off switch. MUSIC blares from a portable radio sitting under the tractor seat.

THE FATHER

is revealed to be in a wheelchair, the victim of a stroke. His right arm dangles to the ground and ends in a rigor-mortis-like fist. The game commentary comes from a transistor radio strapped on the father's chair.

MILT

Don't shut that off.

CLIFF stares a full beat.

CLIFF

(quiet)

It took me forty acres, but I finally figured it out.

MILT

You waste gas. If it's not the government in my pocket, it's my own kid.

CLIFF jumps to the ground in front of his invalid father, picks up a dirt clod and throws it.

MILT (CONT.)

There's two more hours of light. Git a headstart on tomorrow's milo.

Cliff's clod hits the yard light pole. Father and son then look to each other.

MILT (CONT.)

Well, you gonna stand there all day?

CLIFF

I'm pleadin' guilty.

MILT

What's that got to do with . . .

(annoyed at radio)

. . . that damned punker music. You should be hearin' the game. What's yer accident got to do with milo?

Cliff leans, snaps the portable radio's volume knob to off, then rocks upright to continue the face-up to his eroded father.

CLIFF

It's got to do with my life, which I know ain't as important to you as milo.

Milt MacPherson gestures about.

MILT

What's all this for? What did I git in this wheel-chair for? For you if you need tellin'.

CLIFF

(flat)

I been told.

MILT

Well, git movin'. It was an accident. Rich is dead. You're not. Keep your head up.

Cliff spins, takes three steps, kicks the ground, whirls back, and rushes out words.

CLIFF

I gotta pay.

(holding out arms)

I should have died too. If I'd had doors on that pickup . . .

Milt holds out his arm to his hurting child. Cliff sits on his lap in the wheelchair and cries. The men embrace. Milt looks to the back porch. The mother, GAIL MACPHERSON, nods to her husband and tears. The Scotch Collie whines. The game audio continues. Nebraska scores.

CUT TO:

EXT.—MIDVALE REGIONAL CENTER—DAY

An ordered collection of brick buildings, ivy, and trees with leaves turning colors for winter.

SUSAN (V.O.)

I don't want to be here.

DR. GARGON (V.O.)

I don't either. Or is it neither?

CUT TO:

INT.—DOCTOR GARGON'S OFFICE—DAY

The decor is circa 1980 Sears catalog. A "Have a Happy Day" poster is Scotch-taped to the vacant portion of one wall. Mrs. Garber sits in a straight-backed chair, nervously pumping a nylon-sheathed crossed leg. Susan Ellen Garber is confronted by Dr. James E. Gargon, 44, overweight, cautious, and cynical.

SUSAN

I don't . . . CARE!!!

Mrs. Garber claps her hands together.

MRS. GARBER

Susan! None of that!!!

DR. GARGON

Mrs. Garber, *that* is what I need. *That* is why I asked you to join us.

SUSAN

Yes, mother. How else can he know if I'm crazy unless I show it? The more he gets into word association, the more disassociated the responses become, and the more apparent my schizophrenia is.

(to GARGON)

Come on, Dr. Gargon. More. Let's give her a real show.

Gargon smiles and shakes his head, tching. Susan doesn't like this.

DR. GARGON

You want to be the doctor?

SUSAN

Fuck!

DR. GARGON

Love.

MRS. GARBER

(embarrassed)

Susan Ellen!

Susan ignores her mother and picks up Gargon's lead.

SUSAN

Midvale.

DR. GARGON

Nuthouse.

SUSAN

Gargon.

DR. GARGON

Gargoyle.

Susan giggles. Gargon overlaps.

DR. GARGON

Silliness.

SUSAN

This.

DR. GARGON

Father.

Susan's eyes dart to her mother, then to Gargon.

SUSAN
(soft)

Crail.

MRS. GARBER
(to Doctor)
See . . . that's one of those words she makes up.

DR. GARGON
(to Susan, hard)
Mother!

The girl slowly folds her arms behind her neck and places her head between her knees. GARGON repeats.

DR. GARGON (CONT.)
Mother!

No response. MRS. GARBER is embarrassed once more.

MRS. GARBER
Susan, you come out of that. I'd like to hear exactly what you have to say.
(to Doctor)
When she does that, I normally make her wash the dishes.

Susan rises and exits to the outer office. Gargon's secretary is watching this Saturday's game with Arizona State on a portable TV. As Susan pulls the door, Gargon calls after her.

DR. GARGON
We'll be right out, Susan.
(to the mother)
Mrs. Garber, come next Saturday. We'll find out things she wants from home and call you.

MRS. GARBER
You mean, just leave her here? Now? She's been . . . accepted?

DR. GARGON
(small, ironic smile)
Yes, she's been accepted.

MRS. GARBER
And you'll handle her personally. Like the governor promised.

DR. GARGON
Personally.

MRS. GARBER
But this is all part of the legal procedure. She's not really sick.

DR. GARGON
Mrs. Garber, your daughter is *really* sick.
(Mrs. Garber shocks)
It's been very hard on you, hasn't it?

Mrs. Garber rises.

MRS. GARBER
My God. Really sick? You mean . . . in the head?

Gargon nods. The woman's eyes flutter, then solidify as she chooses to disclose a dark family fact while jamming on red and white gloves.

MRS. GARBER
(hushed, hurried)
A distant, you understand, cousin on my husband's side is in that . . .
(motions to the North)
other section. He's a hydro . . . you know, a pinhead.

DR. GARGON
A *micro*cephalic.

MRS. GARBER
Yes, that's it. Nothing like Susan, thank God. That would really be terrible.

She crosses to and stops in front of Gargon.

MRS. GARBER
Doctor . . . did *we* do anything wrong?

Gargon looks at the floor speechless. Suddenly, Mrs. Garber's gloved hand claps to her forehead.

MRS. GARBER (CONT.)
Oh, no! Her father and I have tickets to the football game next Saturday. That's why he couldn't come today. You know how hard tickets are to get.

Gargon can respond to this as he opens the door.

DR. GARGON
I've heard.

Susan looks into the carpet as she's sitting on a chair by the secretary's desk. Nebraska scores again.

MRS. GARBER
(reacts to touchdown)
Oh, good. We're beating the point spread.
(back to business)
We'll work something out, Doctor. You know our daughter comes first. She's all we've got.

The mother goes to and hugs the nonresponsive daughter. Mrs. Garber smothers a sob and leaves. Gargon studies Susan then reaches out to touch her but stops before contact as Susan's head rises.

SUSAN
I still don't want to be here.

CUT TO:

EXT.—WEBSTER COUNTY COURTHOUSE—DAY

Cliff, Mr. and Mrs. MacPherson, a BAILIFF, Cliff's lawyer GEORGE ALEXANDER, and the county attorney MARLON HARRIS, fidget before JUDGE BARRON. VELMA OLSON's fingers manipulate the court reporter keys. The judge, 69, is tired and anxious to help lifelong friends.

CLIFF

Yes, sir. It's the worst thing I ever done. Like I told Dad. I gotta pay. I should have pulled over. I mean, I really liked him. He was our quarterback when I was a kid.

JUDGE BARRON

(to reporter)

Velma, let's slip off the record here. Rest them fingers.

(to Cliff)

Couldn't Rich have pulled over?

CLIFF

I guess so.

JUDGE BARRON

(to Milt)

You think your boy should do this, Milt?

MILT

After my damned stroke, I just ain't myself, Homer.

The judge nods and then considers GAIL, who won't wait for his question.

GAIL

(to Judge)

He's been taught the commandments, Homer. There doesn't seem to be any "except" after "thou shalt not kill."

The old man sighs and studies his intertwined, coarse fingers.

JUDGE BARRON

It's up to me then. Afraid of this. Wonder how the game is comin'.

The bailiff points to a plug in his ear.

BAILIFF

Big Reds's up by thirty-one, Homer.

The judge nods and looks to the lawyers.

JUDGE BARRON

Anything else, George? Marlon?

GEORGE

We keep on restin', Your Honor.

MARLON

Outta my hands, sir.

JUDGE BARRON

(barks)

You both talk together, I can't hear nothing'.

(to Cliff)

I could put you in the penitentiary for seven years and a half for bein' good. That's normal vehicular manslaughter . . .

The judge reacts to the COURT REPORTER's throat clear.

VELMA

(hands poised over keys)

Should I . . . ?

JUDGE BARRON

Just clean it up for us, Velma. Don't make it sound like my tongue's loose on both ends and wigglin' in the middle.

(to County Attorney)

For the short life left in me, I can't see what's to be gained by nailin' him in with them hardened criminals at Lincoln.

MARLON

(hopeful)

A societal assignment, Your Honor?

JUDGE BARRON
(smiles)
That's what they call it now?
(to Cliff)
He's talkin' about puttin' you someplace where you can do some good.

MILT
Is that like them "con . . ."
(gives up)
. . . "C.O.s" durin' the war?

JUDGE BARRON
Except you can't be a medic today. I thought about the fish and game . . . or parks department. Like out in Chadron.
(to Cliff)
You still talk about Idaho, Clifford? Like when we went fishin' when you was a kid?
(Cliff nods but the Judge aborts the answer)
Well, it don't matter. All they had was, uh . . .
(hates to say it, then . . .)
You gotta go to Midvale.
(to Milt, quickly)
Jiggs Hadley'll do the chores?

All are stunned.

MILT
The nuthouse?

CLIFF
(pleads)
But I don't . . .

JUDGE BARRON
(interrupts)
. . . have a choice, son. You had one before by pleading "not guilty." Not now.

GAIL
A year and a half, Homer?

JUDGE BARRON
'Probably work out about that, Gail.
(to both parents)
Still better'n the pen. Unsatisfactory things happen to young men up there. Even AIDS today.

JUDGE BARRON (CONT)
(to Cliff)
You'll make it all right, Clifford. I always said you'd be the best of the whole lot around here.

MILT
But, Jesus, Homer. Midvale?

CUT TO:

THE END OF THE BEGINNING

And that's the beginning of *The Glass Hammer*. Cliff's sentence to the mental institution. The page 17 point.

You can't tell because of the book printing reduction but the actual script page count for this first act is eighteen pages. I blew it by one. But well remember, I said it's a "floating" page 17. It's the concept that is valid, not the specific.

The acts, as they pertain to screenwriting, relate only to the Aristotelian beginning, middle, and end concept. The Hunterian act references are situation, complications, and conclusion. The situation here is Cliff going into a mental institution.

When you reveal the situation to your audience, you have reached the end of the beginning. How does your beginning look to you? How does *The Glass Hammer* look to me?

Will the audience get the joke? The premise? The situation? Good. Well, smile for a moment. But not too long. Cinch up your belt. Lay in an extra supply of No Doz and coffee, because the longest work is coming. The story is the hardest but Act Two will consume the most time.

OK, maybe one more smile. Wait. Reread your first act. I'll do it too. Right now.

Did you? I did. Are you still smiling? So am I. I tell 434 to burst through the first draft as quickly as possible, then go back and make it good. Maybe great. But for now, settle for "not too bad." And keep on with the smiles. You'll need them. So will I.

Chapter 6

THE ACT TWO SCRIPT

(The Complications–to page, maybe, 85)

Now we separate the women from the girls, the men from the boys. This is the blue collar time of screenwriting: the laying of the pipe, the grunt work, the *second act.*

Perhaps that's what F. Scott Fitzgerald meant when he said Americans don't have second acts. We don't want to work hard enough. We want the glamour. The glow. The buzz. And we want it yesterday. French novelist Gustave Flaubert lamented about his contemporaries who wrote so easily and incessantly, "Like a stream. With me, it is a tiny thread of water. Hard labor at art is necessary for me before obtaining a waterfall."

How you obtain your own waterfall is something you'll *have* to determine, or else you should consider a career in real estate or sawing Mark Twain's wood. For you it may be hunger. Anger and love are also good, but normally those emotions are too temporary to run the second-act race. Best of all, just do it. Writers write. Write on.

All the other needed achievements in the screenwriting process depend primarily on inspiration. For Act Two, it's perspiration. But don't check your inspiration at the door.

1. Thick Plots

The second act is where the plot must thicken. Actions stimulate reactions which stimulate further actions. Those actions become complications. Complications cause conflict, and conflict is born in character. Lajos Egri: "If we wish to know the structure of conflict, we must first know character. But since character is influenced by environment, we must know that, too. It might seem that conflict springs spontaneously from one single cause, but this is not true. A complexity of many reasons makes one solitary conflict."

Your job in the second act is to unfold the complexity of reasons. Characters getting into trouble because of their own actions or the actions of others and the conflict exacerbated by the character's reactions and subsequent actions.

The second act is when you particularly focus on that wall credo: LIFE IS WHEN THINGS HAPPEN ONE AFTER ANOTHER. STRUCTURE IS WHEN THINGS HAPPEN *BECAUSE* OF THE OTHER.

2. Killing Darlings

Every scene's life must be born inside the womb of a preceding scene. Yes, you should have fully dealt with that issue when you were stepping out your Act Two at the outline level. But, now's the time to again check if an extraneous scene slipped through, or if there was a wonderful scene you just couldn't cut before. Now your objectivity will allow you to see how the scene doesn't fit. Be tough.

To put it succinctly, even brutally, don't get too wonderful. Remember William Faulkner's commandment: "In writing, you must kill all your darlings."

3. And Kill the Chitty-Chat

I first heard the words "chitty chat" from Richard Walter. From his book in script form:

```
                    MARGE
      Hi, how are you?

                    RALPH
      Fine, thanks. Yourself?
```

MARGE

Not bad, thanks.

RALPH

The family?

MARGE

Just great, though the baby has a rash. You?

RALPH

Excellent. Say, would you like a cup of coffee?

MARGE

Sounds great.

RALPH

How do you take it? Sugar? Cream? Milk? Low fat? Skim?

MARGE

Black, thanks. Have you any Sweet 'n Low?

RALPH

No, but I have NutraSweet.

MARGE

This is some beautiful day, isn't it?

RALPH

Sure is, but they said on the radio that it might rain.

There is a full page of script wasted. You only have a precious 100 to 110 pages. An aggregate of ten of these turkeys would constitute approximately ten percent of your script.

Yes, we chatty chat in real life. But never forget, you're a screenwriter. You stride in the world of movies. And movies give the *illusion* of reality, not reality. Cut all the hi's and the please and thank you's. Get to the pinnacle of the scene with dialogue or action that directly leads to that pinnacle.

Less is more, and chitty chat is *always* more of more.

4. Exposed Exposition

At this point, you'll be tempted to start scenes with a deadly phrase you've heard ad nauseam. "Let me get this straight." Then you hear a character recapping the plot or blathering on about something coming up, or describing an incident that happened off-camera between scenes. It's a weak, static, and lazy way to disguise exposition. When tempted to use "let me get this straight," or have your characters "run over it one more time," don't.

To disguise your exposition, be inventive. Create something out of nothing. Use character, sets, locales, events, babies, sex. At the very least, bring on Humphrey's humping camels or arguments, or lovemaking. I often think of ducks.

I wanted to introduce and expose two significant characters to my protagonist in a love story called *Chasing Rainbows*. I immediately perceived a sleep-inducing scene if I wrote the equivalent of Eileen's saying, "Denny, this is Clive. Clive, Denny. Oh, and here's my housekeeper, Mrs. Baynes."

I thought, how can I get Denny to know these characters and something about them without expository blah-blah? Let's see. Eileen lives in a high-rise condo. The window could be open. Wait, a bird could fly in. No, a duck's funnier. Yes, Denny's from Nebraska, he would know how to handle a loose duck in her apartment. The city people could be freaked. Denny would be the momentary authority. That would help his character and well start his relationship with the other three. We could introduce Clive here and get everyone's reaction to Clive's out-of-the-closet personality. That would be good for character and comedy. By now, the audience will know Eileen is an ultra-high-priced "companion." We'll use this scene to start Denny questioning her profession and show her reluctance to tell him. And we'll do all this with a duck.

CUT TO:

EXT.—DOHENY TOWERS ENTRYWAY—DAY

Eyes searching, voice humming Johnny Paycheck's "Take This Job and Shove It." Denny's fingers move down the building directory board. STOPPING at PHILLIPS, EILEEN,

Denny jabs an adjacent black button. He mildly startles when Eileen's VOICE shrieks from the boards' speaker.

EILEEN
(voice over; excited)
Yes??! Oh, my God! Over there, Mrs. Baynes!

DENNY
(to speaker)
I'm Denny. Uh . . . Mr. Dennis Anderson.

EILEEN
(voice over)
Mr. Dennis Anderson? My God, our white knight! Come up quickly, Mr. Dennis Anderson!

Eileen disconnects. Denny is tense, wants to comply. But how? A BUZZ emits from the huge double glass admittance doors. Denny startles at its sound, then tentatively advances.

CUT TO:

INT.—DOHENY TOWERS LOBBY—DAY

The BUZZ stops as Denny enters. A SECURITY MAN sits before him, studying a bank of in-house TV monitors. Denny is nervously compelled to explain himself while passing the stoic guard.

DENNY
I'm Denny? Mr. Denny Anderson? I'm up to see Eileen Phillips.

Nothing. The man doesn't seemingly relate to anyone three-dimensional. Denny continues on by a lobby fountain and reflecting pool to the twin elevators. He pushes the heat-respondent summons button, rocks on his heels, resumes humming, then notices something above eye level in the elevator entry corner.

HIS P.O.V.

A TV camera.

DENNY

moves one step. The camera moves, adjusting. Denny quickly moves back, the camera mimics the shift. Another human move, another electronic shift. The elevator doors whoosh wide, Denny doesn't resist a small wave as the doors close.

THE SECURITY GUARD

rolls his eyes.

CUT TO:

EXT.—EILEEN'S APARTMENT—DAY

EILEEN

is on her apartment's balcony.

EILEEN

Clive! Help! Quick!

CLIVE

rushes onto his adjoining balcony. A small Japanese-styled bridge has been built to span the two balconies. Clive Cloven is 35, gay, a dancer for stage productions. Eileen's best friend. Clive, in shorts, tugs a sleep mask from his head.

CLIVE

Eileen, I know I'm redundant but you'll wake the dead . . .

(head motions into his apartment)

. . . and Harold, too.

EILEEN

Please, Clive, no one-liners. I need you.

CUT TO:

INT.—DOHENY TOWERS—DAY

Fourteenth floor. Denny studies her card for the correct number, looks back and forth, chooses to exit right after another small, more confident wave to another overhead tracking camera.

CUT TO:

INT.—EILEEN'S APARTMENT—DAY

CLIVE AND EILEEN

look O.S.

CLIVE
(joy)
Oh, my God, a cock!

EILEEN
No such luck, Clive. It's a duck.

MRS. BAYNES

sprays Windex at a very agitated duck hunched atop a surreal desk.

CLIVE
(mock hurt)
Well, day *has* just broke for some of us.

MRS. BAYNES
(concentrating)
Hush now, Mr. Cloven.

EILEEN
(stage whisper)
The plan is, when the ammonia in that window spray hits, you'll grab him and . . .
(pantos)
. . . you know, back out the window.

CLIVE
(protesting)
I'll grab . . .
(softens in mid-sentence)
. . . how do you know it's a "he"?

EILEEN
Clive, *will* you . . .

She is interrupted by her DOOR CHIMES. The duck reacts to the sound and again goes mad, flapping against the ceiling.

EILEEN
(continues)
Oh, shit.
(remembers)
Oh, Denny.

As she stalks to the door, Clive fully awakens.

CLIVE
Denny?

EILEEN
(bursting open the door)
Denny!
(gestures to hysterical duck)
You are needed!

CLIVE
(leering)
For suuurre.

The PHONE RINGS.

MRS. BAYNES
Clive, shut up!

DENNY
(to Eileen)
What's the story?

EILEEN
This poor duck came in through . . .

DENNY
Excuse me, but . . . the phone?

EILEEN
Oh, the service'll get it.

DENNY
The service?

EILEEN
Mrs. Baynes was trying to . . . oh, Mrs. Baynes . . . Denny Anderson. Denny . . . Clive.

DENNY
Hullo . . . hullo.

MRS. BAYNES
Mr. Anderson.

EILEEN
(overlaps)
Not a word, Clive.

CLIVE
Where *did* you get *him,* Eileen?

DENNY
(John Wayne time again)
Okay, I know your problem.

CLIVE
You do?!

DENNY
Who's got a flashlight?

The PHONE RINGS again (and INTERMITTENTLY CONTINUES throughout the scene.)

EILEEN
A penlight?

DENNY
Oughta do it.

Eileen seizes a penlight from a near drawer as Denny slowly advances on the duck.

DENNY
(continues; receiving penlight)
Okay, now. Everybody hang loose.

CLIVE
I will. I will.

MRS. BAYNES	EILEEN
Clive!	Clive!

DENNY
It ain't the problem you might think.

He shines the penlight at the duck's eyes. Denny looks about. Impressed.

DENNY
(continues)
This place is really somethin', lady. What do you do for a living?

CLIVE
You mean you . . . mumphf.

Eileen clamps a hand over her friend's caustic mouth.

EILEEN
Freelance business woman, Mr. Anderson.

DENNY
Don't s'pose you have to make out from one payday to the next.

CLIVE
Denny . . . mumphf.

Again, the hand.

EILEEN
The duck, Mr. Anderson. The duck.

Another PHONE RING.

DENNY
(advances on duck)
No problem, ma'am, no problem. I'm from Nebraska. I know some about livestock.

PHONE CUTS OFF in mid-ring. Denny quizzes.

DENNY
(continues)
Tell me, what branch of the service takes phone calls?

CLIVE
(shrieking)
I love him! I love him!

The human scream startles the bird who swings its wings, then arcs out of the open balcony doorway.

DENNY
(sheepish; to Eileen)
Well, that was easier'n we figured.

Each admires the other. Clive muses words of prophecy.

CLIVE
(soft)
Not hardly, my friend. Not hardly.

Worry grays Mrs. Baynes' refined features. Something's coming.

CUT TO:

See how much came across with that berserk duck? And the Denny-Eileen love story even started at the scene's end.

Loose ducks in rooms for humor. Hitler screaming at Goebbels about invading Poland from one direction when the dummkopf wants to come in from another. The Godfather and Citizen Kane coolly explaining to someone about their abilities to destroy people and things with the resources of their explanations. All excellent ways to get around characters flatly blurting out the blah-blah or running over it one more time.

SECOND ACTS AND THIRD PARTIES

Sometimes in the second act, you'll have two people waiting for a shoe to fall or an obligatory scene. Worse, both can be the same scene.

A trick, when confronted with any one of these three possibilities, is bringing a third party into the scene.

Let's show with a scene from *To Die For.* My script about a forty-ish couple who lose their young son due to medical malpractice. The scenes in question have the couple waiting to learn about their son's condition, and then being informed he has died. These are two potentially boring, obligatory scenes. I heighted the drama and the interest level by using the third party trick. You see, generally when someone else is in front of your two people, they can't be so on-the-nose with their dialogue. Restrained subtext is what the scene's dialogue must contain.

Notice how much a security guard can give to such a scene.

CUT TO:

INT.—HOSPITAL CORRIDOR—NIGHT

The mother moves. Springing to the door. A posted nurse, experienced in parental vigils, steps out to block Sonia.

POSTED NURSE

I'm sorry.

SONIA

It's our son in there.

THE NURSE'S FINGER

pushes a silent alarm.

NURSE (V.O.)
It's important for everybody that you keep calm.

NURSE JEAN

from the emergency room comes out and starts to sidestep past.

BARRY
Look . . . what could it hurt . . . ?

Sonia interrupts, remembering Nurse Jean.

SONIA
(to Nurse Jean)
Nurse . . . you were with him earlier. Please . . . please, what's happening?

Jean knows the truth, but again, that damned white dacron veneer.

NURSE JEAN
Dr. Mason will discuss it with you.

Nurse Jean quickly hurries off.

BARRY
(to the retreating nurse)
We just want to know if he's OK!
(to posted nurse)
What's so against the rules about that?

Sonia starts to push by.

SONIA
(rushing words together)
We'll stay in the back, we won't talk. . . .

The nurse holds her position against Sonia and speaks to a summoned, large, black security guard.

POSTED NURSE

Fred . . .

THE SECURITY GUARD

spreads his huge arms high as an onrushing defensive lineman trying to block a buttonhook pass.

SECURITY GUARD

Folks, we all got jobs to do. This nurse here's supposed to be someplace else but here. You're supposed to be out here instead of in there. And I'm supposed to see to that.

(compassionate)

Whoever's in there surely already knows you love them. You just gotta love'm out here . . . for now.

TIME CUT TO:

INT.—THE CORRIDOR—NIGHT

Thirty minutes have passed. On a hard bench, Barry holds and rocks the seated, catatonic Sonia.

The security guard sits in a tin folding chair placed at the hallway's other side. He pages the newly printed early morning paper and rambles to the traumatized couple.

SECURITY GUARD

(just talking aloud)

. . . and I had them dressed to the nines . . . all lined up in front of their granny. My momma. I said, "What do you think of your first grandchildren, momma?" There's five brothers and sisters in my family. Well, she looked over them half specs and says, "Son, they look all right to me . . . but they're just kids." That made me *so* damned mad. . . .

Dr. Sheila Mason wearily comes through the significant door. The story, then the rocking stops.

In this human moment, the mother has the most strength to summon words.

SONIA

How's our boy?

After an endless second, Dr. Mason replies in a self-preserving, near-rote manner. She's said these words before.

DR. MASON

I'm sorry. He's dead. We did all we could. Your son . . . had the finest care.

The security guard starts to say something, then apparently remembers another of his "momma's" wisdoms and doesn't. He half folds his paper and walks off. Slump-shouldered. Dr. Mason also starts to say something, then doesn't. Her wisdom comes from experience. She does turn to reenter the door that is no longer a parental barrier. Barry and Sonia cling together. Tableau. Nothing can prepare a human for this. The most dramatic grief of all.

CUT TO:

Imagine those two scenes without a guard. Boring! On-the-nose! The guard works better than a hallway sandwich vendor or meter reader because of his authority posture. Good choices are simply the heart of writing.

Bring third, fourth, fifth parties, even crowds, into your choice process when scenes are less than compelling. Such choices could give you the needed edge to push a scene from OK to good to excellent.

MAKING SCENES INTERESTING

We certainly want all scenes to be fabulous. But they won't be. It took Oscar Hammerstein years to realize every word of his lyrics could not be a pearl. He became far more contented with his life's lot when he accepted that reality.

At the very least, though, each scene you write for any screen should be interesting. If you're having trouble getting a scene to stand up as interesting in your objective opinion, here are more trade tricks.

Throw away your first attempt and come at the scene's needs from a markedly different physical direction. Writer/director Billy Wilder *(Some Like It Hot, Sunset Boulevard)* recommends: "If you see a man coming through a doorway, it means nothing. If you see him coming through a window, that is at once interesting." If you're not inspired to change the locale or have someone come in through a window, vary the protagonist or antagonist's attitude. Shift from angry to loving, or perhaps back and forth within the same scene.

Dredging the scene bottom is another technique. Often you just haven't gone deep enough with the reasons for the scene's existence. Warning, though. Keep in mind that when you dive in the darkest dramatic waters, you will often have to restrain the scene from going on too long. Somerset Maugham admonished: "Do not overexplain too much." A caveat for emotional subtext as well as exposition.

Finally, rush it all out. Whether you're angry, happy, or passionate, rush it. Write quickly. Let your soul take over. It will often be wonderful and exactly right.

1. Scene Pinnacles

Some directors will ask for the pinnacle of a particular scene. That's a very useful and clear way of pinpointing the "why" a scene is even in the outline. Irving Ravetch *(Hud, Norma Rae)* believes scenes themselves have three acts.

Obviously the end of a scene should be its third act or pinnacle. So when you're into the script's second act and a scene lies there without life or quiver, determine the pinnacle, the dramatic information you most want to get across in the scene, be it plot, character point, or both. From there, think and restructure backwards. Then from the pinnacle to the scene's conclusion, rethink again and maybe restructure more.

This will make perfect sense to you who look for convolution in screenplay writing. For those who don't, you might simply have placed your pinnacle too early in the scene. Or the scene's pinnacle just isn't as significant as it should be.

For exceptional study of the beginning, middle, and end of scenes, refer to the screenplays and video tapes of *Hud; The Long, Hot Summer; Norma Rae; Murphy's Romance; The Reivers; Stanley and Iris* and any other movie written by UCLA alums Irving Ravetch and Harriet Frank, Jr. Irving says they like the work to speak for itself. Their superlative work does not speak, it shouts.

2. Touches

A great and loving influence for many screenwriters was director Jan Kadar. Jan would softly rub his Czechoslovakian fingertips together and coax "touches" out of scenes, writers, and actors. Jan once said it would be an "honor" to direct a particular script because it had so many wonderful "touches." "Touches" are a major differentiation between good and excellent in any art form.

One could define "touches" as details, but such descriptions risk diminishing this dimension of the art process. Fred Astaire was incredibly focused on detail. Rembrandt on light sources for his oils. In motion pictures, "touches" translate into the brief moments that speak to the characters in your drama or comedy.

Deborah Kerr played a sheepherder's wife in *The Sundowners.* While she looks off to see an elegant woman, one car down, directing porters to luggage, Deborah quickly turns back, as if she were afraid of being caught. She then notices her reflection in the passenger car's window glass and wistfully straightens a loose strand in her functional hair arrangement. A touch that says everything about the past and present of her character.

In another window, this one an exclusive Manhattan restaurant, sits the object of a police stakeout. This criminal, with a high-fashion model, pleasantly accepts a plate of steaming lobster. The camera pulls back to reveal the Gene Hackman detective devouring a slab of cold, greasy pizza while waiting for the next movement of *The French Connection.* Touches.

Whenever the *Fallen Angel* pedophile was pressured or had sexual tension, he would twist his large turquoise ring. Once, in protesting his innocence, he reached out to touch his lawyer. The lawyer perceptibly shrunk back. Touches.

Touches like, "You do the thinkin', Butch. That's what you're good at." Offers that can't be refused. E.T. going trick-or-treating. Charles

Foster Kane calling most people by their last names but the loyal Bernstein always *Mr.* Bernstein. Rick's anger at hearing "As Time Goes By."

All touches that do not *have* to be in these memorable movies, yet a major reason why they were memorable. Such moments of dialogue or business are rarely essential to plot but always essential to *good* character. Look for and include touches throughout your first draft and *all* of your rewrites. Generally they're "throwaway" moments. If you accent them too hard, they float like lead.

If you're a beginning writer, you might give one rewrite totally to adding or elaborating touches. After experience, you'll look for touches with every line you write. It's often a major difference between good and excellent. If you're going to work as hard as you've got to work to be good, take just a turn more to be the best you can be.

3. Transitions

How many more times do we have to see someone setting something on a surface, then in the next scene someone picking something up from another surface? New writers and directors love to have a door to close end a scene, followed by the sound and sight of another door opening. It was all clever and innovative the first time. Now it's just "cute."

While avoiding the "cute," look for fresh ways to get from scene to scene. One of the most brilliant transitions was the leap of thousands of years when the simian flung the bone to the air and Stanley Kubrick did a direct cut to the *2001* spaceship. Equally memorable is Charles Foster Kane's deteriorating marriage, with cuts of Kane and his wife at different breakfast settings—the space between them, and their marriage, growing apart with each transition.

The story usually creates a sufficient transition, best indicated by a direct "cut to." Forget the old-fashioned flips, clock wipes, fade outs, fade ins, and even dissolves. MTV and commercials have conditioned the audience to accept information so quickly that anything other than cuts slows the pace of your script and your subsequent picture.

When you devise a transition that is visually clever, go ahead. Succumb to the inspiration. But most of your transitions should be direct cuts that continue the unfolding and escalating of the story and character development. For *The Glass Hammer,* I may occasionally weaken and put in a visual attempt to carry the audience, and more specifically the director, from one scene to the next. In post-production, if these attempts make it that far, a clever technique *may* help maximize the storytelling. The goal is always *to maximize the story.* If your inventive transition does not relate to the telling of your story, kill the darling and use a direct cut designed only for leading the audience's emotion, which is goal enough.

STOPWATCH TIMING

In my teaching, I am drawn each quarter to the John Brady interview with Paul Schrader. When I talk about second acts and the overall flow of writing the script, I let my 434 audience hear aloud this Brady/ Schrader Q and A:

> BRADY: Do you know where you're going when you sit down to write word number one in your script?
>
> SCHRADER: Before I sit down to write, I have all the scenes listed. What happens in each scene. How many pages I anticipate each scene will take. I have a running log on the film. I can look down and see what happens by page thirty, what happens by page forty, fifty, sixty and so forth. I have the whole thing timed out to a hundred and five, a hundred and ten pages. To what I *think* it will play, so that two, three pages ahead or behind, you may add or drop dialogue or scenes. But if you're two pages ahead or behind, you have to work that into the timing. Especially if you get five pages ahead, or worse, five pages behind. Then something you had planned to work on page forty may not work the same way on page forty-five. Because what the audience sees as an intriguing development on page forty may be a predictable development on page forty-five. And if you start slowing down your script, you have to accommodate the fact you're getting there five minutes later.
>
> BRADY: So it's stopwatch timing.
>
> SCHRADER: Completely timed out. You can see how the characters interplay. Like in *American Gigolo,* I have the characters meet eight times in the movie. And I can see what pages they would meet on

those eight times and the different things that happen between the times they meet, so that there's always something to talk about when they meet. Something to develop. They don't just meet and talk. The viewer wants them to meet because things have *happened* and the viewer wants to see how they will deal with them later.

BRADY: You always have a character on the ascent.

SCHRADER: You try to time these things out. It's like running the mile. You start to recognize signposts peripherally, and you know as you're running past this house, this corner, whether you're ahead or behind your time. And if you're pushing too hard, you back off; if you're not pushing hard enough, you speed up. Because you have to reach that point at the end of the mile where you are *totally* spent. If you have no energy left you have failed; and if you run out of energy *before* the end, you have failed. You have to calculate while you're running how much reserve you have and how much farther you have to go.

The same thing applies to writing a script. You have to calculate how much juice is left in the story and how much you've used up. If you're behind, you have to speed up; and if you're ahead, you have to go back and cut. When I block out a scene and I say three and one-half pages on a scene, I'm very shocked if I write the scene and it's four, four and a half pages. It means that something new has come in. Because if I say A meets B in a restaurant, they discuss C and D. X walks in, another bit of exposition, and another event happens . . . boom, boom. I will list these things and calculate how long that will take. Then I figure out in the structure of the script how long I can support that scene. Often you'll come across a scene you feel has enough interesting material to support four or five pages. But the structure will only support two or three. So you have to find other places in the movie to put that dialogue. Because the audience only wants to sit and watch that scene for about two minutes; then it wants to get on to something else. If you make them sit for five, you slow them down and you hurt yourself. Better to cut out the good stuff, find another place for it and keep the pace going. A viewer cannot set a movie down. He can set a book down. He can stop, take a break, pick it up later. But when a viewer is bored for *more* than three or four minutes, the movie is irreparably harmed. The flow is broken. He will never be able to accept the movie as innocently as he could before. Whereas you can bore the reader of a book, because he'll stop. Or he may even skim a section if he's not interested. If you're not interested in whaling in *Moby Dick,* you can skim that section. You can't skim anything in a movie. You have to sit through it.

That Schrader/Brady back and forth is first-rate information for a beginning writer. Not so much for what it specifically says, and it's saying "structure," but mostly for what it implies. It implies that movies, writers, and especially audiences have rhythms.

Though I've abandoned charting, I too can tell if a scene has the material in it for two, three, or more pages. I can go through my outline, putting the page count behind each step and be within five pages of the actual total. Unless, as Schrader says, "something new has come in" at the story development level.

Whether you use Schrader's rhythm or mine, or your own, it makes no difference. *Having a rhythm* is what is important.

WRITING YOUR SECOND ACT

Now's the time to shut off the phones, and warn your friends and lovers you're going to be impossible for a few weeks. Pledge declarations of love to be resumed in the foreseeable future. Right now, you have to attend to a passion you hope will be much more consuming than anything human. Forget about appearing self-sufficient. Beg for extra fuzzies, full refrigerators, sex whenever you wish, and nothing but love. Screw devil's advocates, constructive criticism, or "input." This is your time in the second act sun. Cry for help. Be vulnerable when you're into the second act. People will also like the idea of being part of your artistic process.

I'll do it, you do it. Up F. Scott Fitzgerald's pantleg! We do have second acts!!

THE GLASS HAMMER SECOND ACT

CUT TO:

EXT.—MIDVALE REGIONAL CENTER—INNER COURTYARD—DAY

Susan is escorted to her ward by a 19-year-old bearded TOM CRAWFORD. Tom carries a soft, constant, ethereal smile. He always speaks slightly above a whisper. The couple moves in silence. Tom reaches a door handle as an inhuman SCREAM exits from a second-story window across the overgrown rose garden. Tom does not respond. SUSAN startles.

SUSAN

Jesus Christ Almighty!

A flash of irritation betrays Tom's inner thought. Outwardly he consults a wristwatch.

TOM

Harriet. Every day at two.

(assuring)

You won't hear it in A.

SUSAN

(pointing)

That's . . .

TOM

(opening door)

F . . . Ward F.

CUT TO:

INT.—WARD A—RECEPTION ROOM

Twelve people. Two at Ping-Pong, two talk, three read, one stares out a barred window, two at cribbage, one paints, and one is asleep on the floor before an artificial fireplace. Susan is flanked by a husky black middle-aged nurse, MRS. HAPSBURY, who blows a referee whistle that normally rests on her sagging bosom. Activity freezes.

MRS. HAPSBURY

Okay, here's a new one.

She nods at a twitching, middle-aged BLONDE.

MRS. HAPSBURY (CONT)

You start, Lorraine.

The "introducing" ritual commences. Each says his name with no expression, all by rote, all in rhythm.

ALL

(individually)

Lorraine Graham. Ellis T. Franklin. Jean Badham. Richard . . . not Dick . . . Warner. Robin Ohmsteade. Mary Moranville. Erv Young.

They have come to the woman, still asleep, near the hearth.

MRS. HAPSBURY

(pointing)

Paula Kinscher.

The next person continues.

MAN

Charles Gruber.

WOMAN

I'm Paula, too. Paula Kennedy. P.K. here to tell her and I apart.

MAN

George Wright.

They have gotten around to Susan and look for her to continue the cadence. She gratuitously adjusts her hair.

MRS. HAPSBURY

(demanding)

And?

SUSAN

Me? Oh, me. Susan . . . uh . . . Suzy Garber.

The last name is the trigger for all to resume their prior occupations. Susan and Mrs. Hapsbury are alone and together.

MRS. HAPSBURY
(gesturing)
The men sleep at that end, the girls up here. I'll show you . . .
(interrupts herself)
. . . Didn't Tom bring your things?

Susan starts to answer, but Mrs. Hapsbury has already perceived the situation.

MRS. HAPSBURY (CONT., O.S.)
I get it. That's all right. We have old clothes from the penitentiary. No problem. Your mom or dad or whatever'll bring 'em next Saturday, right?

Mrs. Hapsbury strides to the female quarters, not waiting for an answer.

SUSAN

starts to pull in.

MRS. HAPSBURY (O.S.)
Right?

SUSAN
(tight)
Grobel.

CUT TO:

EXT.—MEMORIAL COLISEUM, LINCOLN, NEBRASKA—DAY

Seventy-six thousand, one hundred forty-three people vault to their feet.

SPORTS ANNOUNCER (V.O.)
Well, there you have it, ladies and gentlemen! The big plays that made Nebraska number one last year, are *still* being made!!

CUT TO:

EXT.—MIDVALE REGIONAL CENTER—DAY

Mrs. Garber tearfully leaves the main building. The V.O. of the sports announcer continues, emanating from various radios in the area, an aural presence consistent with every urban Nebraska setting on football Saturday afternoon. Mrs. Garber gets into an empty powder-blue Mercedes. Behind this expensive car, Cliff stands beside his parents' green Ford. Two stuffed pillowcases in each hand. He nods to his mother, then father. Mrs. Garber pulls into traffic. As Cliff turns to walk to the entrance, Harriet's two o'clock SCREAM is clearly, chillingly heard over the sportscast.

MILT

looks to his wife, rubs his weathered eyes, shudders, then looks back to the ominous building that is about to swallow his first and only born.

CLIFF

slowly mounts the weathered steps, pauses, enters.

CUT TO:

INT.—ORDERLY QUARTERS—DAY

Cliff looks about his new "home." The door opens and Tom Crawford walks in, startling Cliff.

TOM

I'm Tom Crawford. They want me to orient you.

CLIFF

I was just hopin' somebody'd show me the sights.

Cliff swings his pillowcases on a bare mattress. A Bible falls out of one pillowcase top. Cliff puts it back in and stammers.

CLIFF (CONT.)

Mom wanted me to use Dad's suitcase or even grocery bags. Dad 'n' I thought these pillowcases would hold more than them bags.

TOM
You wouldn't be a brother?

Tom gives "the way" sign. A forefinger pointing overhead. Cliff looks up the ceiling, then back to Tom. He doesn't understand. Tom shrugs off disappointment.

TOM (CONT.)
Well, I saw the Bible . . .

CLIFF
(shy smile)
Mom sorta slipped that in.

CUT TO:

INT.—DOUBLE SWINGING DOORS—DAY

Tom and Cliff have paused at the entryway to Ward A. Cliff receives a towel from Tom.

TOM
Always have one of these small hand towels in your belt. If you're attacked . . .

He demonstrates by whipping the towel from his own belt, stepping behind the young farm boy, putting it around Cliff's neck and twisting. Cliff starts to choke and struggle before Tom releases his hold.

TOM (CONT.)
See, just cut off their air a *little* bit. That'll slow them until help comes.
(motions to the doors)
Of course, if you start out in A Ward here, you won't have to worry much.

CUT TO:

EXT.—FENCED-IN PLAY YARD—DAY

Physically and mentally handicapped adults play like kindergarten children on teeter-totters, swings, sand piles, etc.

Tom and Cliff wander through their strange joy to a far door. Cliff stops, looks back.

CLIFF

We had a two-headed calf born once, but these . . . these are people.

Tom holds the door knob and frowns.

TOM

(serious)

These are sins. Sins of the fathers manifested upon the children.

Cliff doesn't hear.

CLIFF

Jee-sus. Something to write home about.

CUT TO:

INT.—WARD A—RECREATION AREA—DAY

Most of the ward's inhabitants are cheerfully decorating for the Halloween season. Grotesque masks and paintings are being taped to walls. Paula, though, is in her constant slumber before the fireplace. Cliff smiles at their obvious pleasure. He talks low.

CLIFF

(to Tom)

This's my speed. They don't even look *in*-sane ta me.

Tom reacts and wryly head-beckons Cliff. Tom goes to the women's restroom door and knocks.

TOM

All clear?

No reply. He enters. Cliff reluctantly follows.

CUT TO:

INT.—RESTROOM—DAY

There are two stools and two tubs with shower curtains drawn across their enclosures. Over two sinks there is a four-by-six sheet of stainless steel. The metal is pocked with dents. Age has dulled its finish. The two boys enter and stare in this unusual mirror. Tom fingers the textured surface.

TOM

There's no glass in these wards. No pumpkin-carving knives. No mirrors. This one is steel. It was smooth . . . clear. They see themselves and hate and hate and pound and pound.

SUSAN

sits behind the plastic shower curtain, in the tub. Fully clothed. Listening.

TOM

(voice over)

With shoes, books, spoons they steal from the mess hall. Some of them even smash their heads here.

CLIFF

is anxious to go, as it's the women's bathroom. He swings the door open for Tom.

CLIFF

Things still make more sense for me here instead of that freak farm on the other side.

SUSAN

sees them leave by staring through a shower curtain tear at the dented metal mirror.

TOM

(voice over)

That's probably where they'll put you first.

CLIFF

I s'pose it's wrong, Tom, but I can't hardly look at 'em.

CUT TO:

EXT.—MIDVALE DAIRY QUEEN—NIGHT

A QUASIMOTO HEAD

licks a "Dairy Queen" cone.

CLIFF

smiles as he waits in line to be served. The Dairy Queen is surrounded by trick-or-treaters of all ages. Everyone has been on the door-to-door rounds and the parents are giving their children a final ice cream or hamburger treat for this Midvale Halloween night. Cliff looks at everyone with new eyes. The grotesque humans with costumes, the grotesque adults without. "Who is crazy, who is sane?" thinks Cliff. As he turns, he startles.

AN ADULT FRANKENSTEIN

waits behind Cliff. The man takes off his rubber head and smiles. He has rotting teeth, disheveled hair, a twisted smile. He is more bizarre than his mask.

MATCH CUT TO:

EXT.—HANDICAPPED PLAY YARD—DAY

ANN GREENFIELD

a ten-year-old "flat-headed" hydrocephalic, giggles.

CLIFF

is doing yo-yo tricks for her. Specifically, "walking the dog." Dr. Gargon is in the b.g. talking to a nurse. An orderly hurries up and whispers in his ear.

CLIFF
(to Ann)
I was thought ta be choppin' weeds out of the corn when I learned this.

Ann licks her lips, rubs her stomach.

ANN
Ummmm . . . corn.

CLIFF
Oh, yeah? Sure like to pull and cook some good ears from our bottomland. Oh, I forgot. It's "gone by" now.

Dr. Gargon approaches.

DR. GARGON
MacPherson.

CLIFF
Oh, yes, sir. I was just showing Ann . . .
(decides his action is obvious and will just respond)
. . . what can I do for you?

DR. GARGON
Crawford says you want Ward A.

CLIFF
Oh, Ward A.
(to Ann)
Ann, jump on that swing. I'll be right over to push.

She smiles and moves to obey.

CLIFF (CONT.)
(to Dr. Gargon)
Like my Dad used to say, "I feel truly foolish."
(motions around)
These people are . . . better'n most outside. The couple days I been here, we've kind of got on.

Gargon is interested in this unusual young man.

DR. GARGON

Look, there's a job for you over there right now.
See Mrs. Hapsbury, do it, and then say yes or no.
Take a pail and a sponge.

Cliff studies the area. Ann waits in her stationary swing.

CLIFF
(to Gargon)

Fair enough.

CUT TO:

INT.—WARD A—RECREATION ROOM—DAY

MRS. HAPSBURY
(stern)

Where's your towel, young man?

Cliff holds the pail and sponge before the imposing woman.

CLIFF
(shy)

I was a linebacker in high school, ma'am.

She jams her own towel in his belt.

MRS. HAPSBURY

You read up on adrenaline . . . then talk to me
about linebackers, young man. OK, go on.

She motions to the women's closed restroom door. Cliff reaches for the knob, then stops.

CLIFF

. . . All clear?

(then knocks)

Anybody in there?

No response. He cautiously edges open the door.

CUT TO:

INT.—WOMEN'S RESTROOM—DAY

Cliff looks about. Puzzlement. The restroom walls are smeared with rudimentary printing. A brown substance. The letters form "fuck the universe!" Cliff sniffs, screws up his nose, and straightens his brow. He approaches the walls and examines.

CLIFF
(softly)
Hoooo-ly sheeeiit.

Cliff startles at a giggle behind the shower curtain stretched across the bathtub. Now, silence. Cliff's eyes swivel. He thinks, then sets the pail down, and apprehensively eases the curtain back.

Susan sits, knees drawn up, again fully clothed in the dry bathtub. She giggles once more.

SUSAN
(coy)
I always thought mine went to the pie factory. Maybe it should go to the Vatican. You know? Holy shit?

CLIFF (CONT.)
You mean ta tell me you did this?

Instead of crying, Susan hysterically laughs. Classic manic-depression. Cliff flares and yanks her out of the tub.

CLIFF (CONT.)
You keep hold of yourself, young woman.

He picks her up and paternally jams her on a stool. She quiets.

CLIFF (CONT.)
That's what you're supposed to use. You know it, too.

Susan erupts, runs to a wall and tries to rub the brown stuff on her face, then on Cliff. He stops her.

CLIFF (CONT.)

You oughta get my hand right on your bare ass.

SUSAN

(quickly)

Oooh, do it.

Quiet. Cliff is clearly embarrassed.

CLIFF

Don't talk like that.

More quiet. Susan starts to tear. Cliff rises, goes to the sink, looks at her via the mutilated metal mirror, and lets the water run while reaching for a washcloth. He tests the water, looks back at her, smiles, then again tests.

CLIFF (CONT.)

(to Susan)

Takes a month of Sundays to get warm water up through these pipes.

Then, it comes. He rinses the cloth, moves to Susan, and washes her face as a teacher does a child after recess. He finishes.

CLIFF (CONT.)

There. Anybody as ugly as you needs all the help possible.

Susan's eyes quiz.

SUSAN

I don't like you.

CLIFF

You ain't alone.

SUSAN
You use bad English.

CLIFF
You use dirty English. Omaha talk.

Susan thinks on that.

SUSAN
(taunting)
Yes, you're a hick. A country stick.

CLIFF
(rising)
Well . . . better do what I was sent here for. Then we'll get you in a proper bed.

Susan seductively squeals and Cliff ignores. He retrieves the sponge, dips it in the pail of water, and starts to wash the walls. Susan is irritated at his inattention, rises, lifts the toilet seat cover, then her dress, and sits. Cliff's eyes roll to the ceiling and back.

CLIFF (CONT.)
Come on. Don't do that with me here. Let me get outta your way first.

He starts to leave. Susan grabs his passing arm and takes the sponge from his hand.

SUSAN
I'll help.

CLIFF
(warm smile)
Now you're talkin' fine.

DISSOLVE TO:

INT.—WARD A—DORMITORY—DAY

Susan's head sinks back on her pillow. Cliff's farm hands tug a sheet and blanket up to her neck.

CLIFF

Ain't this better'n any cold tub?

SUSAN

(sexy twinkle)

I'd rather have a hot . . .

Cliff slides his hand over her mouth.

CLIFF

Let's bypass any more Omaha talk.

Susan clouds. Cliff quickly tries to change the mood.

CLIFF (CONT.)

Next time you take a notion to decorate the bathroom, holler for me first.

As he starts away, she grabs at him. Her finger hits his midsection, she draws it back in slight pain.

CLIFF (CONT.)

What's the . . . oh, that darn buckle.

Cliff lifts his orderly smock to show a large three-by-five rectangular brass belt buckle. She holds her finger and studies the ornament. It has the engraving of a stagecoach and the words, "Wells Fargo—Omaha."

SUSAN

(reading)

Wells Fargo . . . Omaha?

CLIFF

Wanted one sayin' Beaver Crossing.

Susan questions.

CLIFF (CONT.)

You know there was a Beaver Crossing, Nebraska?

She shakes her head.

CLIFF (CONT.)
(twinkle)
How long do you s'pose it'll take him?

Susan sputters out a laugh and punches him above the buckle. Cliff enjoys the joke he's "pulled" many times. He starts to move out.

SUSAN
(abruptly)
What's your name?

Cliff stops.

CLIFF
Clifford. "Cliff" MacPherson.

SUSAN
I'm Susan. Suzy Garber.

CLIFF
Susan *Ellen* Garber.
(points to chart on foot of her bed)
According to here.

Again she aborts his exit.

SUSAN
If I "holler," will you be around?

Cliff rubs the back of his neck.

CLIFF
Yep, Sue Ellen. You talked me into it. I'll be around.

Susan smiles and contentedly settles.

CUT TO:

EXT.—TRASH BIN AREA—DAY

Cliff tips a garbage can of leaves into a dumpster as Dr. Gargon pulls from a Bronco four-wheeler he just parked in the center's adjacent lot.

DR. GARGON
Hey, Clifford. The big game's in a half hour.

Cliff looks and responds.

CLIFF
My dad used to say "No rest for the wicked."

DR. GARGON
"So you must be wicked." We had the same dad.

He starts off.

CLIFF
Oh, Doc?
(Gargon looks back)
Doc, Ward A'll be fine and dandy.

DR. GARGON
Why'd you change your mind?

CLIFF
Just trying to be agreeable.
(grins)
Maybe thought I could get out from under all these leaves.

DR. GARGON
You got it. Start Monday. Don't ever forget, they may act totally sane but they're a little bit or a lot madder than you and I.

CLIFF
(grins)
That's pretty mad, Doc.

DR. GARGON
(serious)
It can be, Clifford. It really can be.

CUT TO:

EXT.—CENTER'S INNER COURTYARD—DAY

Cliff rakes more leaves. The promised Nebraska game comes from his transistor radio hanging on a near limb. He notices someone O.C.

P.O.V.

Susan rushes away from the Mess Hall doorway and half-runs to the Ward A door, as if she's walking for safety. She licks at a popsicle.

SPORTS ANNOUNCER
(voice over)
Well, it's a beautiful fall day here in Nebraska on this Saturday before Thanksgiving. A perfect setting for another classic showdown between Nebraska and Oklahoma.

CLIFF

studies Susan. He actually stares.

SPORTS ANNOUNCER
(voice over)
Both teams again undefeated. Both teams again playing for the Orange Bowl.

Cliff quickly looks away in near terror. Caught.
SUSAN has paused by the Ward A door. She commits deliberate fellatio on the phallic popsicle.

CLIFF

will not look, as the embarrassed young man rakes and rakes.

SUSAN

smiles, then enters her building.

SPORTS ANNOUNCER
(voice over)
It's the biggest game in the country, but it's always been the biggest game since I've been on board these Cornhusker broadcasts.

CUT TO:

EXT.—QUICK STOP CONVENIENCE STORE—DAY

Cliff is pumping ten dollars of gas into a Dodge van that bears "Midvale Regional Center" on its side panels. Cliff simultaneously admires an empty, jacked-up new Chevy pickup. Obviously given a "turn" similar to his wrecked pickup. Its doors are open and the Nebraska-Oklahoma game blares from its radio. Cliff looks over to the Quick-Stop store.

P.O.V.

Inside the small building that used to be a service station bay, six teenagers scream and yell at a television set that features a different sportscaster.

SPORTSCASTER
(voice over)
He's across the twenty, the thirty, forty, fifty, forty, thirty, twenty, ten!!! Eighty-five yards for a go-ahead Nebraska touchdown!!! Yes, Cornhusker fans, there *is* no place like Nebraska!

The University bands strike up the song "There Is No Place Like Nebraska" as they do after every Cornhusker touchdown. The Quick-Stop customers pound each other and shout in victory. A big blond teenager the most vocal and most physical.

CLIFF

shakes his head and smiles. More "who is crazy and who is sane" thoughts. Snaps the gas nozzle back in its cradle.

CUT TO:

INT.—WARD A—RECREATION ROOM—NIGHT

Cliff's hands place an angel on top of an artificial Christmas tree. The inmates applaud. Susan is beside him, apparently happy and healthy. She hugs the farm boy.

Tom enters and glances about, pleased at the seasonal transformation. His eyes narrow at Cliff and Susan happily talking.

CLIFF
(pointing)
Slip in the bathroom, fetch water for the stand. I'll start throwing tinsel.

He stoops for the box of aluminum strands.

SUSAN
(sobers)
Cliff . . .

He straightens.

SUSAN (CONT.)
(hard)
I want your ass here when I get back.

CLIFF
(exasperated)
Sue Ellen, you and that damn Omaha talk.

SUSAN
(seriously)
I'm not shittin'.

CLIFF
Me neither, young lady. Do as you're asked.

He smooths her cheek with the knuckles of his fist.

CLIFF (CONT)
Then I'll give you somethin' when you get back.

Susan holds his fist, nervously smiles, and moves off. Tom comes to Cliff.

TOM

You're playing with the devil, Cliffy, the absolute devil.

Cliff considers his reply while placing a shred of tinsel.

CLIFF

(ignoring)

Tom, this old plastic tree ain't looking bad, all things considered.

TOM

(righteous)

Cliffy, I am my brother's keeper.

CLIFF

Tommy, I *ain't* your brother.

TOM

Keep your eyes open, Cliff. You'll see there aren't any sharp ornaments on *this* tree.

Tom moves off. Cliff looks at the tree, spins a ball, and thinks on Tom's dire warning. Susan approaches. A urinal filled with water in her hand.

SUSAN

(teasing)

Super water. I've seen studs before but that Ellis T. Franklin . . .

CLIFF

(tight)

Sue Ellen, you went in the men's room?

SUSAN

It was on Mrs. Hapsbury's desk. She said it was okay.

Cliff is embarrassed for his thought.

CLIFF

That's my girl.

The three words sober Susan. Cliff takes the urinal.

SUSAN

Where's my something?

Cliff doesn't understand.

SUSAN (CONT.)

You said you'd give me something when I got back. Here I am. Back.

Cliff pocket-digs.

ON A MINIATURE MANTELPIECE CRÈCHE SCENE.

Tom's fingers lift out a cross someone placed in the tiny manger.

TOM (V.O.)

Who did this?!

CLIFF'S HAND

presses his Omaha belt buckle into Susan's open palm. Cliff and Susan are oblivious to Tom's rage.

TOM (V.O.)

Who did this?!

TOM

brandishes the tiny cross in front of the fireplace. Paula sleeps at his feet.

TOM

Sacrilege! High sacrilege!

(accusing all)

You are stepping further and further down the road to Hell. You must see God's love. You must feel God's love. You must know that God loves you.

MRS. HAPSBURY

and an AIDE enter. The black matron throws her eyes to the ceiling.

TOM (CONT.)

. . . and God's love is most *perfectly* exemplified by the gift of his precious, precious child at Christmastime.

MRS. HAPSBURY

Tom . . .

TOM

(ignoring)

Oh, *when* will you read the scriptures, God's holy, holy word, and *find* the comfort and love he has for each and every one of you. God loves you *so* much.

Mrs. Hapsbury sees the urinal resting on an end table by Cliff and Susan, who continue to ignore Tom's tirade. Mrs. Hapsbury strides to the table, seizes the urinal, and confirms the contents.

TOM (CONT.)

If you could only feel the blessing of receiving the Holy Spirit . . .

Mrs. Hapsbury dashes the water in his wild face. Tom shocks, stops, stares. The tiny metal cross drops from his fingers and tinkles on the hearthstone.

MRS. HAPSBURY

Go clean up, Tom. Right now! The rest of you keep decorating or go to bed.

The rock-still patients still peer at Tom obediently stumbling off on the order of this strong woman.

MRS. HAPSBURY (CONT.)

Right now!

The inmates resume their activity. Mrs. Hapsbury softly snaps to her aide.

MRS. HAPSBURY (CONT.)
Some days, I can't tell who's craziest.

The two move off. Susan and Cliff are seated cross-legged at the base of the decorated tree. Cliff has made a "cat's cradle" from a double-length strand of tinsel. He holds it up for Susan's admiration. She reaches out and tears it apart. Cliff reacts by sprinkling the broken strands in her hair. She laughs and grabs his offending hand.

CLIFF AND SUSAN

almost kiss.

CUT TO:

INT.—DR. GARGON'S OUTER OFFICE—NIGHT

Cliff is looking through an F-H cabinet drawer. He finds Susan's file and starts paging through it. His concentration is shattered by Dr. Gargon's voice.

DR. GARGON
(voice over)
Susan?

Cliff blushes with guilt and fright.

DR. GARGON

takes it from the young orderly and returns it to the file after verifying the answer to his question.

CLIFF
I know I wasn't supposed to do that, sir.

Gargon locks the cabinet.

DR. GARGON
They tell me you've been more effective with Susan than anyone else.

CLIFF
It's . . . not been planned.

DR. GARGON
Keep going. See what happens.

CLIFF
I'm not qualified, sir.

DR. GARGON
And that's probably why you can help her. Just watch your heart, Clifford. You're not playing with fire, you're in the fire.

CUT TO:

EXT.—MIDVALE REGIONAL CENTER—DAY

A new snow lends the accumulation of brick buildings a benign beauty.

CLIFF
(voice over)
Dammit, Sue Ellen you keep doin' that, I'm gonna get on edge.

SUSAN
(voice over)
Is "on edge" the same as "pissed"?

CUT TO:

EXT.—SNOW-COVERED INNER COURTYARD—DAY

Cliff and Susan have shuffle-stepped a circle with quartered sections in snow and now play a Midwestern child's game of "fox and goose." Susan is walking through a quarter.

CLIFF
No self-respectin' goose kitty-corners.

SUSAN
(winded)
All lazy brown foxes overcome devious traits by lesser adversaries in their quest for spiritual enrichment and physical nourishment.

Susan points a finger at Cliff.

SUSAN (CONT.)
For getting pissed . . . boom.

Cliff topples as a falling tree into a bank beside the happy girl. He lies facedown in the snow. Seconds pass. Susan shakes his shoulder.

SUSAN (CONT.)
Cliff, come on.

No response as the boy can hold his breath an abnormal period of time. Susan gets serious.

SUSAN (CONT.)
Cliff, that's enough.

A loud electronic BUZZING violates the air. Cliff lifts his face. They both look around.

SUSAN (CONT.)
Good old Harriet. Her once-a-month breakout. Neither wind, rain, snow, or lack of imagination stops her.

CLIFF
You're not supposed to know about her.

SUSAN
To know a crazy, ask a crazy.

CLIFF
You're not crazy.

SUSAN
(seriously)
I'm crazy the rest of my life, Cliff. The duration.

Susan glances away. Cliff is embarrassed.

CLIFF
(looking to Ward F)
Wonder how Harriet gets loose? Every month, every which way. And Ward F's supposed to be the toughest.

Susan continues her stare away.

CLIFF (CONT.)
Must give her something to do. Keeps her from goin' nuts totally.

The BUZZER stops. Some distant YELLING, nothing articulate. Cliff muses, not consciously expecting an answer.

CLIFF (CONT.)
How do you figure someone becomes that way?

SUSAN
(to a void)
Pain . . . loneliness . . . contrast . . . a soul reaching into the marrow of hell that lives in the center of a teardrop.

CLIFF
(uncomfortable)
I think I understand.

SUSAN
The lesser colors of a rainbow can bloom and buzz . . . cry and ache . . . the night dreams fade . . . the day grows to a specter that throws you out, up and backward, slipping in your own desperation . . . your own liquid shriek as the life of promise smolders, sparks, smolders, flames . . .

During this, Cliff compresses a handful of snow, leans over Susan, and faintly caresses her forehead with the cold.

CLIFF
(interrupts)
Sue Ellen?

The girl focuses.

CLIFF (CONT.)
(gentle)
That's real creative. I don't know about you, but it makes me real nervous.

The girl stoically takes the boy's face and pulls his lips to hers. Their first kiss is long. After the release, Cliff tilts back slightly. Susan smiles in love.

Cliff rolls on his back and stares at the blue sky.

CLIFF (CONT.)
It don't seem right.

SUSAN
(nods)
Because of what I've done.

CLIFF
(tightens)
I don't give a shit where you been or what you done.
(softer)
I mean taking advantage of you. Here. It don't seem right.

SUSAN
(slight imitation of his delivery)
'Course, on the other hand, it *does* seem right.

Cliff thinks, decides, then looks about. No observers. Cliff slides off his gloves, blows warmth in his bare hands and pulls her face into his.

CUT TO:

EXT.—COURTYARD—DAY

CLIFF'S GLOVED HANDS

break off two icicles that hang from a Chinese elm.

CLIFF AND SUSAN

are still in the snowbound inner courtyard. They proceed to lick them like ice cream cones.

SUSAN
(giggles)
Kind of phallic.

CLIFF
Huh?

Susan flusters as she realizes Cliff doesn't even know the word. ANOTHER BUZZER SOUNDS. The youngsters ignore it.

SUSAN
You know, lick. Like a popsicle?

CLIFF
(grins)
Only wish they came in cherry.

Dr. Gargon approaches, running.

DR. GARGON
Step to, Clifford. They're looking for us.

CLIFF
How's come?

By now, Dr. GARGON has passed and replies over his shoulder while continuing to run.

DR. GARGON
Harriet got outside this time.

Susan takes Cliff's arm.

CLIFF
(to Susan)
I thought it was all sort of a game.

He quick-kisses her on the lips.

CLIFF (CONT.)

See you inside.

Cliff breaks away from Susan and starts trotting away.

SUSAN

Cliff.

He doesn't hear.

SUSAN (CONT.)

Cliff!! Don't go!!

Cliff pauses at the door that opens into Ward F.

CLIFF

It's okay, Sue Ellen. Back quicker than you can shake a lamb's tail. Okay?

She doesn't respond.

CLIFF (CONT.)

OK!!??

SUSAN

starts to pull in, faintly trembling.

SUSAN
(soft)

Crail.

The BUZZER stops.

SUSAN'S P.O.V.

The distant Cliff doesn't hear but assumes her agreement, waves, and ducks through the entrance.

CUT TO:

INT.—WOMEN'S RESTROOM—DAY

Susan glares into the battered restroom mirror. She traces the outline of her reflected face with a quivering forefinger. When her hand gets down to the neck, she breaks. A desperate grimace. As suddenly, she slashes at her throat with an object in her cruel fingers. Blood spurts. Her hysteria is mute.

ON THE RESTROOM FLOOR

Susan's dripping fist opens and Cliff's Wells Fargo belt buckle slides to and CLANKS on the octagonal porcelain tiles. One of its metal edges has been honed to a knife-like sharpness. Her hand is still.

CUT TO:

EXT.—COUNTY HOSPITAL—NIGHT

A building whose drabness is distinguished by white, piled snow. Visitors and employees come and go from the main entrance.

CUT TO:

INT.—COUNTY HOSPITAL RECOVERY ROOM—ROOM

Susan lies in stark white. A slightly bloodstained bandage conceals her throat wounds. The young girl's lashes flutter and open. She focuses. The eyeballs swivel, then stop as Cliff rests a forefinger on her lips. The girl's body, arms, and legs are bound to the bed.

CLIFF
(quiet)
You're gonna be fine. None of that Omaha talk now.
(he thinks)
They asked me if I could give shots. I used to vaccinate heifers for blackleg. That's good enough, they said.
(holds up hypodermic needle)
Are you afraid of these?

(then remembers)
No, don't say nothing. It don't make no difference. I'm supposed to give you this when you wake up.

Susan's eyes question and look around.

CLIFF (CONT.)
(understands)
Oh, yeah. We came to town. You know, Midvale. You needed a real hospital.

He removes the alcohol jar from the near night stand.

CLIFF (CONT.)
Best do my job.

He swabs her arm with the chilling liquid, then readies the needle.

CLIFF (CONT.)
(gentle)
Think of picnics and parties. That's what mom would say. I know what. Dad 'n I used to slap 'em on one end 'n' stick 'em in the other.
(smiles)
Oughta work on people.
(gentle)
You sure are people.

Susan breaks her initial smile. Cliff sobers.

CLIFF (CONT.)
(choke in throat)
I'm sorry . . . for all my part.

The understanding girl's lips purse in a faint kiss gesture. Cliff slaps her thigh with one hand and darts the needle in Susan's arm with the other. He pushes the syringe plunger, then repeats the slap and pulls out the needle. Both smile. Success.

CLIFF (CONT.)
You're supposed to go to sleep with that. Then I'll take you home.

Her eyes again question.

CLIFF (CONT.)
(quiet stammer)
You know, our home for these days.

Her lips again kiss.

CLIFF (CONT.)
(quiet pleasure)
Damn. Even at your worse, you're best.

CUT TO:

INT.—COUNTY HOSPITAL—NIGHT

Cliff wheels Susan out of the elevator, by people who see and whisper in the Emergency Waiting Area, and up the automatic double glass doors.

CLIFF
(to a nearby orderly)
Got a hand?

The orderly nods and they push Susan through the exit.

CUT TO:

EXT.—EMERGENCY ENTRANCE—NIGHT

Cliff and his helper put Susan through the back doors of the Midvale Regional Center Dodge van. Two men, FRED and RALPH, stand outside, chewing and spitting in cups.

RALPH
(to Fred, nodding to van)
All my life this town's carried that funny farm cross.

FRED

You'd think they'd put it in house trailers or something. Move it from city to city every five years or so. Sort of spread out the load.

Cliff and the orderly glance to each other.

RALPH

Not bad. Bet it could stand on its own two feet by charging admission to see some of 'em.

FRED

Like the old freak shows.

RALPH

(nodding)

They're like vegetables anyway.

Cliff closes the van. Hard.

FRED

Gets 'em off welfare. Gives 'em pride.

A NURSE puts her head out of the door.

NURSE

Mr. Stebbins.

Ralph empties his cup in a planter.

RALPH

(apprehensively)

Oh, Christ, now what?

They go inside as Cliff tightly walks to the driver's door. He nods to the orderly.

CLIFF

Much obliged.

ORDERLY

Any time.

CUT TO:

INT.—MIDVALE DODGE VAN—NIGHT

Cliff drives the deserted main street of Midvale. Only night cats move. They hold to the shadows. In the town's commercial center, a swaying, four-way signal flashes red over the intersection. Susan, sedated, sleeps full-length behind the driver's seat. Cliff considers running the light, then stops. The earlier seen jacked-up new Chevy pickup wheels around the deserted corner, runs the light, then spins a full circle about Cliff's van. It's filled with the same teenagers, all drinking beer. The driver is ROD HARRIS. Big and blond, the local quarterback.

CUT TO:

EXT. INTERSECTION

After a second taunting circle, the pickup pulls even with the Midvale van. Most of the teenagers are down to thirty-four in the "Ninety-nine Bottles of Beer on the Wall" song.

CUT TO:

INT.—VAN

Cliff breaks a slight grin as he looks to Rod Harris gunning his motor. Challenging. A shadow draws over Cliff's face. He returns to driving, pulling across the intersection, not responding to the gauntlet.

CUT TO:

EXT.—INTERSECTION—NIGHT

The youngsters taunt Cliff.

FAT TEENAGER

Another load for the loony bin?!

SKINNY TEENAGER

Hey, maybe he's one of "them"!

PIMPLED TEENAGER

Come on, Rod! Take his ass!

CUT TO:

INT.—VAN—NIGHT

Cliff's jaw is marble. He's now angry. The pickup pulls even again. Cliff accelerates. The pickup accelerates. Still even. The kids continue to taunt. Rod presents a middle finger. Up your ass. Cliff checks Susan. She's out of it. Cliff looks back to the road. They are through the Midvale business district. He decides.

CLIFF'S BOOTED FOOT

floorboards. The "Ninety-nine Bottles of Beer" singers stop. They chorus, "All right!!!" "Go for it," etc.

CUT TO:

EXT.—MIDVALE OUTSKIRTS—NIGHT

City limits sign in f.g. The two vehicles approach it, then race by to the waiting countryside.

CUT TO:

INT.—VAN—NIGHT

Cliff frowns. He simply hasn't the machine to be competitive. An empty beer BOTTLE from the adjacent pickup CRASHES off the metal van. Cliff ANGERS and looks back to Susan. Still asleep. Drugged. Cliff then considers the speedometer.

It winds up and up to eighty.

Cliff decides, then turns from the reading to the still paralleled Rod Harris, and slows. The pickup moves on and by. As its tailgate clears, Cliff steers behind it and to the far right side of the blacktop. The teenagers in the bed of the pickup fizz beer on Cliff's windshield. Cliff looks again to the speedometer.

The red-tipped marker drops to exactly seventy-two and holds.

CLIFF

looks back to the unconscious Susan.

CLIFF
(to Susan)
Hang onto your hat.

The country mouse inhales, now.

CLIFF'S LEFT FOOT

slams, then lets up on the brake as the right foot simultaneously foots the accelerator, then releases.

CLIFF

spins the steering wheel counterclockwise.

CUT TO:

EXT.—ROAD—NIGHT

Rod Harris is going away but slowing down in the b.g. The f.g. is awesome. TIRE SCREAM and smoke. The Dodge van whirls on a near dime, tips, regains its four wheels and careens in the opposite direction it was going—three seconds earlier at seventy-two miles per hour. A moonshiner U-turn.

CUT TO:

INT.—NEW PICKUP—NIGHT

ROD HARRIS
(looking back)
Jeeeesus H. Christ!!!

CUT TO:

EXT.—ROAD—NIGHT

Rod Harris makes a conventional U-turn to pursue.

CUT TO:

EXT.—ROAD—NIGHT

A mile distant. Cliff makes a similar "normal" U-turn.

CUT TO:

INT.—NEW PICKUP—NIGHT

Rod Harris comprehends Cliff's approaching van. The gauntlet is returning.

ROD HARRIS
(awed mutter)
He's crazier'n the crazies.

CUT TO:

INT.—VAN—NIGHT

Cliff studies the oncoming pickup. In the final second, *both* vehicles veer and whip by. No one in the truck misses Cliff's upraised middle finger in front of a tight victory smile.

CUT TO:

EXT.—ROAD—NIGHT

The pickup, though, in making way for Cliff's van, hits the road shoulder and catapults into an eight-foot-wide irrigation ditch, spectacularly but safely, spraying water twenty feet in the air for a distance of forty yards.

CUT TO:

INT.—CLIFF'S VAN—NIGHT

Resumes normal speed. Cliff checks Susan and erases his victory smile. Reality has returned.

CUT TO:

INT.—MIDVALE REGIONAL CENTER—NIGHT

Double doors identify Ward F—Room 3.

CLIFF

closes his eyes and inhales deep. The farm boy rolls the still unconscious Susan through the entrance to the most feared ward.

CUT TO:

INT.—WARD F—ROOM 3—NIGHT

The L-shaped enclosure is similar to a dormitory but with exceptional distance between beds. Approximately eight feet. The orderly station is at the angle of the L and a lounging area stretches across the room's farthest point. This ward contains thirteen women. The only face familiar to Cliff belongs to the transferred Paula, still sleeping, only now on the floor by her iron bed in a fetal curl about a beaming flashlight. Most inmates listlessly mill, some lie on their beds, all in their own minds.

Normally, there is little mental assimilation with this group. This is one of the exceptional moments, as most are together in their attention on the entering Cliff and Susan. At the orderly station, two muscled ATTENDANTS, one male, one female, peer up from watching television. Cliff is frightened, as this represents the ultimate in terror to all young Nebraska children. He looks about, sees an unmade corner bed, and points.

CLIFF

That hers?

The woman attendant sorts paperwork on a counter, extracts a sheet, and looks to Cliff.

WOMAN ATTENDANT

Susan Ellen Garber?

CLIFF
(affirms)
'Fraid so.

The woman attendant nods. Cliff wheels the gurney to the bed. The two attendants smirk at his rural response. Cliff starts unlashing the restraining straps. A patient, ROBIN, resolutely walks up, puts her face against his, and shouts incoherently. Cliff is shaken. Suddenly, he whirls. The monthly escapee and two-o'clock screamer, Harriet, jerks upright in her bed as rigor mortis would attack a cadaver and rotely screams on a single modulation.

HARRIET
What am I doing here with all these crazy people??!!

MALE ATTENDANT
(by rote)
Lay back, Harriet.

She remains transfixed. Cliff's eyes dart to the attendants, who are back to their viewing. NO response. He slightly turns and comes again face-to-face with Robin. He moves to the foot of the gurney in a vain effort to evade her. She follows and again shouts her secret language an inch from his own mouth. Cliff backs one step and grins in apologetic embarrassment.

CLIFF
Believe I gotta think on that.

Robin looks away and emits a polka whoop. This cues seven of the women to curiously circle Cliff, who self-consciously proceeds with the gurney-to-bed moving of the drugged Susan. Harriet continues her upright position. Paula remains asleep on the mottled tile floor. One of Cliff's observers, BARBARA, is shaking and wrapped in four blankets. A pitiful effort to keep out her perpetual cold.

THE ATTENDANTS

look to each other.

MALE ATTENDANT
I hear he's asking for transfer.

WOMAN ATTENDANT
(incredulous)
To here?

The man nods.

CLIFF

turns down Susan's new bed. One of his spectators speaks. This is MARY. In her dual life, a self-supposed Virgin Mary.

MARY
I am to give birth to a newborn babe.

Cliff tries to ignore.

MARY (CONT.)
He shall be wrapped in swaddling clothes and lie in a manger because there is no room for me at the inn.

To push the gurney next to the bed, Cliff reaches out to Robin.

CLIFF
(takes her by the shoulders and walks her as he talks)
Let me move you over here just a second.

She stoically submits. Cliff rolls the wheeled gurney in place. As the conveyance touches the prepared bed, one of the silent women, SALLY, seizes what is to be Susan's pillow. Cliff reaches out his hand.

CLIFF (CONT.)
She's gonna need that.

The inmate shrinks back, clutching the pillow tighter. Cliff's eyes dart to the attendants station, then back to his problem. The women close in.

CLIFF (CONT.)

Come on, ladies. Let's be for givin' it back.

Sally flings the pillow to Robin. They all play "keep-away" from Cliff.

THE ATTENDANTS

still observe.

MALE ATTENDANT

Whatdaya think?

WOMAN ATTENDANT

Let him have a taste.

CLIFF AND THE INMATES

perform a strange, almost slow-motion-paced ballet with the pillow as a rotating focal point.

CLIFF

(frantic edge)

Come on. You're gonna get me in Dutch.

The pillow splits. Feathers begin to join the air.

CLIFF (CONT.)

Je-sus.

Mary points to Cliff.

MARY

(shrieking)

That's his name! That's his name! How did you know?!

The air shatters with the scream of a WHISTLE similar to the one used by Mrs. Hapsbury.

FEMALE ATTENDANT

Okay. In your beds.

No response.

MALE ATTENDANT

(softly)

Now.

The inmates move, motivated by a mute fear. The attendants stride to Cliff, pathetically trying to collect the drifting feathers. After a few retrievals, he looks up at the man and woman who stand over him.

CLIFF

I'll . . . I'll clean up the mess. Please . . . please don't tell nobody this happened.

Sally, on her bed, smirks, hand over mouth. Harriet ethereally drops back to a supine position.

CLIFF (CONT.)

Sure appreciate your help.

(slightly harder plea)

Means a lot to me.

CUT TO:

EXT.—ORANGE BOWL—DAY

The Nebraska rooting section celebrates as the Cornhusker football team takes the field.

SPORTS ANNOUNCER (V.O.)

And here they come, Nebraska fans. The Cornhuskers are in red with white trim today.

CUT TO:

EXT.—MIDVALE REGIONAL CENTER—DAY

The buildings are now locked in winter.

SPORTS ANNOUNCER (V.O.)
The last time they were in the Orange Bowl, they lost to mighty Miami.

SPORTS ANNOUNCER (V.O. CONT.)
Today, the team voted to break the white with red trim tradition, hoping to break out some good luck for everyone connected with the Big Red. And that means, of course, every man, woman, and child in the great state of Nebraska.

CUT TO:

INT.—DR. GARGON'S OFFICE—DAY

The sports announcer, on Gargon's outer office portable TV, can almost be heard. An intense Dr. Gargon and Cliff are not aware.

DR. GARGON
It's been said since nineteen seventeen, when these walls were built, *no one* in his right mind wants to go to F. Pun intended.

CLIFF
Doc, I'm "down to the ground" straight. I still can't see the difference between us out-sane and the in-sane. Maybe being there would help.

DR. GARGON
That's "down to the ground" straight?

CLIFF
And Sue Ellen's there.

DR. GARGON
That's "down to the ground" straight.

CLIFF
I figure it this way. You know how sometimes you give someone a pet to help them think right? I've been studyin' our old Scotch collie for years.

DR. GARGON
And Susan loves Scotch collies?

CLIFF
Better say "like." Don't want to get in any deeper than I am.

DR. GARGON
Oh, you're in deep all right. Make no mistake. You know she could be severely schizophrenic the rest of her life?

CLIFF
And she could be totally well the rest of her life.

Dr. Gargon nods, rises, and moves to his window to look out on this New Year's Day landscape.

DR. GARGON
They used to put these people on a ship. The boat would sail the ocean in circles. They would dock every few months for food . . . a new crew . . . and more of these poor, dumb creatures.

CLIFF
Sort of to keep 'em out of everybody's sight?

Dr. Gargon pulls his mind back to Cliff.

DR. GARGON
We're missing the game.

CLIFF
If it's going to get me closer to Sue Ellen in Ward F, I don't mind.

DR. GARGON
You're really serious?

CLIFF
(nods)
"Right down to the ground" serious.

Dr. Gargon goes to his door. Opens it. Stares at the outer office TV game, then decides.

DR. GARGON

OK, Clifford, let's go for the whole nine yards.

Cliff's face nearly bursts with pleasure. Both ignore the game.

CLIFF

Doc, if you weren't so dignified, I'd let out a war-whoop.

Immediately Cliff is startled as Gargon lets out a war-whoop. The doctor shrugs.

DR. GARGON

They'll think we're into the game.

Then Cliff war-whoops. Both beam to each other, and shake hands.

CUT TO:

INT.—WARD F—DAY

A striking match lights a candle speared in a cream puff.

WOMAN ATTENDANT (O.S.)

That's pretty stupid if you don't mind my saying.

CLIFF AND WOMAN ATTENDANT

are at the orderly station. Cliff shakes out the flame and puts the match book in his shirt pocket.

CLIFF

I don't mind.

WOMAN ATTENDANT

(righteously)

The rules say . . .

HARRIET

screams.

CLIFF AND THE WOMAN ATTENDANT

glance in habit to the circular electric wall clock. 2 P.M. Cliff resumes.

CLIFF

I don't know or want to know anything about rules. I'm sure there's a rule somewhere that says you and I ought to be breathin' out instead of in. So don't tell me about any rule that says I can't do some stupid little thing to try and make somebody smile.

Cliff cups his hand over the small blaze to keep it from going out on his walk.

WOMAN ATTENDANT

My, we're paranoid.

Cliff stalks to the Ward's far corner. En route, all patients ignore him but two. LINDA elbows FAITH, nodding to the preoccupied orderly. She jeers Cliff in a sing-songy child's cadence.

LINDA

Societal assignment . . . Assignment societal.

FAITH

(taunting)

We heard, we heard. Rumors fly, sail and grouse. Ward of the court, country mouse.

LINDA

You gonna kill us, too, country mouse?

In the "disturbed wards," the inmates are more inclined to reveal their honest thoughts with little regard for the mask of courtesy. Cliff is aware and doesn't respond. He reaches a sad Susan, sitting on the floor by a bed, knees drawn to her chin, staring as she did the days she lived in the Ward A bathtub. Cliff joins her.

CLIFF
(soft)
Happy Birthday.

No response. He offers the candled cream puff.

CLIFF (CONT.)
(repeats)
Happy Birthday, Sue Ellen.

She focuses, squints down to the flame, then to Cliff.

SUSAN
It's not till April. Seven days after the Fool's.

Cliff is happy. He has pulled her to "her senses."

CLIFF
Hey, fine. You're . . .

SUSAN
. . . not nuts.

She smiles.

CLIFF
In a manner of speakin'. *Your* speakin'.

She warms her hands over the flame.

CLIFF (CONT.)
No, actually this is for us. I get to stay here.

Her eyes flash in fear.

SUSAN
Not really?

CLIFF
(grins)
Hey, whoa back. As an orderly.
(mock shy)
I'll take your bedpan out.

Susan slowly captures Cliff's cheeks with both hands.

CLIFF (CONT.)
(soft)
See, since your mom 'n dad, nor anyone that cares can't be here, I thought I could if I saw hard on red tape. You know, care for you? This could be all right. Like my dad used to say, "Hammers can make steel, or break glass."

Susan bends him backward. Their two heads fold under her high iron bed.

SUSAN
(soft, honest)
I love you, country mouse.

Cliff stuns. He did not expect these words. He would normally war-whoop. The time, place, and person force him to respond more maturely. The country mouse pulls her to his lips and softly warms her face with kisses.

Mary lifts the cream puff and candle, ignoring Cliff and Susan. The light mesmerizes the deeply schizophrenic woman. She preciously carries it to the center of the room.

MARY
(soft)
. . . and he shall be the light of the world.

PAULA'S EYES OPEN.

P.O.V.—THE CANDLE FLAME

PAULA

leaps up and points.

PAULA
(joyful shriek)

Fire!!!

CLIFF

pulls from Susan and springs to Mary.

CLIFF'S HANDS

crush the candle and the pastry, snuffing out the flame.
Cliff, filling oozing from between his fingers, reassures the approaching woman attendant.

CLIFF

It's no problem, ma'am.

Paula, eyes open for the first time in months, Sally, Mary, Harriet, Barbara, Robin, Faith, Linda, and the others hypnotically stare at Cliff. Susan is on her knees. No sound . . . then . . .

SUSAN
(weakly)

Krayvill.

CLIFF
(to Susan)

Don't talk like that, please.

On his walk to her, Cliff pulls free his towel, wipes off the pastry, returns the towel to his belt, and motions her to rise.

CLIFF
(stern)

Susan

SUSAN

Crail.

Cliff bends and takes her by the shoulders. On the touch . . .

THE TOWEL ON CLIFF'S BELT

is whipped off by feminine hands.

THE WOMEN

attack. Their physical blows are accompanied by unearthly, incoherent yelling. The woman attendant flees to the orderly station and activates a shrill ELECTRONIC alarm. The women pull, tear, and claw at every limb and piece of clothing on Cliff's struggling body. Paula takes the matches from Cliff's shirt pocket. Susan is to the side, clutching her knees, rocking in a fetal position, screaming and screaming, going further and further on her journey into madness.

CUT TO:

INT.—REGIONAL CENTER ROOM—NIGHT

Cliff leans over a supine Susan.

CLIFF
(sober)
Hi, honey. You might guess. You're in pack.

P.O.V.—SUSAN'S HEAD

resembles a badly bandaged mummy. Only her eyes are visible. Small holes are apparent for the nose and mouth cavities.

THE "PACK ROOM"

Where hysterical patients are brought, wrapped in cold, wet cloth strips, and strapped on hard white tables. There they lose consciousness via their own inner violence or with the aid of appropriate drugs. Three other PATIENTS are "in pack," giving the room an Egyptian mausoleum appearance. An ATTENDANT behind Cliff moves out and through the exit, obviously to report Susan's "coming-up." The swinging door stops. Cliff leans and lightly kisses the bandages over her lips.

CLIFF
(gentle)
Jesus, this is some note.

Susan blinks.

CLIFF (CONT.)
They say it *can* be best. It gives doc more to work with. Like they can cure pneumonia but not colds. Course, they might have been trying to make me feel better because . . . because I said it was all my fault.

Her eyes twist.

CLIFF (CONT.)
They swear up and down, though, it happens all the time. These patients'll . . . attack an orderly for his sanity. If that makes sense. You know, sort of tryin' to pull 'n drag it out of them 'n stick it in themselves.
(small chuckle)
Guess they had no way of knowing there wasn't none inside this dumb farm kid.

Her eyes protest. Cliff rests his large hand on her cloth-swathed forehead.

CLIFF (CONT.)
(apologetically)
It *is* my fault. I couldn't feel worse. We just gotta get you out.

Dr. Gargon and the attendant enter. The day has been bad. Gargon walks to Susan's head and shines a light in each eye. He glowers at the ceiling, thinks, and walks for the door, shaking his head. Cliff wants to follow but chooses to stay with Susan.

CUT TO:

EXT.—DR. GARGON'S HOME—DAY

More brick. The doctor and his six-year-old son play catch with a red and white football on the front lawn. The child, ADAM, throws the ball over the doctor's head, and into the arms of

CLIFF

tentatively ambling up the driveway. Cliff nervously fidgets the ball, the spirals it back to Adam.

CLIFF
(to Gargon)
Sorry to bother you at home.

DR. GARGON
They say you've been by her side for three days.

CLIFF
She's just . . . layin' there. What's going to happen, Doc? It finally seemed worth gettin' you mad to find out. Bothering you and all.

Gargon catches a return pass from Adam.

DR. GARGON
I guess shock now.

CLIFF
That's not what I wanted to hear.

Gargon laterals the ball to Cliff.

DR. GARGON
But that's what you expected.

Cliff again throws the football to Adam.

DR. GARGON (CONT.)
There are four hundred twenty-three patients in my facility. All I seem to have time for is word games. I'd do *anything* to cure all of them. This is the first time I've played with Adam in six months. And I feel guilty as hell!

Adam end-over-ends the ball to Cliff.

CLIFF
I got the time, Doc. Let me do something. I'm still not qualified, remember?
(plea)
I can't do any worse if I tried. Please?

Cliff now spins the football to Dr. Gargon, who nods.

DR. GARGON
OK. Yeah. You're right.
(throws ball to Adam)
Let's try something. You and her. Forget Scotch collies.

CUT TO:

INT.—REGIONAL CENTER CHAPEL—DAY

Cliff leads Susan and seats her in the front pew. Her movements, her eyes, seem programmed from an alien world. Cliff hunkers on an altar step. A stained-glass, open-armed Jesus looks down from above and behind the altar.

CLIFF
I think this is the best place to do what we gotta.

SUSAN
(to space)
Glavin slov ta gorven trev me forble.

Cliff tries to ignore her schizophrenic language.

CLIFF
We're gonna drop all the doctor talk. All the Omaha talk. Let you hear straight from someone who cares something about you.

SUSAN
Grimeogleboggen.

He rises and walks away, eyes boring into the altar cross.

CLIFF

Sue Ellen, you've *got* to get yourself out of whatever you're at.

(pleads)

Else they're gonna run electricity through you.

SUSAN

Haberfold.

CLIFF

(whispers)

Don't. Jesus, don't.

SUSAN

Comal tov pre vawver itso lamer dre pav calsem. Prpa nomer . . .

Cliff hardens.

CLIFF

(interrupts)

Stop, Susan! Just cut it out!

SUSAN

Barvel.

Cliff returns, seizes her shoulders and shouts.

CLIFF

I want you to . . .

Suddenly, Cliff stops. His hands slide down her body as the young man folds to the floor. After a bowed-head moment, he looks up to her with a soft smile.

CLIFF (CONT.)

I'm supposed to get tough. Slap you around. Give you a . . . I guess a people-type shock. I can't. I just can't. That's not the real me. I love you. That's me.

No response from Susan. She visually moves deeper into madness.

CLIFF (CONT.)
(bewildered)
I love you. Can't you hear that?

Susan's eyelids do not blink.

CLIFF

puts his forehead on Susan's bare knees in despair.

INT.—SHOCK TREATMENT ROOM—DAY

Susan's head lies on a pillow. Her eyes stare to another textured ceiling. The hands of Tom Crawford place inch-and-one-half-round electrodes to each temple.

TOM (V.O.)
See . . . the Lord gave us electricity . . .

SUSAN AND CLIFF

watch Tom conclude the shock treatment preparations.

TOM
(working while talking)
. . . and he gave man a brain. So it makes perfect logic for that brain to employ electricity in a manner to drive the evil from his brain.

Eyes on Susan, Cliff responds, not really aware of what Tom is saying or even his own comment.

CLIFF
Glad you like your transfer to here, Tom.

TOM
I still pray my chaplain's aide application comes through. That's the mainstream of life.

CLIFF
(nods to Susan)
How bad does it . . .

Tom has crossed to a wall phone and dialed two digits.

TOM
(into phone)
Yes, this Tom Crawford. We're ready in shock.
Thank you.

Tom walks to the bed and begins stroking Susan's forehead in pity.
Cliff is irritated with Tom's caressing Susan.

CLIFF
How long does it last?

TOM
Oh . . . less than ten seconds. You see, the patient loses consciousness immediately. Then there should be a brief but very important convulsion. After that . . . sleep. When she wakes, she will hopefully be almost normal and then treated during this approximate normalcy. Actually, the little spasm after the shock is the most important.

Tom rests his hands and studies the still girl. Cliff corrects a strand of Susan's hair that Tom had ruffled.

TOM
(regretful)
Still playing with the devil.

CLIFF
(eyes flash danger)
She ain't the devil.

TOM
(patronizing)
You don't understand, Cliffy. Shock is rarely used now. Except for the very guilt-ridden. It's like exorcising the devil. Perhaps you'll never understand.

The door opens. Dr. Gargon hurries in. He checks Tom's preparations.

DR. GARGON
Good job, Crawford.
(looks at Tom's orderly tag)
Tom, isn't it?

TOM
Yes, sir.

Gargon peers into Susan's open eyes with a light.

DR. GARGON
(to Susan)
Father.

No response. He nods and moves to the shock switch. The doctor looks to the two young men. Tom is loose, Cliff tight, sweating.

DR. GARGON
Clifford, this'll hurt you worse than her.

CLIFF
Doc, I truly believe that.

Gargon stabs the switch. The charge fills Susan. Her eyelids instantly flick shut. Seconds pass. They seem like hours. The three men wait. Gargon concentrates. Tom's lips move in silent prayer. Cliff is near total paralysis. Without warning, Susan starts shaking. Gargon checks his watch and notes on a yellow legal pad. Cliff tries to steady her body. Tom twists and holds Susan's head to the side. Her face severely contorts. Cliff's eyes anger.

TOM
(to Cliff)
So she can't swallow her tongue.

Cliff loosens. So does Susan. She falls into the forecasted sleep. The relieved Cliff dries his forehead with the arm of

his orderly smock and looks to the other men. Gargon is going out of the door, no ceremony. Tom releases her straps.
Susan's still-attached electrodes and her slumbering facial expression project an unearthly specter.

DR. GARGON
(at the door)
We wait. We see.

CUT TO:

INT.—RECOVERY ROOM—DAY

Susan is now without the electronic equipment. At peace. Her eyelids open. The young girl smiles.

CLIFF

backs to the wall phone without losing eye contact. He takes down the receiver, breaks his gaze long enough to dial a number. A pause . . . then . . .

CLIFF
(to receiver; gentle excitement)
She's up. This is Cliff. Yes. Recovery room two four seven. Sue Ellen. Sue Ellen Garber. Okay. Good. Thank you. Got it.

Cliff hangs up and cautiously returns to the bed.

CLIFF (CONT.)
I'm not supposed to say anything. Just give you . . . here. This was my idea.

He reaches to her bedstand, lifts a glass of white substance from an electric baby bottle warmer, and puts a drinking straw in the liquid. Before he inserts the straw between her lips, he speaks.

CLIFF (CONT.)
You sure are a sight for sore eyes.

He places the straw. Susan pulls the mixture into her mouth. Upon first taste, complete lucidity. She spits, sputters, and with the white dripping from her lips, sits up.

SUSAN

What is *that* shit?!

Cliff is stunned. At her language . . . and reaction.

CLIFF

(weakly)

Warm milk and honey.

She nods her head.

SUSAN

You are a hick. A country stick.

Cliff is visibly pleased by her teasing.

CLIFF

(holding up a glass)

You're right. It's what we give baby animals when they ain't got a mom ta suck on.

Susan's eyes go to the ceiling. She then looks again to him and smiles.

SUSAN

Hi.

CUT TO:

INT.—DR. GARGON'S OFFICE—DAY

Susan lies on the traditional couch. Gargon sits in a flipped around straight chair, arms over the high wooden back, chin cupped in his hands.

DR. GARGON

Love.

SUSAN

Happy.

DR. GARGON

Father.

SUSAN

Crail.

DR. GARGON

Mother.

Susan's mouth opens. Nothing. She closes her lips, rubs her eyes.

CUT TO:

INT.—DR. GARGON'S OFFICE—Different Day

Dr. Gargon behind his desk, feet up . . . Susan in a side chair.

DR. GARGON
(chewing pencil)

Love.

SUSAN

Boy.

DR. GARGON

Father.

SUSAN
(slight hesitancy)

Man.

DR. GARGON

Mother.

SUSAN

Magelle.

Dr. Gargon slams his palm to the desk top.

DR. GARGON
(shouts)
Mother!

Susan pulls at her hair and rolls her neck. Gargon rises and holds her head stationary. Severity.

SUSAN
(weak)
Something.

Gargon smiles.

INT.—DR. GARGON'S OFFICE—Different Day

Susan and Dr. Gargon by his office door. He holds it open for her.

DR. GARGON
(loose)
Oh, Suzy. One more thing. Love.

SUSAN
Cliff.

DR. GARGON
Father.

SUSAN
Daddy.

DR. GARGON
Mother.

SUSAN
(slight pause)
Mine.

He frowns, and taps her nose.

DR. GARGON
You hesitated.

She catches and holds his finger.

SUSAN

You know, I'm just your average, everyday demented praecox.

Dr. Gargon kisses her hand. A gallant knight. They smile at his unusual whimsy.

SUSAN (CONT.)

(warm)

Thank you, Dr. Gargoyle. So much.

CUT TO:

INT.—WARD A—RECREATION AREA—DAY

Cliff holds Susan's small bag. The young girls and Mrs. Hapsbury greet.

MRS. HAPSBURY

Well, Suzy Garber.

(they hug)

It's fine, just fine to have you back.

SUSAN

Is my tub ready?

MRS. HAPSBURY

Not when you're on the way out, kiddo.

SUSAN

(agreeing)

It looks good, Mrs. Hapsbury. *Very* good.

The women and Cliff exchange pleased expressions. Mrs. Hapsbury seizes the whistle from between her breasts, puts it to her lip, and blows. Eleven people have a single attention.

MRS. HAPSBURY

OK, gang, here's an old one.

She nods to a bald young man.

MRS. HAPSBURY (CONT.)
You start, Tony.

ALL
(individually)
Tony Clements.
Joy Dansbury.
Ellis T. Franklin.
Elizabeth Harper.
Lorna Nelson.
Robin Ohmsteade.
George Hunt.
Mary Hansen.
Paula Kennedy.
Robert Dawson.

All look expectantly to Susan. She breaks the cadence a half a beat by looking at Cliff, smiling, then back to the assembly.

SUSAN
I'm Sue Ellen Garber.
(warmly)
Hi, Ellis T. Franklin . . . Robin . . . hi, Paula.

The four friends converge and hug like close friends at a class reunion.

DISSOLVE TO:

EXT.—INNER COURTYARD GARDEN—DAY

Susan's hands transplant a flat of marigolds.

CLIFF
Hi.

Susan looks up.

SUSAN
(smiling)
And here's the real farmer, folks. Come to fertilize my inferiority duplex.

CLIFF
This ain't a professional visit to check out your garden privileges.

Susan returns to planting.

SUSAN
Would the professional visitor tell me where he's been since seven twenty-three last night?

Cliff picks up a fresh clod.

CLIFF
(flattered)
They had me across the way. Ann wouldn't eat.

Susan's eyes question.

CLIFF (CONT.)
Ann Greenfield.
(he feels Susan's chill)
She's a ten-year-old hydrocephalic.

Susan's brow straightens. She smiles for an unspoken forgiveness. Cliff splays the clod on a nearby tree.

CLIFF (CONT.)
(shy)
She likes me, sorta.

SUSAN
She's not alone, sorta.

Cliff starts to touch her hand, then is arrested by the approach of an elderly MAN and WOMAN strolling down the curving walk.

CLIFF
(awkwardly changes subject)
Spring practice starts Monday. They got that big Grayson kid from out North Platte way. You know, we need a fullback this year.

SUSAN
My parents are coming Tuesday. Dad's never missed a first day of practice.

CLIFF
(slight worry)
Scared?

SUSAN
I've been practicing my selective inattention.

CLIFF
They're letting me slip home this weekend. Sort of a temporary parole.

Susan is clearly disturbed.

SUSAN
You're coming back . . . ?

CLIFF
You do like me . . . sorta.

SUSAN
(hard)
Don't shit around.

Cliff looks to the bright sky, then back to Susan.

CLIFF
Monday.

At this time, the legs of the old couple walk by. The youngsters stare at the freshly stirred earth.

CLIFF (CONT.)
(after they've gone)
Dad's got a silage crew coming. Want to hunt, too. Kinda miss that. 'Course, pheasant's out of season. But it's on our own land.
(pauses, then)
What I really want . . . is to kiss you.

SUSAN

Do it, country stick.

CUT TO:

INT.—CHAPEL—DAY

Susan and Cliff kiss in the empty sanctuary.

They then walk down the aisle. Each wanting to say, "I love you." Each frightened. Cliff goes for his next thought.

CLIFF

The judge sent me some papers. You know, to go home for good?

Silence. They sit in the front pew.

CLIFF (CONT.)

(looking at Susan)

I'm not filling them out.

SUSAN

You are as dumb as you look. I may stay crazy forever, but I'm not going to be here forever.

CLIFF

(serious)

Helping out at this place, I seem worth more than being at home. 'Course I'd rather be on that mountaintop in Idaho.

Susan shakes her head and hurriedly speaks to surrounding hypothetical spirits.

SUSAN

There must be something the matter with him because he would not be acting as he does, unless there was . . . he does not think there is anything the matter with him because one of the things that is the matter with him is that he does not think that there is anything the matter with him . . . Therefore, we have to help him realize that the fact that he does not think there is anything the matter with him is one of the things that is the matter with him.

Susan expectantly looks to Cliff for a reaction to her Psych 1 tongue twister. He awkwardly smooths the carpet with his boot toe.

Susan stops gaming, blurting out her singular thought.

SUSAN
(earnest)
Cliff, fuck me.

CLIFF
(shock)
Sue Ellen, for God's sake.

SUSAN
(overlaps)
For Him, too.

Cliff dips his head. Susan tries reason.

SUSAN (CONT.)
(pleading)
Found Under Carnal Knowledge. That was the charge in the Sheriff of Nottingham days. Instead of writing out the full thing . . .
(spells)
F-U-C-K. Is that so bad? So dirty?

Cliff could not be more embarrassed.

SUSAN (CONT.)
(recanting)
I'm sorry. Once an Omaha talker . . . always a . . .

She stops as he takes her face. They kiss. Long, hard, deep. Their lips release.

CLIFF

I love you, Sue Ellen.

SUSAN

Oh, how I love you, country stick.

The unusual lovers search the infinity in one another's eyes.

CUT TO:

EXT.—OMAHA MANSION—DAY

Mr. and Mrs. Garber erupt from their antebellum-style mansion. They almost shout at one another en route to their waiting Mercedes in the estate's semicircle drive. Each wears red. Each lapel has a "Go Big Red" button.

MR. GARBER

I really don't want her back here in Omaha, Ellen. I can't handle it. Every time her name comes up, a wagonload of shit's drug in behind.

MRS. GARBER

Roy, she's our responsibility. We love her.

MR. GARBER

Our responsibility first is to our own lives. It's not that I hate Susan, I love her *too* much. The fact I can't do a goddamn thing about the way she is will drive me crazy.

Mr. Garber slams his door and starts the luxurious car.

MRS. GARBER

(getting into car)

Roy, I don't want her back just as much as you do. What will people say if we let her stay in that awful Midvale?

Mrs. Garber closes her door. The two continue their near-screaming M.O.S. within the containment of their soundproof Mercedes as it pulls off and to the distance.

CUT TO:

INT.—VISITOR RECEPTION ROOM—DAY

The door cracks. Cliff and Susan step through. She carries a single rose. Mr. and Mrs. Garber rise.

This room is far better appointed than any of the other hospital rooms.

CLIFF

Like I promised. Here she be.

Roy Garber nervously adjusts his fire red sport jacket.

MR. GARBER

Happy . . . uh . . .

He glances to Cliff. Privacy is in order.

CLIFF

If you don't mind, I'll just get back to my chores.
Real pleased to meet you folks.

Susan touches him.

CLIFF (CONT.)

I'll see you later. Have a good visit.

He smiles and backs from the room. As the door closes, the two parents rush the daughter. Hugs and kisses.

BOTH

(soft singing)

Happy birthday to you, Happy birthday to you,
Happy birthday, Susan Ellen, Happy birthday to you,

MR. GARBER

(adds)

And many moooore. Even though we're one day laaaate.

Now, awkward silence as they all realize this childhood ritual is incongruously ludicrous.

MR. GARBER (CONT.)
(uncomfortable)
Guess you're too big for birthday spankin's now.

The mother ignores the father.

MRS. GARBER
Here . . . sit . . . sit.

The three follow the matriarch's instruction. A moment passes.

MR. GARBER
Well, we've really been through hell.

MRS. GARBER
What your father means is not being able to come down from Omaha to see you. The packing plant and all.

SUSAN
Oh?

MRS. GARBER
You know, Doctor . . .
(gropes)
. . . what's-his-face?

SUSAN
Gargon?

MRS. GARBER
Yes, him. He also thought you'd get well quicker if you didn't have associations from the past. Of course, we could have overruled him, according to the lawyer.

MR. GARBER
(testing)
I suppose if you'd have really wanted us, you'd have asked for us.

SUSAN
I suppose.

Mr. Garber tries another direction.

MR. GARBER
You know, we do realize you've been through hell, too.

MRS. GARBER
(sharp)
Roy, we don't even want to talk about that. We agreed.
(to Susan)
My mother used to tell me "sickness is in the mind." The more you dwell on it, the more you feel sorry for yourself. Feeling sorry for yourself is the worst thing that can happen to you.
(tacks on amendment)
Next to liquor and, it goes without saying, dope.

MR. GARBER
Let's talk about my birthday girl.

MRS. GARBER
(warning)
Only not be self-centered.

MR. GARBER
Right.

MRS. GARBER
(to Susan)
Your father has a surprise for you.

MR. GARBER
I . . . we couldn't wrap it up. I thought about getting a toy one. Putting it in a shoe box or something. Get some wrapping paper . . .

MRS. GARBER
Roy, for Lord's sake, just tell her.

MR. GARBER
(proudly)
I got you your own Mercedes.

MRS. GARBER
A 240 SL like you've always wanted.

Their "birthday girl" doesn't register the remembered glee from childhood. No hand clapping. No jumping. Passive quiet.

MR. GARBER
(soft)
Isn't that great, hon?

MRS. GARBER
(to husband)
Of course it's great. She's just in shock over the present.

MRS. GARBER
(to Susan)
Our favorite color. Red.

Tears begin to streak down Susan's face.

MR. GARBER
(elbows husband)
See. She's happy.
(leans to Susan)
I've got the best news.

Mrs. Garber dramatically glances to her husband, back to Susan, waits a beat and emphasizes each word. Roy looks to the ceiling.

MRS. GARBER
You're . . . coming . . . home. The Judge said it'd be fine. You've served society. It wasn't your fault anyway.

Susan's tears stop. She rises. Moves to the window. She looks out on the inner courtyard and sees Cliff repairing a rose trellis across the way. Susan looks to the flower in her hand. The fist opens. Blood is visible. She has crushed the thorns into her numb palm flesh.

MR. GARBER
(to Susan)
How's that sound, birthday girl?

SUSAN
I wanna go.

MR. GARBER
Oh, you misunderstand. We can't take you today. Doctor . . . uh . . .

MRS. GARBER
Gargon.

MR. GARBER
Yes, the doctor said soon, very soon. He wanted us to, you know, get reacquainted today. I guess to help the adjustment.

MRS. GARBER
When he sees how well we get along . . .
(she whispers in Susan's ear)
I think there's a microphone, maybe a camera in this room . . .
(normal voice and pace)
. . . it should be next week . . . or sooner.

Mrs. Garber rises, looks around, and projects.

MRS. GARBER (CONT.)
There isn't anything we wouldn't do for our birthday girl.

Mr. Garber starts to blot Susan's tears with a Kleenex. On his touch, implosion.

SUSAN
(screams)
Bullshit! Mother-fucking, father-fucking bull-shit!

MRS. GARBER
(shocks)
My little girl . . .

SUSAN
Is an asshole! You're an asshole!
(pointing at mother)
Especially you're an asshole! We're all assholes! You give me enemas when I'm young, shit when I'm old.
(to mother)
You never let me sleep on my stomach.
(mimicking)
Ah, ah . . . we'll drool on Mommy's clean sheets!

MRS. GARBER
(warning, soft)
Enough, Susan Ellen.

SUSAN
You fuck daddy over, me over, it's never enough! Whatever I am, you deserve! The same tearing, cutting, destroying shit your mother gave you!!

Now, her mother erupts. Not with words. Hands. Susan's head whips back and forth with each slap from the larger, older woman.

MR. GARBER
Ellen! Jesus!!

When the silent, pacifistic daughter physically crumbles to her knees, the strong, brutal mother hauls her daughter back to a standing position, then affects the tenderest gentility. She holds Susan's chin with two insistent fingers.

MRS. GARBER
(smiles)
We understand. Finding out you're coming home after all you've been through is, well, we won't dwell on that.
(she lovingly kisses Susan)
We love you.

On a matriarchal nod, the mother and the overwhelmed father move to the visitors' door.

MR. GARBER
(weak)
'Bye, hon. Don't forget, that 240 SL'll be sittin' in the driveway when you get home.

MRS. GARBER
And don't forget, you're all we've got.

Mrs. Garber looks around and smiles to her imagined camera on their exit.

CUT TO:

INT.—REGIONAL CENTER HALLWAY—DAY

Susan glides more than walks. Her fingers trail along the scarred wall. People nod or don't notice her and pass by.

CUT TO:

EXT.—CENTER'S INNER COURTYARD—DAY

Susan moves across the springtime lawn. Fingers rigidly trailing on a parallel low hedge. Cliff is not about, as he's away for proper repair tools. The trellis is still down.

CUT TO:

INT.—ANOTHER CENTER HALLWAY—DAY

Susan continues to glide forward, her fingers now raking a new wall. No one is around this special section of the institution.

CUT TO:

INT.—"PACK ROOM"—DAY

A stiffening Susan comes through the door and into the Pack Room. No one is there. On the tables, however, each of the four is prepared with the cloth strips hanging down their sides. Without hesitation, she sits on a table and lies down. Completely submitting herself to "pack" . . .

DISSOLVE TO:

INT.—"PACK ROOM"—DAY

SUSAN

is as before, the bandages completely swathing her face. Cliff stands over his girl. Waiting, hoping. The farm boy's eyes flicker. In their b.g., an ATTENDANT sits. Chair propped against the wall, reading a fresh paperback. Susan stirs. Cliff softly whistles through his teeth to the attendant, who looks up, nods, and goes out the door. Cliff lifts another bottled blend of milk and honey and inserts the straw in the bandaged mouth opening.

Nothing happens. The liquid starts to come up the straw, stops, pauses, then the flow is reversed, causing the substance to bubble in the glass.

Cliff removes the straw and simultaneously Susan's muffled voice is indistinct but audible. Cliff is paradoxically apprehensive and anticipating. He starts stripping the cloth from her head. As he unwinds it by her mouth, she turns to the side and spits out a stream of the white drink.

SUSAN
(sputtering)
You and that baby cow shit!

Cliff's face almost breaks with an enormous smile. Dr. Gargon enters the uncommon room. He takes out his penlight.

SUSAN (CONT.)
And now folks, the other half of the Dynamic Duo.

The doctor examines her pupils. He then returns his light to its vest pocket receptacle.

DR. GARGON

I pronounce you lucid.

CLIFF

Jesus, that's great.

DR. GARGON

(to Susan)

Was it rough?

Cliff starts removing the balance of the cloth and unstrapping her limbs.

SUSAN

It's . . . a red blur. I guess my selective inattention apparatus went tilt.

CLIFF

(to both)

Look.

Cliff holds up the badly mangled rose he has just unwrapped from her hand.

SUSAN

(to doctor)

I really wanted it to work . . .

She glances to the rose.

Dr. Gargon turns slightly and slams his open palm against the wall.

CLIFF

What's the problem, Doc? She's still well, ain't she?

DR. GARGON

(erupting for everyone and no one)

Time and time and time we cure people to send them back into what drove them here in the first place. Sickness gets to be their only solid ground.

The agonized man stalks to the door, pointing at Susan.

DR. GARGON (CONT.)
Well, it's not going to happen this time, young lady. You're staying here. I've got an appellate judge who'll take care of that!

He rips open the door. Cliff protests.

CLIFF
Whoa down, Doc! She's got a right to be with her folks.

DR. GARGON
Don't give me any of that "gotta right to" country mouse crap, young man! You don't have even the beginning idea of what you and she are . . .

He is interrupted by the escape BUZZER.

DR. GARGON (CONT.)
(reacts)
Oh, shit, Harriet! Well, she was overdue.
(to Cliff and Susan, easier)
Look, it's best here. Besides, you can be with each other more.

An ATTENDANT sprints up.

ATTENDANT
Doctor!

DR. GARGON
OK, OK.

They exit.

CLIFF
(to wooshing door)
Doc, she just can't stay! Please!!

He turns to Susan.

CLIFF (CONT.)
(softer, pleading)
There are, I don't mean this like it sounds, but there are crazy people here.

His strange desperation puzzles the young girl. She tries to comfort by lightening the moment.

SUSAN
I know it, and you know it, let's not tell them.

CLIFF
(decides)
That's it. We're goin'.

SUSAN
OK.

CLIFF
No, no. I mean from here. The whole place. The state, the world if we gotta. I'll make you well.

SUSAN
(shakes her head, warning)
Country stick, I don't think so.

CLIFF
(overwhelms)
Look . . . you've been analyzed, paralyzed, shocked, jolted, revolted, given Metrazol, Amatyl, and all that city crap.

CLIFF (CONT.)
I don't know what's between you and your folks, but I'm damn sick of standing around doing plain nothing. You need to be free! We finally get you well and he says "no"? My ass. Let's go!

SUSAN
(surprised)
Omaha talk?!

CLIFF

(takes her hand)

Right now. Everybody's payin' attention to Harriet. We can slip off and . . .

(abruptly)

. . . I gotta marry you.

SUSAN

Gotta?

CLIFF

Come on, you know. Wanna, gotta.

(soft)

Will you?

Susan smooths her hair, then tilts her forehead to his.

SUSAN

I wanna . . . gotta . . . and will.

Cliff pauses, then swirls around and clenches his fists.

CLIFF

Sue Ellen. I wish I could war-whoop my fool head off. We're gettin' out!

SUSAN

Cliff, I want to, but *think!* Where are we going? How do we get there? We need plans. We need to work it out. If we get caught, Cliff, if we couldn't be together at all, I'd go down forever. I know.

Cliff paces the bizarre room. His mind fragments. The boy stops and looks at Susan.

CLIFF

We got four weeks less or more till her next try.

SUSAN

You're not as dumb as you look, country mouse.

CLIFF
(returns smile)
Maybe Omaha talk is better . . .
(qualifies)
. . . sometimes.

CUT TO:

THE END OF THE MIDDLE

And so *the* decision is made. Butch and Sundance actually go to Bolivia. Eliot chooses to rescue E.T. Rick will use the visas to get Ilsa to safety. Kane begins his move to Florida. Jennifer's mother decides to track the pedophile. And Cliff decides "We're gettin' out!"

Second acts generally end "around" 85. Yet, you can be much more flexible with that number than the floating page 17 Act One end. In *Fallen Angel,* Jennifer's mother gets onto the idea that Howie is the one taking pictures of her daughter on page 88. In this *Glass Hammer* draft, "We're gettin' out" also falls on 88. I think I'm going to go beyond 110 pages at this point, so I will probably trim at the second draft level. The "getting out" decision will probably then be closer to page 80.

The overwritten scripts available of *Kane, Butch, E.T.,* and *Casablanca* do not reflect those films' running times, so page 85 would not literally apply. Yet the key decisions that trigger the third act are made between eighty-five and one hundred minutes into these memorable movies. So a flexible page 85 is still valid at one minute a page.

Have you by now also finished your second? Good. Hopefully very good. How do you feel? Did your libation supply hold up? Were you given warm fuzzies? Of course, you were vulnerable. Is your significant other still significant?

You've come through a long tunnel. Maybe the script's still not quite right. Or a little long. Like mine. Or short. You'll fix the pages in the rewrite. Now's the time to risk breaking your arm with back pats. You did it!

Let your accomplishment be your focus. If this script is your first, you are about to belie that F. Scott Fitzgerald axiom. "The world is full of writers who never write." *You are writing.* Doesn't it feel good? An act two completion is an ACCOMPLISHMENT in capital letters.

At the end of your writing the second act, smile. Maybe laugh. Winston Churchill said: "War is a game played with a smile. If you can't smile, grin. If you can't grin, keep out of the way until you can." Writing is certainly a mental war. So smile. You are writing. And by now, you have written. Aren't you lucky?

Do Churchill one better. Let's laugh. For the best is yet to come. The mountain has been scaled. You're on the downhill run. The finish line is in sight.

Chapter 7

THE ACT THREE SCRIPT

(The Conclusion—to pages 100–110)

If you have a true end to your story, you've now reached the easiest and generally the most enjoyable part of the scriptwriting experience. You know what you're going to say. You let out all the visual or character stops. You don't much have to pay attention to plot. You're working from your gut, then your mind. In Act Two, it was mind-gut.

But don't rush. Don't get too hyper and shorthand without plumbing the farthest recesses of your scenes. No "And the Indians took the town." Or "Jane climbs to the top of the Space Needle, jumps off, pulls a rip cord, and floats down to the outstretched arms of Elmo." Instead of the one sentence, each of those mythical and possibly silly situations could and should be a three-page minimum of exciting script.

Milk your suspense. Raise the audience's level of anticipation. Unless you have a verbal climax, such as the two women having at each other in *Turning Point,* or Spencer Tracy in *Trial at Nuremberg,* less dialogue will always work better in your third acts.

Obviously if you need to get the audience catharsis through dialogue, here is the time for verbal pyrotechnics. Look to masters Chayefsky, Eugene O'Neill, Tennessee Williams, Ibsen, and Shakespeare for models and inspiration. Write that Oscar-winning soliloquy for that superstar actor or actress. Catharsis means "cleansing" in Greek. Cleanse your audience like country Saturday night baths.

Love to write. Love the idea-finding. Love the step outline development. Love the script. Especially love the third act. Paul Newman says, "The final fifteen minutes are the most important of any *movie.*" William Goldman adds that the first fifteen pages are the most important of any *screenplay,* yet "when the end of the movie is the most exciting or emotionally involving part, then the audience troops happily out of the darkness and that's how word of mouth is born."

Egri says Act Three is the time in drama when "a decisive change one way or another unfolds." And *the* third act wisdom from Aristotle: "An end is that which itself naturally follows some other things, either by necessity or as a rule, but has nothing following it."

HUNTER ON THIRD ACTS

The third act is best defined as the conclusion. Since the words "third act" originally relate to theater, using them becomes confusing to most who are not intimately involved in the screenwriting process. "The end," "the ending," or "the resolution" doesn't semantically imply the components of the third act.

The conclusion is the easiest act to dissect, as Acts One and Two exist only to set up Act Three. *Act Three exists solely for itself.* And once again we deal in increments of three. As there is a beginning, middle, and end to existence, screenplays, and lovemaking, so there is a beginning, middle, and end to your third act.

1. The Beginning of the End

The Act Three beginning is the preparation to implement the decision that triggered your curtain drop on Act Two. "We're getting out," says Cliff, and so the beginning of *The Glass Hammer* end will be his preparations for the escape. Sometimes the preparations in Act Three take the form of active reactions by a protagonist like Charles Foster Kane. In most movies though, the third act preparations are active, like Cliff's, the mother's in *Fallen Angel,* or Elliot's in

E.T. A few times these preparations will be action and *re*action from events happening to the protagonists like Rick, Butch, and Sundance.

2. The Middle of the End

The middle of the end will be the action itself. The breakout in *The Glass Hammer* and *E.T.* Butch and Sundance robbing people and places in Bolivia. The capture of the *Fallen Angel* pedophile. Rick giving the letters of transit to Ilsa and Victor. *Kane* is more complicated, yet the ending is still Kane's death; this lack of conventional story structure is one of the reasons *Kane* is a timeless motion picture experience.

But, alas, most of us mortals aren't named Herman Mankiewicz or Orson Welles. Thus, the "middle-of-the-end" action, be it emotional, physical, or a combination thereof, will be exactly what the entire movie has been leading the audience toward: the accomplishment, the victory, the coup de grace.

3. The End of the End

What follows the middle of the end is like the aftertaste of exquisite wine. Or vinegar, if the movie has been less than wonderful. There used to be epilogues tacked onto the end of every play. They were the moments to tell the audience what they've been told.

Perorations are still consciously used at the end of nearly every speech, be it by a minister, politician, or everyone in between. As with epilogues, the peroration's intent is to get what was said across one more, but succinct, time.

The end of your movie end will not have that function, though epilogues and perorations are in exactly the same structural location. All of the memorable last few film frames have a scene that promises the future of the protagonist. We can certainly see it in the Butch and Sundance freeze-frame suggesting immortality for the men, or the children levitating into space with E.T., or the future with Humphrey and Claude walking off together.

In *The Glass Hammer,* after the literal escape, the audience will project the happy future of Cliff and Susan on an idyllic Idaho mountaintop.

THE UNHAPPY ENDING

Not *all seminal* American popular movies end happily: Kane, Butch, and Sundance die, Rick does not get the girl, and Dorothy leaves Oz. And on and on and on down the list of *seminal* American audience movies. Their commonality being a sense of loss *and* gain. I mention this to illustrate the continuous second guessing you can and often should give yourself throughout the entire process.

If I had this non-happy-ending conviction, I would stick with an original inspiration. *The Glass Hammer* couple would literally kill themselves by plunging into their eternity and the Missouri River. Maybe end on a freeze frame, like *Butch and Sundance* or *Thelma & Louise.* Or Cliff could survive and he be committed to the mental institution. The final scene would show him being given a shock treatment, and an eyelid flicker would predict his recovery. But I doubt this existence of my intestines at this, the selling level. I am generally far more interested in being effective than right, and being effective means *selling.* During my thirty years of selling scripts I have been inculcated with a David Susskind admonishment about what *"they"* want: "Happy people with happy problems and happy endings." In *The Glass Hammer,* I can't provide the first two. Maybe I'll negate those responses if I can provide a happy ending.

My hidden agenda is to get a director on my side as we prepare the picture for production. Then together we can talk the people of commerce into a memorable unhappy ending. But for this, the selling script, I will stick to "their" guns.

The ending for you? A football announcer, after a quarterback had thrown a pass to his immediate right or left and it was intercepted, always yammered: "that's the danger of the flat pass." If you wish to throw the flat passes of screenwriting, an unhappy ending, know the peril. Most of Hollywood hates unhappy endings. I recommend the happy, even ecstatic ending to make your script saleable. Later in the process, you can suggest considering the unhappy ending. The purchasing party will probably turn you down but you'll be pleased you tried.

Of course, you could be like the apocryphal guy who goes up to women and directly asks if they'll go to bed with him. Nine times out of ten he gets his head bashed, but that tenth time is a success. Your potential reward *may* be worth the effort. It was reported the man had a fixed smile at death.

THE THIRD-ACT PAGE COUNT

How long should the third act be? As long as it should be. Don't worry about it. In looking at *The Glass Hammer* step outline, the third act projects to run between thirty and thirty-five pages. That'll be five pages or so too long, but I'll write it out and see how it looks for our eyes only.

Most exceptional scripts have substantially varying Act Three page counts. The mother actively goes after the *Fallen Angel* pedophile on page 88 and the draft ends on page 109. Twenty-one pages. In a *Butch and Sundance* draft, from the moment they step on Bolivian soil to the famous freeze frame, we're talking sixty-one Bill Goldman pages. From Rick's decision to give Lazlo and Ilsa the letters of transit to "Louis, I think this is the beginning of a beautiful friendship," nineteen pages. From the moment Elliot decides to rescue E.T. to fade out, fourteen pages. From Kane's Florida move to the incinerating Rosebud, twenty-five pages.

See? Wide variances. From fourteen pages to sixty-four. Ignore the actual third act film-running times, which reflect neither eleven nor sixty-four minutes. These numbers are "selling draft" rather than "shooting draft" page counts. These were the scripts that persuaded people to put down money. That's your goal for now and will keep you alive as a writer.

Let your Act Three page count depend totally upon your conviction that this is the conclusion you want to get across to your *reading* audience. Ultimately, you'll get to the viewing audience, but when writing the third act, remember your initial audience, the reader. Use as many or few pages as you feel you need.

1. Rhythms and Third Acts

You'll love third acts because by then your rhythm is down and *if* your story was well outlined, the third act will flow more gently than Sweet Afton.

Those readers you need to impress will frequently have too much to read, and little patience. They actually subconsciously hate to read (it's too much like homework) and are doing it on their personal time. You're in the hole before the first page is turned.

Be sensitive to those overworked, smart, ambitious humans. Make your third act end between 100 and 110 pages. For television movies, you'll send a shooting draft to the set that is between 99 and 100 pages long. After factoring in commercials, promotional trailers, and station breaks, most TV movies actually run a minute or so one side or the other of 94.

Now that you've decided not to be excessive in your third-act script page count, get to the concept of having fun. Enjoy the writing. William Goldman says in *Adventures,* "Once you start writing, go like hell." That's the equivalent of the Mastrosimone dictum: "It's important to force a writer to write quickly because creativity comes from the unconscious, which I think we all accept as truth."

2. Making It

You're going to make it. Keep in mind Paul Newman's caveat about "writers who think only in terms of three-page scenes" and the eternal "less is more." A balance between those two concepts will produce the best first-draft quality. If it does not work, you still have at your disposal the wastebasket, the eraser, or the delete key.

Try to come in short rather than long. Long means you have to take out, and when you take out, you jeopardize structure. You then must scramble back for the cliff like Wile E. Coyote second-thinking the pursuit of his road-running nemesis.

Short means you must add, but this is not a problem. You can *always* find more passion and tension in scenes throughout the script. The objectivity of time will also show you scenes you can add to heighten the drama or comedy.

Don't worry unduly about page count for now. Worry most about "making it," or better, feel the joy of "making it."

THE GLASS HAMMER THIRD ACT

The feeling some have at this screenwriting juncture was best expressed by Charles Dickens: "I am breaking my heart over this story, and cannot bear to finish it." Others are at the other end of that rainbow. They can hardly wait to finish their third acts because they're mentally quivering to find out how the story *really* ends. They know generically from their step outline, but specific things happen when the reality of writing takes over. Anticipate such things to be magical.

The third act is the moment when you want the road rising to meet you, the wind blowing at your back, the sun shining warmly on your face, the rain falling softly on your field, and God holding you in the palm of Her hand.

CUT TO:

INT.—REGIONAL CENTER LIBRARY—DAY

IDAHO ATLAS MAP

Cliff's finger stabs at a wilderness section.

SUSAN (V.O.)
Idaho?

CLIFF AND SUSAN'S

excited voices maintain a hushed, "library" modulation.

CLIFF
You damn betcha. I was reading on a haystack the summer before last. . . .

SUSAN
(teasing)
When you should have been . . .

CLIFF
Yeah, fillin' up the wagon. Keep quiet a second. Surprise me.

Susan pantomimes a zipper pull across her mouth.

CLIFF (CONT.)
It was a National Geographic. I'd finished reviewin' the African section . . .

(added thought)
. . . the women's underwear pages used to get a good workin' out too when the Sears-Roebuck came.

Susan unzips her mouth, fakes a yawn. Cliff colors.

CLIFF (CONT.)
Sorry. Shouldn't have said that. I get ta feeling sometimes, you're a fella.

SUSAN'S HAND UNDER TABLE

moves to the upper inner section of Cliff's thigh and rubs a tight circle.

CLIFF

looks around. Harder blush.

CLIFF
(to Susan)
Not too often, though.

He removes her disturbing hand, lays and holds it on the table.

CLIFF (CONT.)
(clears throat)
Anyhow, in this article . . .
(looks about)
. . . I bet we could find it here.
(back to Susan)
Some fella claimed parts in Idaho had hardly been seen by human eyes. He said animals didn't know enough to be afraid. You can walk right up to 'em.

SUSAN
Maybe that would be better than Mexico.

CLIFF
Lord, I think so. I got more than enough problem speakin' American, let alone Mexican.

SUSAN

Let's do it.

CLIFF

Land's only a few bucks an acre. When I get home next week, I'll get my seed corn money, oh hey, I can trap as well as raise stuff. We can live better 'n ever before. There ain't nothin' on the farm for me. Nothin' in Omaha for you.

Susan nods. Cliff notices. Dr. Gargon enters the room and walks by without seeing the conspirators. He moves to a stack. Susan quietly closes the atlas and shoves it down the study table.

SUSAN

Let's move it, country stick.

CLIFF

(nods at atlas)

Uh . . . could you hand me that?

SUSAN

It's all right. They'll get it.

CLIFF

(warning)

Sue Ellen . . .

SUSAN

Cliff, you *won't* go to jail.

CLIFF

(blushing)

Honey, I gotta have something in front of me when I stand.

Susan clasps both hands over her mouth, delights, then pushes the atlas even further away.

CUT TO:

EXT.—MACPHERSON FARMYARD—DAY

THE 1982 DOORLESS FORD

contains three autumns of leaves, four laying hens, and the erosion marks of long disuse. Suddenly, Cliff, face and hands greasy, rolls out from under the vehicle. He stands, shoos away the hens and lifts up the hood. Cliff then reaches into an open toolbox on the front fender to begin his overhaul.

CUT TO:

INT.—MACPHERSON BEDROOM—NIGHT

CLIFF'S MOTHER

opens a jewelry box from her vanity table. From it, she picks two rings. One a thin gold band, the other a plain silver circle with a single mounted diamond. Mrs. MacPherson gives them to a waiting Cliff with glistening eyes. The son hugs the mother.

CUT TO:

EXT.—MACPHERSON FARMYARD—DAY

Cliff is sitting in his wheelchair-bound father's lap. Another hug and then he almost springs to the rejuvenated, doorless Ford pickup. Cliff pulls a tarp over the two sleeping bags in the pickup bed, and tousles the nap of his Scotch collie as he swings into the driver's seat. The mother comes on the front porch and waves as Cliff pulls out. His dog whines, sensing finality.

CUT TO:

EXT.—HIGHWAY 136—DAY

The pickup COMES TO CAMERA.

CUT TO:

INT.—PICKUP—DAY

Cliff looks to the sky, sees a Highway Patrol Cessna, looks to his speedometer and pulls it down to fifty-five.

CUT TO:

EXT.—MIDVALE REGIONAL CENTER INNER COURTYARD—DAY

Mrs. Hapsbury starts to pass through the doorway of the Administration Building. The woman stops, looks O.S., and absently fingers the chrome whistle about her neck.

CLIFF AND SUSAN

are hugging each other. Reunited M.O.S. Susan's gardening. Tools at their feet.

MRS. HAPSBURY

smiles, happy for the young couple, and moves into the building.

CLIFF

freezes.

CLIFF

She's gone in.

Susan looks, confirms, then back to Cliff.

SUSAN

Let's go.

The two race to the vine-covered fence and peek through spaces in the green like kids through knotholes.

P.O.V.—PARKING LOT

SUSAN

That's it?

She refers to the doorless Ford pickup.
Cliff nods.

CLIFF
A half dozen old hens'll have to come up with a new layin' place.

SUSAN
All the way to Idaho? You're sure?

CLIFF
Driving here I got a new notion. They'll be after us, you know. I can't be no match for planes, helicopters, two-way radios, radar, and all that.

CLIFF (CONT.)
This new way, all it's gotta do is get us sixty miles to Brownville and drive it in the Missouri. We let everybody think we're drowned, then take a bus to Idaho.

Susan thinks, then sparks.

SUSAN
Get you a wig . . .

CLIFF
(pleased)
Hey, you like it.

SUSAN
(thumbs to pickup)
After seeing that, I like it.

THE DOORLESS PICKUP

waits.

CLIFF (V.O.)
I was runnin' irrigation ditch syphons when I took a notion to back up. Only problem being, I was next to a phone pole. Me 'n that first pickup went north, the door south.

CUT TO:

INT.—CHAPEL—DAY

Susan laughs and nuzzles his neck. The couple are seated on the maroon carpeted steps that lead up to the altar.

CLIFF

Dad was maddern' five greased cats. With his stroke and all, he finally liked gettin' in and out with no door fussing. So, we took off the other one. In a more acceptable manner you might gather.

SUSAN

(adoring)

There just isn't anyone else in the world like you, country mouse.

Embarrassed, Cliff eases a broken windup doll from his pocket.

CLIFF

(holds it up)

Well, we're all set.

SUSAN

(idea)

Cliff . . .

CLIFF

(mind with doll)

I don't feel too right about this part.

SUSAN

We need a name.

He questions.

SUSAN (CONT.)

You know . . . an Idaho name.

CLIFF
Oh, yeah. Could we stick with Cliff and Sue Ellen on the front end?

SUSAN
I think so.

CLIFF
I can't see you no other way.

SUSAN
(testing)
Franklin? Bennett? Volger? Hey, Taylor?

CLIFF
No. That's our damn banker's name. Dad used to say . . . "his motto is 'no.' "

SUSAN
(as she continues)
Washington? Swenson? Laurel? Hardy?
(points)
Bogart!

CLIFF
(shrugs)
We got at least a week.

SUSAN
You know Harriet's last name?

CLIFF
I . . . damn'd if I do.
(slightly angry with himself)
Know someone this long. Can't even call 'em by their last name.

The air shatters.

TOM (O.S.)
(shout)
What's going on down there?

Susan clutches Cliff. Near terror.

TOM

strides down the center aisle. An avenging God. When he recognizes, he stops.

TOM (CONT.)

Oh, you two.

CLIFF

Hello, Tom. We were on our knees but the Lord sorta slipped us around to the backside for a bit. Kinda like a barbecue rotator, you might say.

Tom's face lightens and he sincerely chuckles.

TOM

That's very good. There's a whole sermon in that expression. Excuse me . . .

(flusters)

that's silly. I'm going to pray. I mean, it's silly for me to feel I must excuse myself.

(obvious pride)

I do it three times a day. It helps, but I guess you know.

Tom kneels in front of the altar and mutely commences. Cliff bows in respect.

TOM

(aloud)

Amen.

CLIFF

(agrees)

Amen.

Tom rises.

CLIFF (CONT.)

Say, Tom. You know Harriet's last name?

TOM

Wilson.

CLIFF

(to Susan)

That's it.

Tom walks to the entry.

SUSAN

(to Cliff)

Okay with you? Wilson?

Cliff thinks, then nods. His head movement changes when Tom calls from the sanctuary rear.

TOM

Oh. Sorry I yelled. Once last year a patient and a woman orderly were in here . . . and . . . uh . . . well, let's say the Lord encourages togetherness in His house . . .

TOM (CONT)

. . . but cunnilingus?

(waves)

See you at lunch.

He leaves.

CLIFF

Cunni . . . what?

Susan screams with laughter. Cliff senses the meaning.

CLIFF

(grins)

Think I'll hold that query for the honeymoon.

Susan hugs him with fulfilled joy and love.

SUSAN

Country stick, you're the hick.

CUT TO:

EXT.—BEN FRANKLIN FIVE AND DIME STORE—DAY

Through the window, a pleasant, obese CLERK folds a long black-haired wig into a bag and hands it to a waiting Cliff. Cliff motions a thank-you, walks out front, and is immediately attracted O.C.

P.O.V.

His earlier adversary, blond ROD HARRIS, wheels by on a Harley-Davidson 600 motorcycle. An equally blonde cheerleader is wrapped around his waist. He recognizes Cliff and gives him a middle finger. The companion squeals with teenage pleasure.

CLIFF

nods in response and offers a tight smile. He then looks down to his shopping bag and muses.

CUT TO:

INT.—WARD F—DAY

Two feminine hands light a book of Cliff's matches and hold the flame under a telephone cord. The plastic and wire quickly melt.

PAULA

then turns and throws the blazing matchbook on a pile of sheets from four beds. The white cloth smolders then flames red.

CUT TO:

INT.—ASYLUM—ESCAPE BUZZER—DAY

CUT TO:

INT.—ASYLUM CORRIDOR—DAY

Cliff is on a step ladder changing a hallway lightbulb. He reacts.

CUT TO:

INT.—WARD A WOMEN'S RESTROOM—DAY

Susan is brushing out her hair in the mutilated metal mirror. She stops in mid-stroke and confirms the distant BUZZ.

CUT TO:

CLIFF

climbs off his step ladder. The spent bulb rolls from the top ladder platform and onto the floor, creating a loud POP as it shatters. Cliff startles.

CUT TO:

SUSAN

emerges from the restroom door, into the A recreation area. Mrs. Hapsbury pushes by the girl, into the restroom to close the window so the escape buzzer will be less troublesome to her patients.

CUT TO:

CLIFF

picks up a small paper sack at the ladder base.

CUT TO:

SUSAN

takes a similar parcel from a catch-all table near the Ward A exit door.

CUT TO:

CLIFF

almost runs down a long hallway.

CUT TO:

SUSAN

rushes down another corridor.

CUT TO:

CLIFF

reaches for a door handle. It opens as his hand moves out. Tom bursts through and by. Tom shouts over his shoulder as he jogs off.

TOM

It's Paula!

Cliff is relieved. His guilt had convinced him they were already caught. Cliff then surprises.

CLIFF

The sleeper?

TOM

(twenty feet beyond)

She even cut F's phone line!

CUT TO:

SUSAN

effectively casual, descends a flight of interior stairs.

CUT TO:

EXT.—INNER COURTYARD—DAY

Cliff's eyes search, then worry.

CUT TO:

INT.—MIDVALE HALLWAY—DAY

Susan walks another long hallway. Two nurses and one orderly hurry by. Suspense.

CUT TO:

EXT.—INNER COURTYARD—DAY

Cliff still searches, then finds. Relief.

SUSAN

enters the garden area from a far doorway.
They meet. No joy. Fright, tension.

CLIFF
Everything like it should be?

Susan nods. Cliff starts to a distant door, surveying, one half step ahead of Susan. Both awkwardly nonchalant.

CLIFF (CONT.)
Don't ask me why, but it's Paula.

SUSAN
Not Harriet?

Suddenly, Cliff pulls Susan behind a bush and down. He smooths dirt at its base, attempting to appear busy. Dr. Gargon and Tom go by.

TOM
(in passing; to Gargon)
I guess she made a fire out of something. Then while they were putting it out . . . I better not say any more because I really wasn't there . . .

Tom's last words are lost as the focused men move beyond hearing. Cliff and Susan continue their escape route.

CUT TO:

EXT.—HANDICAPPED PLAY YARD—DAY

The swings, teeter-totter, sand piles, etc., are used by eight boys and girls from the physical ages of four to thirty-five. Cliff and Susan enter. She is visibly shaken. Cliff doesn't notice. He searches. The farm boy nervously tugs and rubs his nose, then decides. He walks to an attendant, GEORGE, who pushes the swing.

CLIFF
(to attendant)
George, I'm looking for Ann. Oh, this is Sue Ellen, she's from A.

GEORGE
I know. Hi, Sue.

CLIFF
(reminding)
Ann?

GEORGE
Helen took her in. Bathroom, you know.

CLIFF
Oh, yeah.
(motions to Susan with forced nonchalance)
Just thought Sue Ellen oughta see another side of life.

Susan is not hearing. His "side of life" has mentally taken her away from their flight. A TWENTY-THREE-YEAR-OLD on a swing speaks to George.

TWENTY-THREE-YEAR-OLD
(petulant)
Andy-over.

GEORGE
No, Jackie. Not on a swing. If you're not happy, go slide.

Cliff pulls Susan away. The distracted Attendant and Jackie continue.

JACKIE

Not happy.

GEORGE

Let's slide.

JACKIE

No slide.

GEORGE

(picking up Jackie)

You start, I guarantee you won't stop.

George almost carries the reluctant twenty-three-year-old Jackie to the slide.

CLIFF'S EYES

recognize. He walks to a sixteen-year-old microcephalic who sits inside a jungle gym.

CLIFF

Hey, Frank. Frank, it's me, Cliff.

FRANK also recognizes and makes an inarticulate joyful noise.

CLIFF (CONT.)

(reaches in his paper sack)

Frank, here. Got something.

Cliff holds out the broken windup doll. Frank likes it.

FRANK

Me.

Cliff is relieved.

CLIFF

Yeah. For you. Come . . . get . . . her.

Frank manipulates his body from the tangle of steel pipes. Cliff looks to Susan, whose eyes are screwed shut, then nervously back to Frank.

CLIFF (CONT)

Come on, Frank. Atta boy. I know this is a girl toy. You'll like it anyway.

Cliff helps Frank over the last bar.

CLIFF (CONT)

There you be.

Frank seizes the doll. Cliff looks to Susan. Her eyes are still closed.

CLIFF

(to Frank)

Oh, now, Frank. Look. It needs fixed.

Cliff flips the doll's limp arm, then pulls it off. Frank reacts in pain.

FRANK

Ouch.

CLIFF

(close to blowing it)

No . . . no, Frank. Not ouch . . . help . . . help.

(points to attendant by the slide)

George help. George . . . help.

Frank glances to George, then to Cliff.

FRANK

Cliff help.

Cliff looks to Susan and shakes her arm, pleading.

CLIFF
Sue Ellen, say the same thing.
(to Frank)
George help. George help.

SUSAN
(weakly)
George help.

CLIFF
(to Susan)
Good girl, keep going.
(to Frank)
George help.

TOGETHER
(articulating)
George . . . help.

Frank bursts a smile.

FRANK
George help.

Frank moves off, holding out the doll and arm. Saying again and again . . .

FRANK
George help . . . George help.

Cliff and Susan cannot nor could they ever enjoy this success. They edge to a door, waiting for Frank to completely distract George.

SUSAN
(numb monotone)
What are we doing . . . what are we doing . . . what are we doing?

CLIFF
Maybe the dumb helpin' the dumb.

The distraught Frank reaches the Attendant. Their planned diversion with a different accomplice is successful. A key shoots out from Cliff's palm. He quickly opens the door. They slide through.

CUT TO:

EXT.—MIDVALE REGIONAL CENTER—DAY

A "Main Entrance" sign is visible. The entryway shadows reveal Cliff stripping off his Pendleton flannel shirt and putting it on Susan. Her hands pull a bandanna from her paper sack and tie it around her head. Cliff tucks her long hair into the back of the shirt collar. The young boy is stripped to a white T-shirt with red "Nebraska #1" lettering.

The two step into the parking lot and over to the MacPherson pickup. The escape BUZZER is far less audible. They duck into the doorless vehicle.

CLIFF

inserts the ignition key. Suddenly, the escape BUZZER STOPS. Silence. They reflect on this, a slight hesitation, the pickup starts.

THE SMOKING FORD

pulls away.

TOM

on a street corner one half block away, looks after Cliff and Susan's departure. The tiny, adult Paula cuddles in his arms as a three-year-old would be carried to bed. Her sleeping head lies on his shoulder. Frowning, Tom walks for the asylum.

CUT TO:

INT.—DOORLESS PICKUP—DAY

CLIFF
(to Susan)
Gosh all fried cakes!
(explaining)
That's what Dad'd say when he was real happy.

Susan hugs Cliff in elation and agrees.

SUSAN
Gosh all fried cakes!

CUT TO:

EXT.—INNER COURTYARD—DAY

Mrs. Hapsbury is in the doorway leading to Ward A, looking O.C.

TOM

is carrying Paula to another door.

TOM
Mrs. Hapsbury, I need Dr. Gargon! We'll be in shock!

MRS. HAPSBURY

moves inside to phone.

CUT TO:

EXT.—NEBRASKA HIGHWAY 136—DAY

The pickup races to and by CAMERA.

SUSAN (V.O.)
Why do you suppose Paula?

CUT TO:

INT.—DOORLESS PICKUP—DAY

CLIFF
Why Frank instead of Ann like we planned? Why everything?

SUSAN
I just about went down on "George help."

CLIFF
Remember Mom. Think "picnics and parties."
(suddenly)
Say, today's the last day of spring practice. You know that Grayson kid from North Platte? Might be the best ever.

SUSAN
Screw football. Pedal to the metal, country mouse.

CUT TO:

EXT.—ANOTHER CITY LIMITS—DAY

The pickup whips by a sign that reads "Tecumseh—Pop. 1926."

CUT TO:

INT.—SHOCK TREATMENT ROOM—DAY

Tom and a NURSE are strapping Paula on the metal table. Dr. Gargon bursts in the room.

DR. GARGON
Good going, Tom.

TOM
Cliff and Susan ran.

DR. GARGON
What?

TOM
When I was bringing Paula back, I saw Cliff driving off in a pickup with Susan.

DR. GARGON

Away from here?

TOM

(nods)

The pickup didn't have any doors. He knows she's not allowed outside.

Dr. Gargon wearily rubs his face with both hands.

DR. GARGON

Thank you, Tom.

The man reluctantly picks up a nearby phone receiver, sighs, then dials zero, and waits a moment.

DR. GARGON

(continues: to phone)

Barbara, I'm afraid we need the Highway Patrol.

TOM

activates the shock machine. Electricity fills Paula. Her eyelids snap shut.

CUT TO:

EXT.—MEMORIAL COLISEUM—DAY

The hard-core Nebraska fans cheer one hundred thirty Nebraska football players as they explode from the dressing room tunnel for the final intra-squad scrimmage of spring practice. Half of the team is in all-white uniform, the other half in red.

SPORTS ANNOUNCER (V.O.)

Welcome to the final scrimmage of Big Red spring practice.

SPORTS ANNOUNCER (V.O. CONT.)

A simulated game that should give our coaches a great deal to think about during the summer preparation for Nebraska's perennial run at the National Championship. We've got Bo Grayson from North Platte on the sidelines because he won't be officially entering the university until the fall. This should be one of the few times this projected All-American will be off the regular Cornhusker playing field.

CUT TO:

EXT.—ANOTHER CITY LIMITS—DAY

Sign of "Brownville—Pop. 200" in f.g. Cliff's pickup comes TO CAMERA.

SUSAN (V.O.)
Think they've missed us yet?

CLIFF (V.O.)
It's possible. Highly possible.

SUSAN (V.O.)
Think anyone cares?

CLIFF (V.O.)
It's been my experience when you don't want someone to care, they care.

SUSAN (V.O.)
I'm as nervous as weak shit.

CLIFF (V.O.)
Nice Omaha talk.

PAN WITH passing PICKUP TO SEE the vehicle slow, drive on the apron, and start across the Brownville Bridge that spans the Missouri River.

CUT TO:

INT.—PICKUP—DAY

Susan is nervous. Hands and legs jiggling. Cliff surveys, neck swiveling, eyes probing.

HIGHWAY PATROL DISPATCHER (V.O.)
Attention all units.
(static)
Harry . . . Carl. Anybody out there?

HARRY (V.O. FILTERED)
Right here, Bob.

CARL (V.O. FILTERED)
What's shakin', Bob?

HIGHWAY PATROL DISPATCHER (V.O.)
Coupla runaways from Midvale. Nothin' serious, both harmless.

CUT TO:

EXT.—BRIDGE—EAST ENTRYWAY—DAY

The pickup emerges, U-turns, and drives back into the steel-work.

HIGHWAY PATROL DISPATCHER (V.O.)
The crazy one's a girl, the other's a kid. Orderly, they say. They got their hands on a '82 to '84 Ford pickup without doors. Headin' east. They may cut up ta Lincoln or Omaha or go for the state line. She's from Omaha. Got the Cessna or you on the ground, Carl?

CARL (V.O. FILTERED)
I'm upstairs, Bob.

HIGHWAY PATROL DISPATCHER (V.O.)
OK, we'll rely on you for the moment. I think we kin all be heroes and take care of it in our own jurisdiction without gettin' all Nebraska involved.

CUT TO:

INT.—PICKUP—DAY

Cliff gears to a near walking speed. Susan notices an egg that has rolled from under the seat and settled next to her foot. She picks up the egg to show Cliff as the air is shattered by a car horn in the rear. Both young people flash terror. Susan crushes the egg in her fright. A four-door CHEVY passes. Cliff is relieved; Susan is not.

CLIFF

And me without a change of shorts.

CUT TO:

EXT.—BROWNVILLE BRIDGE—WEST ENTRYWAY—DAY

The pickup pulls off the apron and turns down a dirt access road.

CUT TO:

EXT.—RIVERSIDE GROVE OF COTTONWOOD TREES—DAY

The truck wheels about and stops.

CUT TO:

INT.—PICKUP—DAY

Cliff rubs his eyes, then blinks them open at Susan.

CLIFF

You know old John Brown used to run escaped slaves up this river? That's how the name Brownville came about.

SUSAN

Cliff, screw John Brown. Let's go, let's go.

Susan bolts out of the truck, Cliff follows.

CUT TO:

EXT.—PICKUP—DAY

Cliff strips the tarpaulin off in the truck bed, revealing the sleeping bags and Rod Harris's Harley-Davidson 600 motorcycle. Susan is surprised.

CLIFF

Them's the bags, my hippie hair's rolled up inside one.

(points to cycle)

I figured we'd have to walk too far to any bus depot of size. You know, in these one-horse towns, people pay attention to everything. This'll get us to Saint Joe.

SUSAN

(looking around)

Let's go to Idaho on that. Like *now.*

CLIFF

The way I drive these things, I'll be happy reaching Saint Joe.

Susan gives him a "come on" hand sign. Cliff tugs out the Harley, then sobers.

CLIFF (CONT.)

Sue Ellen, you gotta know . . .

He gropes. The girl worries.

SUSAN

What, Cliff?

CLIFF

(abruptly)

I stole this bike.

SUSAN

What?

CLIFF

I couldn't feel worse. That's why I didn't say nothing till I had to.

(earnest)

I gotta lock, though. I'm gonna chain it near the Saint Joe police station. Slip a note under their door or something. So the owner gets it back.

Susan throws her hands in the air.

SUSAN

You must be crazy. They're coming and you're doing this country mouse shit.

CLIFF

My old dad says "honesty ain't the best policy . . . it's the only policy."

Susan starts to anger.

CLIFF (CONT.)

Stop that! You just pay attention. Forget you're from Omaha.

Susan settles as commanded. Cliff reaches into his jeans pocket. An unnoticed Cessna appears as a dot on the horizon. Droning closer.

CLIFF (CONT.)

(firm)

I want to do something in case anything happens.

His hand opens, revealing the two rings.

CLIFF (CONT.)

My grandparents'.

(holds up the frail gold ring)

Granddad's farmin' wore his almost through.

Susan takes the diamond.

CLIFF (CONT.)
Mom knows. Seemed almost the worse thing I could do. To have her worry. She'll have to tell Dad when the time comes.

Susan hugs Cliff. Both thrilled.
The plane approaches, still unnoticed.

SUSAN
(soft, in love)
My country mouse.
(brighter)
Can I wear my ring now? In case anything happens?

CLIFF
If I can wear mine.

The plane is overhead. Eleven o'clock. Its height, the moment, the river's rush, all negate the motor hum as they put the rings on each other's fingers.

CLIFF AND SUSAN'S

emotional marriage is complete. Cliff's eyes cloud.

<table>
<tr><td>CLIFF
We gotta take these off before we see a preacher.</td><td>PILOT (V.O. FILTERED)
Bob . . . you hangin' by. We seem ta got something below.</td></tr>
<tr><td>SUSAN
Whatever you say, country mouse.</td><td>PATROL DISPATCHER (V.O.)
Right there, Carl. Don't keep us danglin'.</td></tr>
<tr><td>CLIFF
(looking at his ring)
Dad always bragged he never had his ring off.</td><td>PILOT (V.O. FILTERED)
I make out . . . damn these high-powered mothers . . . they jig-</td></tr>
</table>

gle the piss outta of everthing. I make out a pickup with no doors and two people standin' in a cottonwood clearin' . . . just shootin' the shit.

SUSAN
It's congenital?

PATROL DISPATCHER (V.O.)
Sure that's them?

Cliff questions.

PILOT (V.O. FILTERED)
Everthing checks except . . . fuck in a barrel. They're the damndest fugitives I ever seen.

SUSAN (CONT.)
. . . uh . . . runs in the family.

PATROL DISPATCHER (V.O.)
How's that?

Cliff smiles, nods, takes her ring hand in his.

PILOT (V.O. FILTERED)
Maybe they can't hear me because of the river water, but they ain't runnin'.

CLIFF
Probably a better reason we gotta get going is we can't get caught. If I was broke up from you, I'd lose my mind.

PATROL DISPATCHER (V.O.)
Yeah? We'll take somebody to take care of that. Harry? You on?

Cliff is not aware of any double meaning to his statement. Susan is. She

HARRY (V.O. FILTERED)
I'm thirty minutes

kisses the naive farm boy.

SUSAN
Same here.

away. Remember we decided they'd probably cut up to Omaha.

PATROL DISPATCHER (V.O.)
Oh, yeah. Let's see . . . Carl, you circle high. Try ta keep from bein' too noticeable. I'll call the Missouri Patrol. They might have someone rollin' near the border.

Cliff walks to the driver's side of the truck.

CLIFF
I'll set this old teakettle in the drink, then we'll be outta here 'fore dark.

Cliff climbs in the pickup. Susan takes the passenger seat.

CLIFF (CONT.)
Now what?

SUSAN
I won't just stay here waiting, wondering if you're dead or alive.

CLIFF
Nobody's gonna die. Stay. I told you it's best.

SUSAN
I'm telling you it's worst. Let's move it.

Cliff reluctantly starts the motor and drives the pickup to the paved highway.

CUT TO:

EXT.—HIGHWAY—DAY

Empty. Long. Stretching through the bridge to the Missouri state line.

PILOT (V.O. FILTERED)
They're haulin' out.

The farm vehicle comes out of the dirt access road, drives on the pavement one hundred yards away from the bridge, U-turns and stops on the gravel shoulder.

PATROL DISPATCHER (V.O.)
Hang on, Carl. The cavalry's comin'.

CUT TO:

INT.—PICKUP—DAY

CLIFF
(pointing)
I'll just put her up to full steam, run right through that guard rail, 'n land out in the deep water. When the truck and I go under, I'll come out this side swimming, shoot up to the top, head for the bank.

SUSAN
(nods in comprehension)

She grabs his face . . . then startles back. A car passes by on this nearly vacant highway.

PATROL DISPATCHER (V.O.)
Skyhawk Four? This is the Missouri Cavalry.

She recovers, then starts trembling.

PILOT (V.O. FILTERED)
Hey, 'preciate the help, Rough Rider. For some strange note, our outlaws are just sittin' near the west end of the Brownville Bridge.

MISSOURI PATROL (V.O.)
Roger. E.T.A. Three minutes.

SUSAN
I'm really, really, really scared.

Now Cliff takes her face.

CLIFF
Well, I'm not. Don't that help?

SUSAN
Not one damn bit.

Cliff kisses her.

CLIFF
Okay. Jump out now. This sure can't be seen.
Come on this side. Put your ear on the blacktop.
If you hear a sort of hum . . . something's . . .

Another car appears and speeds by to the opposite direction.
As it passes, Cliff urgently directs.

CLIFF (CONT.)
Quick, get your ear down.

CUT TO:

EXT.—PICKUP—DAY

Susan gets out and complies. She looks up at Cliff, listening.

CLIFF
Still hear him?

She nods.

CLIFF (CONT.)
It's gettin' smaller. The hum?

She again nods.

SUSAN

You sure Tonto got started this way?

Cliff jerks his head to the sky. The far-off Cessna clings to the western horizon.

CLIFF

We might have other problems. Jump in, quick.

SUSAN

I think someone else is coming.

Susan moves and the pickup digs away to cross the bridge.

CLIFF

(voice over the driveaway)

There's a plane over west there. See?

PILOT (V.O. FILTERED)

Headin' your way, Missouri Calvary.

CUT TO:

EXT.—MISSOURI PATROL CAR—DAY

Lights and SIREN BLARE. The lone OFFICER pulls up a short-barreled shotgun, visible on the ride by.

MISSOURI PATROL (V.O. FILTERED)

Much obliged, Skyhawk. We got 'em.

CUT TO:

INT.—CLIFF'S PICKUP—DAY

Through the WINDSHIELD, approaching a lone hill. A mile in the distance, the Missouri Highway Patrol car breaks the crest.

CLIFF AND SUSAN

radiate fear, panic, concern.

CLIFF
Well, Tonto . . .
(looks out the rear window to confirm the plane approaching in the west)
We do have a problem.

SUSAN
(serious, strange calm)
Cliff, I love you . . . forever.

CLIFF
(soft smile to Susan)
Sue Ellen, I wouldn't have it no other way.

Cliff reattends his driving.

THE SPEEDOMETER

winds up.

CUT TO:

INT.—CLIFF'S PICKUP—DAY

THROUGH THE WINDSHIELD. The distant policeman scrambles behind his black and white, then cradles his weapon.

SUSAN

is starting to exhilarate. Cliff is in control.

THE SPEEDOMETER

hits and holds at seventy-two.

CLIFF (V.O.)
Hang onto your hat.

CUT TO:

EXT.—ROAD—DAY

A football field's length in front of the Missouri Patrol car, Cliff's four tires shriek and fume as the pickup correctly spins the moonshiner's U-turn.

PILOT (V.O. FILTERED)
Jeeee-sus. That's some trick.

Cliff's truck returns to the bridge.

CUT TO:

INT.—CLIFF'S PICKUP—DAY

Susan blinks. Cliff smiles.

CLIFF
Slip down on the floorboard, Sue Ellen.

EXT.—HIGHWAY WEST OF BRIDGE—DAY

The plane approaches to land on the highway.

MISSOURI PATROL (V.O. FILTERED)
Watch yourself, Skyhawk. I think the crazy's drivin'. Don't take no chances. Shoot if they get close. The world's got enough crazy people.

Cliff's pickup starts across the bridge. The plane touches down and taxis to the west structure apron.

CLIFF (V.O.)
Like Dad says, "If it ain't one thing, it's another."

CUT TO:

INT.—CLIFF'S PICKUP—DAY

THROUGH WINDSHIELD. Susan is on the floor. Fetal position. Waiting. The plane approaches. Chicken time.

CUT TO:

INT.—PLANE—DAY

THROUGH WINDSHIELD. Cliff's truck isn't slowing.

PILOT (V.O.)

Fuck in a barrel!!!

EXT.—HIGHWAY—DAY

Cliff's truck hurtles off the bridge and onto the blacktop as the plane accelerates to climb back to the sky. The patrol Cessna doesn't have enough speed, yet raises just enough to let Cliff go under.

CUT TO:

INT.—CLIFF'S PICKUP—DAY

Cliff's left foot slams, then lets up on the brake as the right simultaneously floors the accelerator, then releases.

CUT TO:

EXT.—HIGHWAY—DAY

Another "moonshiner" U-turn and Cliff heads for the Missouri Patrol car that has just entered the east end of the one-half-mile bridge. The Highway Patrol Cessna flutters, strains, and lands into the broad Missouri River as Cliff now challenges the black and white. Water sprays one hundred feet in the spring air. Spectacular.

CUT TO:

INT.—CLIFF'S PICKUP—DAY

THROUGH WINDSHIELD. The Missouri Patrol approaches, shotgun out the window. The man FIRES. Shot sprays a perfect circled pattern on the pickup window glass.

CUT TO:

EXT.—RIVER BOTTOM—UP ANGLE—(SLOW MOTION)—DAY

First the law car, then Cliff's pickup easily crash through the light retaining metal. Each vehicle, on different sides, floats in the spring air, then plunges deep into the churning, brackish water, joining the semi-submerged Cessna.

BRIDGE LEVEL

Looking down to the great river. Upstream showers have bloated the ominous, mud-gray beast that sucks at its own banks, spitting up limbs and tree roots. The land moans, waits. Then . . .

PILOT (V.O.)
I been around more'n I care to admit, but I'm here to tell you . . .

TIME CUT TO:

EXT.—RIVERSIDE—DAY

Cumulus clouds rise in fists of thunder behind the two dripping men sitting on the riverbank. The Missouri Calvary and Skyhawk are stunned in wonderment.

PILOT
. . . that was the fuckin'est thing I've ever been through.

MISSOURI PATROLMAN
That includes 'Nam for me.

PILOT
Well, let's get on to town. They can drag the river for them crazy assholes, if anybody cares.

A MOTORCYCLE is HEARD in the Nebraska air.

MISSOURI PATROLMAN
I could care less. I'd hate to see what they look like. My old Winchester pump generally does the job.

PILOT
(upcuts, shouting to distance)
Hey! Hey!
(to Missouri Patrolman)
That motorcycle can git us some help.

TOGETHER
Hey!! Down here!! We need help!!

A motorcycle and its two riders cross the Brownville Bridge. Missouri Cavalry and Skyhawk wave and yell. Nothing. The cycle and riders PASS FROM VIEW. The two officers fling their hands in disgust.

PILOT
Fuck in a barrel.

MISSOURI PATROLMAN
Didn't'cha see that hair?

PILOT
(nods)
Hippies or punkers?

MISSOURI PATROLMAN
All the same.

PILOT
What's this fuckin' country gettin' to?

Wolfgang Amadeus Mozart end title MUSIC hits and cathartically carries the sound track.

CUT TO:

EXT.—HIGHWAY—DAY

Cliff and Susan on the stolen Harley, each in clothing that would even today be typed as "hippie" by Cliff and most other midwesterners. Susan's appearance is sufficiently modified by a leather headstrap. Cliff is less recognizable in his wig. Both laugh. Freedom. Love.

CUT TO:

EXT.—NEBRASKA MEMORIAL COLISEUM—DAY

THE NEBRASKA FOOTBALL SQUADS

wave to their fans as they stream back to the dressing rooms.

SPORTS ANNOUNCER (V.O.)
And there you have it, ladies and gentlemen, boys and girls.

SPORTS ANNOUNCER (V.O. CONT.)
This is not just another spring game but the start of the newest and most potentially powerful chapter in Nebraska Cornhusker football history! Let 'em know you love *The Big Red*!!

MR. AND MRS. GARBER

cheer and applaud with thousands of other Big Red fans.

CUT TO:

EXT.—SAND HILLS—DAY

Cliff and Susan ride their motorcycle through western Nebraska's unique Sand Hills, throwing their "hippie" garb to the roadside. More laughing, more freedom. Mozart continues.

CUT TO:

EXT.—WYOMING HIGHWAY—DAY

Cliff and Susan slowly steer through a broken herd of range cows flooding down the Route 30 concrete ribbon.

CUT TO:

EXT.—YELLOWSTONE HIGHWAY—DAY

Cliff and Susan, on their stopped motorcycle, sail a slice of white bread to a bear, then narrowly squeal away when the huge animal wants the "more" they don't have.

CUT TO:

EXT.—BORDER—DAY

Cliff and Susan cross the Wyoming state line into Idaho. A sign identifies the transition. Both youngsters throw their arms at the sky. The Harley wavers, Cliff sobers, regains control, then, more laughter.

CUT TO:

EXT.—KETCHUM, IDAHO, STREET—DAY

Police station is b.g., Cliff chain-locks the motorcycle to a parking meter. A note is taped over its headlight. Susan tolerantly smiles at her "country mouse."

CUT TO:

EXT.—USED CAR LOT—DAY

A row of vintage pickups. Cliff pulls from under one, slams down the hood, and nods to Susan. She mock-knowingly kicks its tire.

CUT TO:

EXT.—ANCIENT KETCHUM METHODIST CHURCH—DAY

Cliff and Susan skip down its front steps and cross to their new/used pickup. A "Grant Wood" MINISTER and his MATE hand-dip into a package of "Minute Rice" to spray it at the deliriously happy new husband and wife.

CUT TO:

EXT.—IDAHO—DAY

Their pickup drives BY CAMERA.

CUT TO:

INT.—PICKUP—DAY

Cliff and Susan kissing. It's all perfect.

CUT TO:

EXT.—IDAHO HIGHWAY—AERIAL SHOT—DAY

CUT TO:

The new/used MacPerson pickup rolls along the narrow two-lane that serpentines into the Sawtooth Wilderness. The few Idaho ranch buildings appear as tabletop toys surrounded by lush shades of spring green.

CUT TO:

EXT.—NEBRASKA MEMORIAL COLISEUM—DAY

END CREDITS over "Big Red" action and "Big Red" crowds cheering them on as fantasies become realities. Wolfgang Amadeus Mozart concludes.

FADE OUT

The End

THE MOST IMPORTANT DRAFT

George Lucas claims "the most important draft is the first." Your first draft is the scaled mountain. The words "fade out" are like the planted flag claiming the script. You've written things you never knew! After the "fade out" day, you may find how much more you *have* to know, but today is yours.

I'm assuming your "fade out" is now not many hours or days away. When your "fade out" comes, celebrate. That's a hell of an accomplishment.

Producer/writer Harve Bennett received my first draft of *If Tomorrow*

Comes in 1970. He called and said "Congratulations." "Oh," I said, "you liked it?" Harve's reaction was perfect. "No, no, we'll get into that. Congratulations because *you did it.*"

Whether it's good or not is almost away from the point, particularly for a new writer. Doing it is so damned important. If the world is full of writers who never write, you must not be among that accursed number.

William Saroyan submits, "You write a hit the same way you write a flop." Bad is as hard to write as good, sometimes. Saroyan, never at a loss for pessimism, also claimed writing is "the hardest way to earn a living with the possible exception of wrestling alligators."

Now's the time for you to ignore cynicism. Be enthusiastic. Find the glass half-full. Don't be like the boy who cried, after finding his Christmas stocking full of horse droppings, "Christmas is horse manure!" Cry, "Gee, I got a pony!"

You did it! Congratulations! You'll get to whether it's good or not soon enough. In the meantime, massage your writer's ego. Look about you. You are singular in one more way.

The ancient Scots Hunter clan motto is: "Cursum perficio." "I finish the race." For screenwriting and your first draft, you have finished the race. Let the rewrite race begin.

Chapter 8

THE REWRITE(S)

You've scaled Mount Everest and descended its opposite side. But wait, you say you don't feel good? There was that euphoria after you wrote "Fade Out," but it was so temporary. After "doing it," shouldn't the thrill last longer?

Not to worry. You're experiencing the "afterbirth blues." Nothing should quite equal the thrill of having written a first draft. That is *your* draft, your time in the sun, your moment to prove to yourself the script *can* be written. You're not wearing a "How am I writing? Call 848-0616" sign on your posterior.

Perhaps the after-script blues are most related to fear for our baby's future. Who's going to feed it? Help it walk? Get it beyond puberty? Or perhaps it's the down after the first draft high, when we realize nothing can come close. Julius Epstein says that after viewing the "rough cut" of every film he's produced, he's had to rush to the nearest restroom to throw up. Why? "I saw the movie when I was writing the script. Nothing could ever equal that vision." Few sets equal the sets you've conjured in your first draft dreams. Generally the actors fall short. The director is too often a lox.

But let's stop flashing forward in fantasized writer terrors. Let's claim the only responsibility we should accept at this first draft level, authorship. Then let us do all we might to mature the script as well as we can before sending it into the cold world. That's rewriting.

1. Reality vs. Reel-ality

Thus far you've been living a fantasy. Edward Albee *(Who's Afraid of Virginia Woolf?)* once cried: "In the two or three or four months it takes me to write a play, I find the reality of the play is a great deal more alive for me than what passes for reality."

That's absolutely wonderful, and often true. But now you have to kick your motor into the reality gear. Be objective. Be severe. Be everything but cruel in self-reexamination of your pages.

2. Throw the First Draft Away?

Emmy winner Jack Sowards has the most unusual reaction to his first draft screenplays. Jack takes the pages in hand, walks to the nearest wastebasket, and dumps them. For Jack, his original first draft is a warm-up for the real first draft to follow. Most flinch at Jack's procedure with the same reaction males would give someone proposing to use a Bowie knife to render them eligible for harem guarding. Most could *never* allow themselves to destroy a first draft *or* reproducing organs (in that order). You may be a eunuch when your script is being shot, but right now you have the power to change your words and, as importantly, the power to not change your words.

3. Know Thyself, No One Else Will

New writers should dissect themselves personally before examining the first draft. Why are you writing? Joy, anger, or money are good and lasting motivations. Proving things to loved ones is merely a temporary impetus. John Gardner has excellent thoughts on that: "In my own experience, nothing is harder for the developing writer than overcoming his anxiety that he is fooling himself and cheating or embarrassing his family and friends. To most people, even those who don't read much, there is something special and vaguely magical about writing. It is not easy for them to believe that someone they know, someone quite ordinary in many respects, can really do it."

Well you can really do it or you wouldn't have these pages of filled paper nearby. And now's the time to forget about family and friends.

You're beyond that. Remember Jesus telling a multitude: "A prophet is without honor in his own house."

REWRITING FOR YOURSELF

After you come down from your "fade out" high, and work through your "afterbirth blues," you'll generally accept and even welcome the chance to rewrite for yourself prior to letting the script go out.

Professional writers work their pages over a little or a lot prior to "turning the script in." I rework my script pages on the day of writing, just after they're written, *and* before I go to sleep. Then, I give them a once-over as a warm-up before writing the next day's original pages. That's three opportunities to rewrite and polish during my first draft process.

Accept the axiom "scripts are not written but rewritten," as fact and an opportunity. Somerset Maugham claimed "only a mediocre writer is at his best." An exceptional writer is never satisfied. He or she is always playing with the pages. Even after the script *must* be turned in and the film *must* be shot, most cry "oh for one more chance to make it better."

Richard Walter says, "Rewriting is like finding focus on a camera. You never hit clarity exactly on the first rotation. You rack from out-of-focus to focus and on beyond a touch, then rotate the lens back to the clearest possible picture." That's particularly true if you've "pushed" the drama or "gone over the top" in comedy. Unfortunately, most scripts don't even get up to focus; they "rack" short of the clearest possible picture and are less than their potential. Go "through focus." Go to extreme, and then bring the drama or comedy back to its most effective level during your rewrite.

Just as scripts do not write themselves, they certainly do not rewrite themselves. You, the author, must be present and experience every single birth pang and joy. John Irving *(The World According to Garp)* says, "Half of my life is an act of revision."

1. Be Clear

There are so many choices to make in screenwriting. You have the constant opportunity for using the extreme swings of the dramatic pendulum or any point in between. But what you should be, above all, is *clear.* Perhaps initially your story or characters will be intentionally vague or mysterious, but they must be well revealed at some time in the narrative. The eighteenth-century French novelist Stendhal clearly believed: "I see only one rule. To be clear. If I am not clear, then my entire world crumples into nothing."

Neither Stendhal nor you can have Elmo jamming an elbow into the nearby Henrietta and wondering, "What'd that mean?" You *must not* take your audience out of the emotional flow of your story with lack of clarity, because you may never get them back. They'll switch to another channel or pop in another video tape or start worrying about how they're going to survive the next onslaught of bills.

2. But Don't Be Obvious

It may seem paradoxical to the "be clear" admonition but *don't be obvious,* in dialogue, description, or storytelling. You want to give your audience the opportunity to argue about something in your script on the way to the parking lot. Being obvious and heavy-handed generally means you've let your grinding axe irreparably slice through the story's fabric, so be subtle. Gustave Flaubert, a French novelist, passionately claimed: "In his work, the artist should be like God in creation. Invisible and all powerful. The artist should be felt everywhere and seen nowhere."

Often scripts are so clearly manipulative you can visualize the story-meeting people pushing, shoving, and maneuvering every twist and turn of character and plot. As you disguise your exposition, disguise your prejudices, while being clear. In the end of superlative movies, audiences know exactly what they want to know about Butch and Sundance, Rick and Ilsa, Charles Foster Kane, and E.T. And they'll be clear about that knowledge. Such clarity starts with the writer.

Joseph Conrad: "A work that aspires, however humbly, to the condition of art, should carry its justification in every line." Justification can only be achieved in writing if clarity is present. If something's not clear in your script, rewrite. Or cut. Elimination of elements that do not fit in scripts is also an essential part of rewriting. Often cutting scenes or dialogue is better than reworking existing words that fail.

3. What's Wrong

Most people in the entertainment world focus on what's wrong. An overworked executive or producer doesn't have time to "make nice." You *should* know and appreciate what works in your scripts. But fortunately and unfortunately, at the rewriting level you'll mostly be concentrating on what's wrong.

Be masochistic. Be tough on yourself. Be pleased with the pages you like, then let that pleasure go. Focus on the pages you dislike or make you reach for the medicine chest antacids. Don't be cruel, just demanding.

BEFORE THE MADDING CROWD

When you have concluded your own examination of the so-called first draft, you can do more rewriting, or subject the script to a limited outside world. The professional writer generally finishes off the script and kicks the beast to the madding crowd. The new writer should get some feedback before rewriting or showing the draft to more gimlet-eyed humans.

Now's the perfect time to evaluate your friendships. You need three. Three's also the perfect number for story conferences. Two can be talking while one thinks. That's not quite the concept in my asking you to choose three friends. The theory, though, can be tested and proven by getting the lucky three together to have them discuss the script, with yourself an interested bystander. If this happens, do not say a word. Listen. You'll learn. Literally.

Then through your friendships, identify the ones who tell you what you want to hear. To paraphrase the movie pioneer Sam Goldwyn, "Include them out." Also weed out those brutal "let me be frank" friends. That will be too hard on your fragile writer's id. Try those who'd take you to the airport. Friends who will tell you what you need to hear and what they feel, but kindly. They can help you be better than you are and, just maybe, the best you can be.

They most likely won't be the same three for every script. Some may give you better thoughts on your comedy, others on your love story, and there may be another threesome best for the historical piece. Of course, some may be good for all. Cast individual friends to your individual script. Then let them read copies.

Give them well-typed photocopies. The script doesn't have to be as perfect as when you offer it to professionals, but you're asking them for a minimum of two hours of their lives for this "read," so you should make their effort as visually easy as possible.

And don't have them read the same script copy. There are two financial things you'll worry about initially: the agent's ten percent and the photocopy costs. The agent's ten is just inevitable. Don't even think about it. Treat those dollars as you would treat a parking ticket. Pay it. Forget self-flagellation; it's a waste of good emotion you should be putting into your scenes. The identical concept applies to copying your script pages. Do it and forget it. You have such minor expenses as a writer. Thank God you don't have to get film, actors, and crew together to produce or direct. We writers can always write. We may not be getting paid, but we can always work. Not so for anyone else in this collaborative art called filmmaking.

Now give those three friends a good weekend to read your script. Please warn them, for the sake of your sanity, screenwriters hate the words, "I'm half through your script and . . ." Nothing can follow to help the minor shock. No, not even ". . . and I'm loving it." For when someone says they're half-through your script, that means they *could* put it down. We screenwriters cherish, "I loved your work so much I couldn't put it down," as much as novelists.

After that and similar admonitions configured to your own psyche, wait. I know it's hard. The only thing worse is having them reading the script in front of you. Your eyes and soul perceiving damnation in their every body twitch and itch. After the wait, they'll call.

Then, hear what your appointed critics have to say. When Bill Goldman goes into a studio story conference, he disarms the people nervous at being in the same room with the renowned Bill Goldman by saying, "Tell me what you want to tell me." That's smart at any level of meeting about scripts. Be open. Though you may be seething inside, don't be defensive. Though they are destroying your love child, be quiet. Though you want to scream and justify, don't.

Listen. Then ask some "what if's": "What if I make the lead black?" "What if she had slept with him before they landed the helicopter on the Brooklyn Bridge?"

Get what you can from these people, who hopefully will still be your friends afterwards. Take supreme advantage of their good nature.

You'll never have a better excuse for being a user, because they'll actually like being part of your scriptwriting process. For some, the intimacy may be more than any exchange of body fluids.

Then sort through their thoughts, passions, hates, loves, and carpings. Take what you want what you think will help the script reach its potential, and throw the rest away, or put them on a shelf to be reexamined downstream if need be.

1. Table Reading

Assembling the trio and others for an evening of reading aloud the entire script would be perfect for optimum input. In the table readings, you read the description and pass out the roles to those whose personality best fits the characters. That's what you should do with amateur actors. With professional players, you're often safe with more arbitrary assigning.

RE-REWRITING

Now it's time to rewrite your rewrites for yourself. Couple your own instincts and intellect with what's been tallied from the different sources. Then recall Ernest Hemingway: "The most essential gift for a good writer is a built-in, shock-proof shit detector." Apply that detector to every breathing aspect of your script and the friends' suggestions. Show no mercy, only self-honesty with a dollop of compassion.

Consider Dr. Samuel Johnson's words to a fellow writer: "Your manuscript is both good and original. The part that is good is not original and the part that is original is not good."

1. Being Objective

Rewriting is often like looking through a microscope and seeing yourself. You'll find the you under the microscope is no longer the you looking through the eyepiece today. Just as you personally change from year to year, your writer-self changes from first to second draft and beyond. You can now be more objective than during the days of original creation. You can criticize your loved ones and still love them.

With writing, the end result of similar criticism can be even better. You can rarely change loved ones, but you can change scripts.

Being objective in rewriting is exactly like being objective in all problem solving. It is seeing the entire picture, the forest *and* the trees.

2. Rewriting Questions

Does my hero have something at stake? Is my heavy a good heavy? Is the hero or heavy split? Is conflict or tension in every scene? Is my dialogue less to be more? Do the spoken words illuminate what my characters are *not* saying? Do things happen after the other or *because of* the other? Did I protect my spine? Did I let the comedy come from character? Did I disguise my exposition? Will my audience suspend their disbelief throughout? Is my unbelievability believable? Did I "push" it?

One of my yesteryear 434'ers was the most grateful to me for making her "push it." She extended the script's drama far beyond her instincts and inhibitions. I admonished one 434 woman to let herself sexually go on paper, because she was far too restrained. When I read her rewrite, asbestos gloves were needed to turn the page.

Write or rewrite outrageously. That will often translate into interesting scenes for the audience. If you don't catch yourself going "over the top," rest easy with writer Arte Julian's belief there'll always be someone around to "help you dull it down."

Don't hold back. Tam Mossman's recommendation for novelists is applicable to screenwriters. "Never save anything for your next book because that possible creation may not be properly shaped to hold the thoughts you're working with today. In fiction especially, anything that could happen, should happen." Catch any and all "holding back" in your rewrite. Don't compromise. Compromises in storytelling generally result in scenes that are neither fish nor fowl or any other cliché you shouldn't use.

3. Clichés

In dialogue or description, if you've seen it before, don't use it. Simple? Yes, there's nothing new under the sun, but you can freshen clichés. Put new verbal clothes on clichés so they seem new. Instead of "slipping one by" someone, have a character try to "sneak daylight past the rooster." But don't be so exotic that Elmo will again elbow Henrietta.

4. Going Deep

Emily Carr believes, "You often feel, when you look it straight in the eye, you could have put more into it. Could have let yourself go and dug harder."

Go deep, dig harder. Look for the gold beneath the tinsel. Discover and allow the audience to also discover what your script's really about. *E.T., Kane, B & S, Casablanca,* and *Angel* go far beneath the dimensions of those five film surfaces. Use their quality of thought on your own subject, story, and characters.

Use your experience, your research, your soul, and the best dimensions of your mind when rewriting your people and story to their deepest potential. Henry James emphasizes: "The deepest quality of a work of art will always be the quality of the mind of the writer. No good novel will ever proceed from a superficial mind." No good screenplay will ever proceed from a superficial soul. As you need instinct, story, *and* character in your first draft, you need mind *and* soul very specifically in rewriting.

5. Gender Writing

Virginia Woolf felt, "It is fatal for anyone who writes to think of their sex. It is fatal to be a man or woman pure and simple. One must be woman-manly or man-womanly." A writer must be omnisexual. Homosexual or heterosexual, man, woman, girl, boy. Everyone.

At some moment in rewriting, climb into the sexual skin of your characters and see if you're maximizing that valuable potential. Yes, Virginia Woolf, *their* sex, not your sex. Some will be tight, some loose, most in between. *All* must be sexually considered. Especially in your rewrite. Now is when you have the perspective and the overall insight.

THE FIRST READ-THROUGH

Now you've thoroughly thought out the story or you wouldn't have gotten to a full script. But you can't think it out enough. Here's when you think more and more.

After a few days perspective, sit down and read the script straight through. You may want your "ride to the airport" friends to read your script during this time. Whatever seems best for your script and your writer's id.

How many days you need for perspective depends either on your own psyche or on how much time you have before a deadline. On this first read-through, pretend you are the audience. Divorce yourself, as much as you can, from the decisions, joys, and pains remembered in the days of creation. You can't totally block those memories, but you'll come closer if you have even a single day of perspective.

Your optimum read-through reaction is "that's going to be just fine." If you're much more expansive, you're on the precipice of self-delusion.

On this first read, try not to make changes. Get the straight-through reading and imagined "viewing-a-movie" experience. After that two or so hours ask: Did your storytelling goals hold up? Was the page-turning flow even? Was the conflict continually rising? Was the entire script any good?

Make mental and physical notes of changes you might try during the next levels of examination so you can pick them up later. For now though, try to find affirmation that the script can turn out to be a baby worth raising.

OK, we've read through our scripts. For me on *The Glass Hammer,* it is a baby worth raising. 1. I have a strong, valid love story. 2. Mental illness is a subject well worth exploring in this context. Actually the audience will see and feel sides to insanity fresh and revealing to most. 3. I've got some good beats of humor throughout that come from character. 4. My story has a nice progression. Rising conflict. Continuous tension. 5. A fulfilling third act. Good.

1. The Dialogue Read-Through

Let's look at the dialogue next. That's where most will be focusing when they read your script. The majority will skim the descriptions to get the essence. But everyone who reads the full script *will* read dialogue. Ergo, I recommend work on dialogue right after your initial read-through while you are fresh. If you spend a lot of your initial time on description, you may not be as attentive to your dialogue examination. And since that's what readers most react to, get your dialogue best first.

In your dialogue read-through, READ THE WORDS OUT LOUD. Give yourself all the parts and read nothing but the dialogue. ALOUD. You'll get a much better impression of how the out-loud words will play and even read. Yes, you'll have pages of descriptive action but skip those pages to the next piece of dialogue.

Now make all the dialogue changes you want during or after the read-through. This should be a two- or three-day process. You're not reading this time for story or even much character logic. This read is for dialogue flow. Is it awkward? Smooth? Too punchy? Not punchy enough? On-the-nose? Obscure? But most of all, does it play? Will it read well on the page and spring well from the mouths of imagined actors? All of these questions are best considered and achieved when you read *aloud.*

2. The Descriptions Read-Through

Now, to the second rhythm of rewriting life. Spend the next two or three days on your description read-through. Again, aloud. Read and rewrite for rhythm, comfortability when appropriate, shock when you can.

As much as anything in descriptions, be literate. Even literary on occasion. Here's where you try for a touch of Cather, Steinbeck, Hemingway, with a strong bit of yourself. Here's where you best use ordinary, economical phrases with a word or three of delicious description for color.

Take page one of *The Glass Hammer:* Instead of, "Fans cheer as the Nebraska football team goes to the dressing room," "Seventy-six thousand one hundred and forty-three cheer the University of Nebraska football team fighting their way through adulating fans toward the dressing room." "Adulating" and "fighting" are words of action and emotion which liven up that initial terse, ordinary, boring description. The exact crowd count because that's likely never been done before. It also implies the stadium is sold out, which further implies the football-mad state of Nebraska.

On page two, instead of, "A boy throws a second watermelon at Cliff's truck," "The football player has another melon above his head, taking a weaving aim on Cliff's truck." Instead of, "end credits over Nebraska football games," "END CREDITS over 'Big Red' action and 'Big Red' crowds cheering them on as fantasies become realities."

But don't let "color words" be so self-conscious they get in the way of the script's effectiveness. To keep the reader, your first audience, informed, awake, interested in the story and people, and periodically excited is the immediate goal of description. In description, though, less is only *nearly always* more. When in doubt, go for less.

To accomplish your own out-loud description read-through and concurrent rewriting, you might take additional time. A chase sequence can use up two or three days rework alone to get it fresh and exciting. A couple making love should always be more writing effort than "Cliff and Susan make love."

3. The Characters Read-Through

By now, we want to believe our characters are rich, vibrant, and with edges. We first fleshed them out during the story development. They grew and some even spurted in different directions throughout writing the script. They're a little different from your first conception? Yes, they often seem to mature on their own though your fingers actually did the keyboard pressing. That's good.

Their new life, and especially old life, should give you cause to pause. Are they rich and vibrant, or did your story provoke a dull, stereotypical character or two? Perhaps the less-than-wonderful characters can be attributed to your inattention, or laziness. It can happen to about one character per script. But fear not.

This is the time to inject uniqueness into that less than wonderful role by tracking your characters. Look at each individual part with nothing but a creative eye to writing him or her the best the role can be written for its perimeters.

Fasten paper clips on the pages where each character has something to do or say. Don't bother clipping the pages in which characters appear in but one scene. Those roles should have been maximized in the dialogue and description read-throughs. Also, don't paper clip the pages of the protagonist because he or she will normally be on nearly every page. To prevent repeatedly riffling through the script to clip each character, page through once and paper clip a specific part of the paper for each role. Like the top left clips pertain to Tom, top right to Susan, top right side for Dr. Gargon, middle right for Susan's mother, bottom right for her father, etc.

Then flip through each character's paper clipped pages, "tracking" that part through the entire script. READING ALOUD words that relate to only him or her. Total character isolation. Total focus.

After the first read-through, you will occasionally believe the character is wonderful. An excellent role. Optimally your writing will make the role "actor proof." That's show business shorthand for characters that are so good even the most unskilled actor can't screw them up.

You will as occasionally feel characters are flat, boring, and merely functional. Now's the time to give them special idiosyncrasies. Perhaps they should have a regional accent. Make the person obese or thin? Maybe they can be hyperactive or sleepwalking. Use irony, like a doctor who nurses a cold throughout the story, a cobbler whose children need shoes, or a heroic Indiana Jones afraid of snakes. Anything you can devise, consistent with the character's characteristics, to make the role wonderful, identifiable, or at the very least, good.

Most of your paper-clipped characters you'll like or you wouldn't have gotten this far in the scriptwriting process, yet keep yourself open. You might discover an extra twist that can push the role's potential up to your "excellent" perception. That special twist may be any of the characteristics you've considered for the parts that need strong help or Lourdes. You may enjoy this "tracking" best of all in the rewriting process because you have a limited and rewarding focus. Nothing else matters but those people you've lived with for weeks.

Go over the paper-clipped pages of all of your roles again and again individually, until you're satisfied they're as good as you can make them at this point. Remember, audiences remember characters even more than story. Salt the mine. *Make your characters memorable.* Here and now.

4. The "Touches" Pass

When you become an experienced writer, you'll possibly skip this rewriting step because you'll have hopefully gotten so good you lace "touches" into every scene. Those touches will get there through your highly developed instincts or calculations.

You've seen negative reviews shrilling about movies' being "contrived?" *Every movie is contrived!* The cutting edge is whether the contrivances are good or bad. Do the contrivances seem organically natural to the story and characters? Or do the contrivances seem arbitrary, forced, and unnatural to those same story and character components?

So it is with "touches." Is it logical a character would study himself whenever a mirror is in the room? Would she tiptoe or clomp by her snoring husband's TV chair? Be consistent, logical, and inspired with those touches that so enhance stories.

You will find you already have many well-contrived and even accidental touches in the story, characters, and ambiance. You will also have already put in many touches when you tracked your characters. There will probably still be much more you can do with background people, animals, and locales.

Especially consider rain. Rain for every scene that could be enriched with the emotions showers generally evoke. Romance and tragedy particularly. Remember Audrey Hepburn holding the cat in the drenching rain in *Breakfast at Tiffany's*? The James Gardner–Julie Andrews rain scene by Gardner's plane that would take him to D-Day in *The Americanization of Emily*? Rain on George's wedding day in *It's a Wonderful Life*?

Director Louis Malle *(Au Revoir Les Infants, Atlantic City)* and his writers consciously barrage us with wonderful touches far beyond weather. There will often be moments with background characters while the main action for the scene plays out in the foreground. Malle will also have the scene's main character walk out of frame and he'll have the camera hold for bit players to say something or have a piece of business that subtly relates to the movie's tone or texture. Or occasionally Malle's minor characters will start a scene and the protagonist will then enter the frame with his or her dominant action. They're all wonderfully "contrived" techniques by writers, not directors. Take advantage of these and similar dimensional possibilities. Overtly look for such moments.

With antique cars, after the major restoration is complete, the refurbishers "detail" the vehicle. Every single inch of the automobile is microscopically brushed, polished, repaired. This "touches" pass for your scripts will the equivalent of "detailing" antique autos. It's the precise attention just before the anxiously anticipated test drive.

5. The Final Read-Through

Now the test drive, the final read-through. Here, play the role of people in the outside world. Separate yourself from the rewriting steps by an overnight. Pretend you're an interested person who wants to read a quality script.

Isolate nothing. You're done with your dialogue, the descriptions, the characters, the touches. They all seem right and occasionally wonderful.

On that fresh day, be the person who will soon be reading your script. He or she is gimlet-eyed because they've read so many scripts that have been an eventual waste of valuable time. The scripts have not fulfilled any promise. You want yours to be different. You want their eyes to expand to the size of children's on their first look under the tree Christmas morning.

Right now, just roll through your script. Give a small, impertinent wrist flip with every page turn. In these minutes, forget about more rewriting. Enjoy. Oh, maybe turn down a page or two to remind yourself of a place you'd like to polish or play with, but overall, just concentrate on having a good read.

THE POLISH

OK, I've again read *The Glass Hammer*. I liked it. Loved it in many places. What to do, what to do. I want at least a polish before sending my love child into the world. I'm twelve pages or so long so I do want to cut. Yes, I'll do it now as I admonished you.

I also want more humor. And more "touches." During the writing of *The Glass Hammer* I liked Cliff saying "Hang on to your hat," so I put that in his car action scenes. A "touches" runner that should work.

I originally thought I'd go to Bruce Springsteen and try to persuade him to compose an end title song for the film. Would that be on-the-nose? Too predictable? Maybe, maybe not. His voice and lyrics could be wonderful. During the Springsteen deliberation, classical music came into my thought process.

Maybe it bubbled up from the deep of Harlan Ellison's swamp of the subconscious. Yes, I want classical music. Beethoven? Too dark. Chopin? Too light. Handel, too religious. Mozart. Maybe. Yes. Because of *Amadeus*, Wolfgang's now familiar beyond the classical music freaks. As importantly, I can find a piece that would be perfect to counterpoint

Cliff, Susan, Big Red Football, and my "what's it about," the simple overcoming the complex. Public domain classical music will be cheaper but money should *never* be a consideration at the "spec" script level. *Think only of what would be best.*

I'll also pull out ten to twelve pages, and try to get more humor for the audience and for tone. Then do one more "touches" read-through and help some of my characters become even better.

I really like and identify with Cliff. Susan seems pretty full, even frightening at times. Her parents are somewhat stereotypical but I don't have many scenes to get more into why they are what they are. Both reflect parents far beyond their own parents. Susan is breaking that cycle. I sense her parents have to be the most stock of my characters. Tom I know, loathe, and simultaneously love. Tom will kill himself or other people inside of two years. In the name of Je-sus. Tom is a real-life person from my church years back. Ten people were stabbed for Je-sus. Two died. I know Tom.

Everyone else is fine, but Dr. Gargon will probably never be good enough. Part of me wants him to be the protagonist because I so care about his daily dilemmas with the mentally ill. I want to say so much about Dr. Gargon, and through Dr. Gargon, I'm in danger of making him more than he should be for this story. Perhaps in the future I'll write a Dr. Gargon script. Right now, he must serve Cliff and Susan's story. To do more with Dr. Gargon is to add pages and I *have* to cut. I'll just examine each scene he's in and give the most I can possibly give to this tortured man. I'll track his character through one more time. That will help him be the best he can and should be.

You should have similar musings about your people and pages after your final read-through. Oh, it *was* a good read, wasn't it? If not, firmly ask your mirror if you're being too hard on the script. If you don't think so, rethink your story. Then, repeat the dialogue, description, and character isolation steps one more time. After that burst of work, if you're still unhappy, maybe you're right. Pull the chain. Go onto another project. Or poll your ride-to-the-airport friends for confirmation or encouragement.

THE ECSTASY

Hopefully you'll be pleased, even ecstatic, with your script. Try very hard to have your ecstasy firmly grounded in the pleasure of completion and the pride in your abilities, not the anticipation of dollars and fame. Remember? "The end is nothing, the journey is all."

As soon as humanly possible, make the most objective self-appraisal you can on your writing talent. The talent for your current story and your talent in the overall. Sometimes you just can't break the back of your story. Sooner or later you may have to accept the fact that your ability does not best reside in comedy or drama or action adventure or whatever. It's all right to lack strong aptitude for certain story forms, but deluding yourself is *not* all right. Identifying your strengths and weaknesses in writing is as important a self-recognition as you can have as a beginning *or* established writer.

When you get your talent somewhat sorted out, then play to your strength. Try hard to be pleased with what you write as you are writing and rewriting. You can most easily be pleased if you're writing what you like to write. And that's generally what you'll best write.

THE REWRITING TIME FOR YOURSELF

After you finish the first, first draft, how long should you take to rewrite yourself?

Every professional writer and every script will dictate their own answers. Some writers and scripts will be close right off and need a mere few days of polishing. Others, like the aforementioned Jack Sowards, will rewrite from page one. You'll likely fall somewhere between the extremes. And that will depend upon one's maturity as a writer and the hell or happiness provoked within us by the story. *E.T.*, *Butch and Sundance,* and *Fallen Angel* are much easier scripts to write than *Citizen Kane* and *Casablanca.* Multiple character stories like *The Big Chill* and *MASH* are especially complex. Adaptations from sprawling *Gone with the Wind* and *Doctor Zhivago* novels are also very time-consuming in each of the three efforts of screenwriting: story, script, and rewriting.

Take as long as rewriting takes. Not one hour more or less. New writers often have a harder time determining if something's good. They more easily distinguish bad. Another danger is that after much rewriting and rethinking, everything starts to seem bad.

Writing a script, especially a speculative script, is like telling a joke. You want to express the joke so people get the point. That's also the most important element in your scripts. Do people get the point? The joke? You must be very objective on that question. After your answer becomes yes, then only rewrite to the degree you're satisfied, pleased, or a combination thereof. Don't rewrite it to death.

You certainly don't want to let anything escape from your sanctuary if you risk shame. But in the fullest overview, please yourself. Be genuinely proud. Not stubborn or ego-filled, but proud. Then you can fend off most slings and arrows from without.

SHOULD YOUR TITLE BE YOUR TITLE?

You'll question most of your script titles until the moment you go to your grand reward. Just prior to the premiere airing of *Fallen Angel,* a well-meaning friend, Doug Duitsman, the publicity vice-president of Columbia Television, the movie's producing studio, called me into his office.

"Lew, I'm worried about the title. I don't think *Fallen Angel* says anything." I shook my head, smiled in appreciation for his genuine concern, and said: "Doug, I agree. I've come up with at least a hundred possible titles. All I can say is that they're just not any better. *Gone with the Wind* and *Of Human Bondage* have been taken. Peter Frankovich at CBS gave the script that title and, well, I guess we're stuck with it."

Fallen Angel was the highest-rated movie of the 1980–81 television season. Forty-two percent of America wasn't deterred by the title we were "stuck with." All I can say is "Thank you, Peter Frankovich."

Julian Myers is the movie marketing legend who wrote "TEN COMMANDMENTS FOR GOOD BOX OFFICE" in a UCLA Writer's Block newsletter. Myers commandment #6 is:

> Start with a strong title and keep it. A title such as "Sudden Impact," "Scarface," "Guns of Navarone." Avoid inscrutable monikers like "Heart Like a Wheel," "Streamers," "Merry Christmas, Mr. Lawrence."

The great majority of *popular* movie titles relate to a person or place. *E.T., Butch and Sundance, Casablanca, Citizen Kane,* and *Fallen Angel* are good example films to illuminate teaching precepts. Their titles certainly prove out that theory, as do *Mary Poppins, Norma Rae, Batman, When Harry Met Sally,* and on and on to ad nearly infinitum. Theory becomes fact when you examine weekly *Variety*'s listing of all-time top box office movies. Seventy percent concern places or people.

But for the "spec script" do *not* select titles for marquees. Your titles are *desktop titles*. You're trying to entice someone to take the script home for their night's primary reading by 1. your name on the cover and 2. the title. *E.T., Casablanca, Butch and Sundance,* and *Citizen Kane* obviously work extremely well for public word of mouth and marquees. They wouldn't be particularly enticing titles if they were on scripts lying about on your desk if you're the president of a motion picture studio. *Go for the desktop title*. Entice. Intrigue.

AND NOW, THE MADDING CROWD

Let's flash forward. The time has come to present your script to the world. You've detailed the car, fine-tooth-combed, beaten, caressed, loved, and self-debated every word in your script. That's enough. Stop.

Now think of yourself as a proud mother bird. Apprehensive, yet aware she must bump her fledgling from the secure nest. You may be sure the mother bird has done her best to help the baby fly, and so should you.

1. Turn Out Perfect Scripts

But first, the mother bird will examine her child's feathers. Are they just right? Properly fluffed? Aerodynamically skewed? So it must be with your scripts.

Hopefully you have relatives or friends as precise and wonderful as Sherwood Anderson: "Fortunately both my wife and my mother-in-law seem to love digging up mistakes in spelling, punctuation, etc. I can hear them in the next room laughing at me."

2. The First Blush

Producer Warren Bush used to have a facile stock phrase when meeting Rubin Carson after reading his turned-in draft. "Not bad for a first blush, Rubin." Carson summoned forth every Nautilus muscle fiber to restrain himself from leaping across the desk to strangle him.

After all the original, then rewriting, work Rubin and we have done to get to this "kick-our-babies-out-of-the-nest" time, "first blush" would not be the most cherished designation of such toil. "Not bad" is only a little better.

But whether the script is perceived to be good, bad, or whatever in between, it's ours. We *must* claim parenthood.

Reverend Wayne Ulrickson used to have a sermon that suggested we go throughout life with hearts in open palms. Don't clutch your heart so close no one can see it. Expose it. Sure, some will come along and beat on your heart with figurative sticks, stones, and ball bats. Most people though will stroke and give that heart love, care, and nourishment.

So it exactly is with our scripts. Some will loathe. Some will like. And you need but one to *love* who has the ability to get the script produced. You can't get any of the good reactions unless your heart and your script rest in open palms.

3. Write Four to Six Scripts

Flashing even further forward, don't risk damaging the fragility of your writer's id until you've written four to six scripts. Premature exposure to the world can be very hard on the heart in your chest or palm if you've got but one or two drafts in the marketplace. Four to six scripts out diffuses the potential pain, so a single rejection isn't as devastating. You just know one of the others will strike fire. Also, the experience of writing four to six hundred pages of script strengthens your confidence.

4. The Calling Card Script

When you present your scripts to the world, at best you hope their quality will persuade someone to want to transform your work into motion pictures. At worst, you want this same sheaf of work to be good calling card scripts, strong samples of your ability. Scripts that can evoke, "Gee, we don't want to buy this but we like the writing. Let's put the writer on something we do want to shoot."

John Milius wrote *Apocalypse Now* while a U.S.C. film student. For ten years, his script was one of the most talked-about unproduced works in

Hollywood. Milius got job after job off that calling card script before Francis Ford Coppola committed to shoot the resultant movie.

5. The Selling Script

Another reality you must quickly accept is that your final draft should be for selling to whoever is reading. You certainly don't want to be excessive but you *will* say a touch more than is needed for your final script or the "spec" draft. Hopefully in your rewrites you'll have an aware director who will encourage you to take out the excessive verbiage.

REWRITING FOR OTHERS

Let's expand your knowledge of "how to" write for others. Be they friends, supposed friends, or Steven Spielberg, they are still "them." It's all pejorative, all true.

A script that does not go through the rewriting mill is rarer than sandstorms around the timberline of Mount Everest. All of the rewriting for "them" is based on the convictions of the person who has the most power in the process. Some requirements may go beyond subjective opinion and have strong, Aristotelian validity. Other requirements may be invalid, unnecessary. Whatever the swing of the rewriting pendulum, you *have* to deal with any and all such requests. Yet take care the pendulum doesn't swing all the way around and hit you in the backside. Hopefully, you'll handle the rewriting meetings with intelligence, not petulance. The latter will get you to quickly assimilating into your father's plumbing operation.

1. Loving to Rewrite

Everyone, even your parents, knows a writer writes. And now *you* must understand that a writer rewrites.

Many who love to write hate to rewrite. It's often torture. They put so much into the first draft they find rewriting hell. Many others, like Jack Sowards, who throws his first draft away, *love* to rewrite. They don't consider rewriting to be anything less than pleasurable or necessary.

Believe in your subconscious, your first instinct. Try to get it right in the first place. That attitude can cause you to experience near euphoria in the writing of the first draft, yet much despair and subsequent agony later. Everyone with a criticism will be seen to be more horrific than any opera phantom. But, *we must hear what they have to say.*

Most importantly, they *may* have good ideas. Walt Disney used to put cartoon situations on his company bulletin board. Like Mickey Mouse, as the sorcerer's apprentice, going up a flight of stairs with two buckets of water. Employees were encouraged to submit sight gags that could be funny for Mickey's movement, and there was a five-dollar prize if their idea was used in the film. The janitors and secretaries won five-dollar bills as often as anyone, excepting the animators.

Though we may be tempted to disparage people's opinions or feelings on our first drafts, be as open as you possibly can. Look within yourself for the ability to *listen.* One of the more valuable assets of writers is their ability to *listen.* Listen in meetings. Listen to ideas, suggestions, criticism. Sometimes after the rewrite that springs from a meeting, it's clear some writers consciously or subconsciously do not *listen.* Few of the mutual meeting decisions are reflected in the rewrite pages, and thus time was wasted by all. Such writers will surely have fewer supporters for future employment.

Yes, some in those meetings are *not* knowledgeable. Some will also be posturing. Others will be unfeeling or simply dumb. You've got to block all of those layers out and *listen* to what they say only as their words relate to the script. They may represent the anticipated audience for your produced screenplay.

Best you figure out what that audience might say at the rewrite level than anytime later. It can be far less painful than bad reviews and far less expensive than reshooting scenes.

2. Hating Criticism

It's hard. Criticize our children, spouses, dogs, homes, and even ourselves, but be easy with our scripts. John Sayles was once asked why he mortgaged everything he owned to shoot movies like *Return of the Secaucus 7* and *The Brother from Another Planet.* His reply was, "Because

I couldn't take one more meeting with those fuckers and their notes."

I often agree. You might be able to do that when you're as secure, well-known, and good as John Sayles, but right now, you probably can't. You'll have to take that meeting. And as long as you're there, be open to getting something from the very same meeting. You may pan creative gold. There were no blind gold panners, and that's what you'll be if you sit in those gatherings with arms folded and ego filling the room.

Agent Jon Brown warns not to go to meetings with an "attitude." And this is fine advice. Of course, no one wants you to go in and be a script whore; that's an attitude in reverse. Don't be an "anything you like I like" writer because you will be as undesirable to those persons able to buy your wares as a writer who won't listen at all. Walt Disney used to loathe the writers that would take down verbatim what he dictated, and give it back to him in the rewrite. Walt called those writers "secretaries."

3. Attitudes

Many writers who have been working a long time have huge attitudes, yet blame their lack of employment on ageism. Often that's real, but as often their attitude in meetings is simply insufferable. They're almost always dealing with people younger and less experienced than themselves. They find it hard not to come off as "the teacher." Quinn Martin said: "We're not doing Shakespeare. It's a game. Play it, enjoy it. If the day comes when you can't, get out."

How true. Yet people rarely get out. They go into meetings angry, resentful, or bitter.

Neither wealth nor experience will likely be an immediate problem for you, but you *can* develop an "attitude." Younger, inexperienced writers often write "visions" instead of screenplays. Their reactions to script suggestions so often begin, "Well, my vision is . . ." or, "But the story I want to tell is . . ." "I" and "my," all said with an "attitude." Writing maturity often proves that timeless belief, "the more you know, the less you know." Sir James Barrie *(Peter Pan)* once said it well: "I am not young enough to know everything."

4. Listening to "Them"

There are writers who consider their first draft written in stone, and the writers who act as creative secretaries. The best posture is generally in the middle. Listen. Accept a good idea even if, or maybe especially because, it comes from the morning bus driver, or a director. Reject their ideas if you don't feel they're organically appropriate for the script.

You say, "How can I reject anything if the suggester's my boss?" Well, it's very necessary to walk a tightrope between practicality and aesthetics. Unlike books, oils, or even theater, screen entertainment is the most collaborative art in history. A director beginning a film is a general leading an army to war, and your script is the battle plan for that war. You, the screenwriter, must understand that concept to accommodate the various components of the army without rewriting the plan so that it would lead to defeat. In less allegorical words, making your screenplay lead to a dull, confusing, or silly movie.

Irwin Allen often used the words: "I'll examine that." Generally, that meant "no," but his response was less confrontive and it gave executives the encouragement that they might have a good idea for improving the script. Telling your "boss" you'll consider his or her suggestion will more likely lead you to an acceptable compromise, or conversely some inspiration that will satisfy the note but simultaneously make the script better.

If you must say "no," make sure you're not destroying your future relationship with that person. You'd rather be effective, and not be replaced by another writer, than be right. In this business of show, you can be "right" but wrong in the long of the haul. Do not be "wrong by being right." You can't win anything when you get that devastating "we've decided to put another writer on the script" phone call, so do what you can to stay on the script without being a "secretary."

Sometimes tell employers you're skeptical of rewriting a scene, or a character, or adding another scene, but you'll try it. They are sometimes absolutely right. Or your "trying it" will clearly show your concern was justified and you can quickly use your friend, the wastebasket.

5. Free Writing and Rewriting

Whatever comes from showing scripts, don't rewrite yourself or others for free. Beyond the casting couch, the biggest scam involving show business personkind is, "We don't have money now but you'll get a lot when we shoot the picture." You'll be shoveled dialogue about Brink's trucks eventually backing up to your front door when producers ask for a free "run" with your or someone else's original material. Beware. Mayo Simon: "Some producers don't rest easy at night unless they've fucked at least one writer by day."

On your original scripts that have been lying fallow for a while, you may feel "why not." But if you're going to write or rewrite without pay, use your valuable time for yourself on your own "spec" script. Remember, you're creating a "property" that is yours. Something someone, sometime, somewhere may want to buy. Something that can also be a strong "calling card" which might lead to professional employment.

6. Short Storks and Long Ducks

This screenwriting progression is like night following day. Rewriting for others follows writing. Take refuge in the ancient Japanese proverb, "You cannot make a stork's legs short, nor a duck's legs long."

H. G. Wells had a most realistic perspective. "No passion in the world is equal to the passion to alter someone else's draft." Accept it as fact. Accept it, even with gritted teeth, as beneficial. Your life and heart will be easier, your shrink bills less, and your marriages fewer.

Turn the rewriting process into a positive. Your ego is not what's important here, for your script holds God. We screenwriters sometimes personally assume the deification but what we are trying to give, through the medium of our scripts and our souls, is a glimpse of God. No matter how light or frivolous you or others might perceive the heart of your story to be.

Sometimes you can improve that heart enormously through listening to others, whether they sign your paychecks or not. Other times the benefits are small, but even those can be helpful. They may stimulate a handful of "touches" that can make the eventual film even more effective.

If the suggestion comes from the financially vested, and that suggestion is terrible, try to talk him or her out of the "note" gently. Maybe the sponsor, in return, can talk you into the thought. If that back and forth is not helpful to the script, resort to a final ploy. Say you'll "examine it." Or even commit to "try it."

Generally you'll develop a thought that can "satisfy" the original suggestion. If not, not. Most often though, you'll help the script if you try to accept such input as potentially beneficial.

7. But Do We Like the People?

Humorist Rubin Carson suggests that producers and directors must, prior to assuming their positions, learn how to say "needs work" and "do we like the people" in ten different languages. "Needs work" is simply a smokescreen response to cover up the person's lack of articulation and creative ability to comment on scripts. "Do we like the people" is a phrase one needs to less facilely challenge. *We do not need to "like the people".* We need to *understand* the people.

We do not need to like Citizen Kane, most of the Humphrey Bogart characters, or the pedophile Howie in *Fallen Angel.* We need to understand them. To understand them means to dimensionalize them. To develop the character beyond the stereotype. To make Butch and Sundance more than robbers. To make E.T. not a monster from outer space, but lovable and loving. To understand why Scarlett O'Hara loves Tara over Rhett Butler.

Don't worry about making the character lovable. Worry about the role's having dimension so that "they" and the audience understand why the character is what the character is. Put in "pet the dog" scenes. Literally giving him or her a dog will be a giant stride forward in getting the "do we like the people" people off your script's back.

8. Walking Away

Don't ever settle for less than what you strongly believe. If you feel the script will be irreparably hurt by some outside suggestion, don't make the change. Walk away from the "note," or walk away from the script if you believe the requested change would be important to resist.

But do everything you can to walk away without hostility or petulance. You do, and should, want to maintain the relationship. People on both sides of the creative barrier recognize and respect *honest* differences. Differences founded in integrity, not ego. Many times WGA colleagues have said, "I just can't do it. I know what you want. I can't make it work for me. I'm sorry." Generally studio and network buyers respect and strongly appreciate the writer with such integrity.

People, and young writers, misinterpret these creative differences. They so want to believe the other side is either the company president's relative or dumb. Rarely is either true. Such people want to also believe the writer is the pure, white knight, and this is also rarely true.

9. I'm Afraid We'll Have to Get Someone Else

Sometimes the words are exactly that blunt. Other times the phrase will be: "We need another perspective." Or, "You're not able to see the forest for the trees." Or, "We're just not crazy about it." Or, "We want to give it some top spin. You want it to be good, don't you?"

Any variation of those words of horror are the precursor to the darkest days most writers experience: being rewritten. It's simply the worst. It's the equivalent of your significant other blatantly cheating in front of you with all God's children watching and aware.

What can you do? First you cry. Inside, outside, or both. You've a right if you care about your script, and the hurt is so hard.

No matter the circumstance, smile off your pain and *GO ON TO ANOTHER SCRIPT.* If for no other reason but to save your psychological buns. It's much like death, but death is permanent. Being rewritten reruns into infinity. But you will survive. If you write on, you can even prevail.

THE FINAL REWRITE

After the script rewrites, try to be around for the post-production editing process. Where the editor puts the closeup or the director's rearranging of a scene in the story progression can be disastrous or heavenly. In fact, everything "they" and those influences around "them" do can potently affect your screenwriting. Editing is truly the final rewrite.

Try to learn as much as you can about editing. The cutting of scenes to help pace, performance, and story clarity is invaluable information *that is writing.* Such editing knowledge will help you immeasurably when you write.

Start by asking the editor and the director if you can sit in on their sessions and observe. When the editor is alone with the scenes, can you still hang out? Learn so much about editing information and the available choices that the editing experts will actually *want* to hear your reactions to their work. Then and only then will you be part of the final rewrite. And you'll enjoy the experience. Best of all, your involvement *should* be good for the movie.

AFTER ALL IS SAID AND DONE—AND DONE

'Tis quite an obstacle course. Getting the idea. Developing the story. Building your characters. The step outline. The three acts. The rewriting. The nitpickers. "Them" and "they." We now come to getting your script *done.*

Getting *done* is key. Many new writers hate to get done. Like they hate to leave the school womb. They rewrite, rewrite, and rewrite in the rewriting womb, mostly because of their own paranoia. They can often be like one small child who was asked, "How was your first day in kindergarten?" The boy visibly shrunk to accompany his timid response: "They looked at me."

"They" will look at you through your script. And you must survive. Your specific survival on each script is what's important now. The draft you've just finished, and are proud of, needs armour for the inevitable storm.

1. The Hollywood Triangle

The most damning reaction you can give someone is apathy. To scream, yell, and exhibit even negative passion is far less emotionally destructive than *not* giving someone acknowledgement they even exist. So it is with your love-children screenplays. People profess to be "dying" to read your script, then never react. As planes disappear into the supposed Bermuda Triangle, Hollywood seemingly has a mystery spot for submitted scripts.

When "they" ignore you by their lack of response, do unto them the same. Forget them. Every person finds time to do things they want to do. "They" didn't want to really read your script. They were just "making nice." Let the matter go. Concentrate on those who do read.

2. The Morale of Your Script

The responses of those who read can often hurt. But sometimes overt acceptance can be *too* joyful. UCLA's John Wooden was and still is the most successful coach in college basketball history. He constantly tried to psychologically condition his team to have as close to the same demeanor when they lost as when they won. He believed if the lows were too low and the highs too high, the slams at each end would be destructive to the team's season-long morale.

That's a wonderful principle for screenwriting. For specific scripts, for your overall writer morale. Say a quiet "thank you very much" if someone doesn't like your script, and a similar "thank you very much" to those who write garlands of ecstasy across the cover page.

3. You Must Like Your Script

After you've written four to six scripts, you will hopefully reach an able degree of skill in writing. When you do, *you* will be the best judge of your script. You are the one who must maintain the conviction that your script is worthwhile when others would imply otherwise. If someone "loves" your script, that is equally valid *and* invalid. When you suffer a criticism, cling to the George Burns truism "one person's laugh is another's yawn."

"It is a vulgar and barbarous drama which would not be tolerated by the vilest populace of France or Italy. One would imagine this piece to be the work of a drunken savage." That's Voltaire reviewing Shakespeare's *Hamlet.* Any questions?

So think of Shakespeare and George Burns when the survival of a script seems futile. *Believe in your script* until time and consistent negatives tell you to stop believing. Then write another. Quickly.

William Goldman says, "Nobody knows anything." While this is true, everybody knows something. They certainly know what they know but rarely what audiences know. We all guess. Some of us guess better because of our instincts, experience, education, or luck. We want all four but if you ever have a choice, take luck. Branch Rickey maintained, "Luck is the residue of design." And a script is all design.

4. The Twenty-Five Cents on the Dresser

Mostly, we should want integrity in the rewriting of our scripts, in our souls. Our physical needs, and even greed, may temporarily overpower the quest for integrity. Keep courage whenever you can. Forgo anger, petulance, and ego. Recall Molière's, "Writers are like hookers. We start out doing it for ourselves. Then for a few friends. Then we say, 'What the hell? I might as well be getting paid for it.' "

Your integrity is at the most crucial juncture when that twenty-five cents is on the dresser, when your hand is over the quarter. That's the moment of decision. Not when the customer's in the midst of the service after your having accepted the twenty-five cents.

If you think you can maintain your integrity, pick up the money and submit. If you don't feel you can get out of the rewriting experience with the script's integrity intact, *don't* pick up the quarter. Let the customer go down the hall. Otherwise, you'll pocket the quarter, close your eyes, spread your legs, pretend it isn't happening, and hate yourself in the morning. And the long run will be significantly less long.

Generally, you'll pick up the quarter. Sometimes the earth will move. That possibility can be worth it all. But no matter if you're new at rewriting, or a wily vet, recall your first instincts, then Billy Wilder's painfully funny observation: "As soon as we take out the improvements, we might have a good script."

FADE OUT

The most significant mentor after my mother was Dr. Enid Miller, the guiding light of Nebraska Wesleyan Theater. On "Doc's" deathbed, she tried to speak to me. I put my ear next to her lips and asked "Doc" to repeat what she had said, that being her first attempt at words in hours. She repeated, "When you go up to get that diploma, I don't give a shit about seeing a good actor up there. I want to see a good man." I heard. And I'm still hearing.

It's not enough to try to be good. You *must* be good. You must be alive to be a wonderful screenwriter. You must *see* life to be a wonderful screenwriter.

Drama critic George Jean Nathan was emphatic about life. "What interests me in life . . . is the surface of life. Life's music and color. Its charm and ease. Its humor, its loveliness. The great problems of the world . . . social, political, economic, and theological . . . do not concern me in the slightest. I am concerned about life."

L'chaim.

You must be significantly a part of life. You must be a good man. A good woman. Alice Walker (*The Color Purple* novel) has the perspective: "I'm not sure a bad person can write a good book. If art doesn't make us better, then what on earth is it for?"

To be artistically good is important. To be humanistically good is most important. And to be good in either dimension, you must know love, love, and be loved. Love at all depths will be your very best screenwriting technique. Truman Capote passionately believed, "Any work of art, provided it springs from a sincere motivation to further understanding between people, is an act of faith and therefore is an act of love."

Ray Bradbury's been onto this forever. Ray delivered the invocation to a Humanitas Prize gathering and every 434 man and woman since has been blessed with Ray's words. It's your turn.

> Dear Lord. . . . Help us to remember the gift of excellence that lies with us if we but call and bring it forth.

Help us to recall that in excellence is surprising profit, for the soul, for the mind, and for the life we live, beside that soul, and with that mind.

Help us to know that only in our loves can we create, and out of that creation change some stray, small part of the world we touch.

Remind us to know that the more we create out of love of an idea, the better our work, our lives, our influence, becomes. Tell us again, for we forget, that work done without love is stillborn, mindless, and lost in the very hour of its deliverance.

Help us to love ideas and their creation, even as we love our neighbors, and, because we are proper creators, ourselves.

Tell us to lie down with that one inescapable person, our lonely selves, knowing that if the work of the previous day was a surprise of joy that we stumbled upon through curiosity, true need, and rare zest, and the energy that comes from wild discovery, we are good company for the night.

Teach us not to hesitate atop cliffs, but to leap off into our writing without wings. And teach us, with passion and love, how to build wings on the way down, hoping for a soft landing.

We ask these things because, poor creatures that we are, we do forget, and must remind ourselves, as you remind us, that love is the final answer, and excellence its hallmark, and profit, which is peace of mind, its everlasting residue.

Please, Lord, hear this, amen.

Students, people on streets, even the rotten kids next door continually wonder if they have talent. For most it seems the ultimate question. "Do I have talent?" usually means "will my life count for anything?"

During one final class gathering at my manse, we were going on and on with one student, telling her how close she was to a wonderful story. We continually urged her to "push it" one more notch. Her classmate Mitch Hara interrupted this with his own special astonishment. To everyone. "The most amazing thing about Lew is that he *really, really* believes we all have talent!"

I blinked in puzzlement. Was that a compliment or insult? The subsequent applause from the class seemed to indicate the former. So many professors, professionals, and others in the midst of life seem to be locked in the mode of *not* believing a majority of people have talent. They espouse that most dreamers just struggle in failure rather than realistically recognize they are failures and immediately go into real estate or log sawing.

Reject such negativism. It's dehumanizing, demoralizing, denying for the God within us all, and just plain wrong. We *all* have talent. How we use it and don't use it is what the game is about in writing, and in life itself. We must not get beaten down by those who choose to simply take up space on this planet, by those whose lives risk counting for nothing.

> I think one's talent is a growth inside one. I do not think one can explain growth. It is silent and subtle. One does not keep digging up a plant to see how it grows. —Artist/writer Emily Carr

As a screenwriter, you can never have enough growth. And you can always *not* have growth. That choice you must resist. Sadly, the choice is most often made *not* to try. Let your tombstone read, "I tried."

Another growth choice is less obvious. Seventy-year-old screenwriter Sol Saks barked at sixty-four-year-old writer Rubin Carson, "Will you ever *shut up!* How are you going to learn?" He's right. At sixty-four you can and should continue to learn. Always be a student, even if you're teaching yourself. *Particularly* if you're the teacher. American poet Wystan Hugh Auden believed: "When a successful author analyzes the reasons for his or her success, they generally underestimate the talent they were born with, and overestimate their skill in using that talent."

Believe in your talent for screenwriting. Talent is the expression of your soul. Who would deny their soul? Who *should* deny their soul? Absolutely no one, not you or any human within sniffing distance of 434.

George Orwell *(1984, Animal Farm)* claimed: "There is a minority of gifted, willful people determined to live their own lives to the end. Writers belong in this class."

Live *your* life to the end. If you choose to live life as a screenwriter, you will be in that lot of "gifted, willful people." Doesn't sound like bad company.

I aspire to expire in the exact manner of Anton Chekhov. On his deathbed, that brilliant Russian playwright held a goblet of vintage champagne aloft and with his beloved wife toasted to a life well led. My beloved Pamela and I have a magnum of Mumm's at the ready.

I promise our final toast will include you . . . and 434. Write on.

FADE OUT

THE END

INDEX